Passionate
Judaism

Published by

THE JUDAICA PRESS, INC.

Passionate Judaism

An Inspirational Guide
For A Happy and Fulfilling
Torah Life

By Rabbi Moshe Meir Weiss

Weiss, Moshe Meir.
Passionate Judaism / Moshe Meir Weiss.
p. cm.   ISBN 1-880582-33-3
1. Jewish sermons, American.
2. Spiritual life—Judaism. 3. Hasidism. I. Title.
BM740.2.W46 1998
296.4'7—dc21   CIP 98-40489

THE JUDAICA PRESS, INC.
123 Ditmas Avenue
Brooklyn, New York 11218
718-972-6200 / 800-972-6201
JudaicaPr@aol.com

Visit us on the web at: **www.judaicapress.com**

ISBN 1-880582-33-3

The author warmly welcomes your comments or suggestions.
Address: P.O. Box 140726 Staten Island, N.Y. 10314
Phone: 718-983-7095
E-mail: 73552.3477@compuserve.com

Manufactured in the United States of America

RABBI MOSES FEINSTEIN

455 F. D. R. DRIVE

New York. N. Y. 10002

ORegon 7-1222

משה פיינשטיין

ר"מ תפארת ירושלים

בנוא יארק

בע"ה

כו׳ שבט תשד"מ

לכבוד קהל אגודת ישראל בסטעטן אייל נד, ה׳ עליהם יחיו.

בשמחה שמעתי איך שבית הכנסת אגודת ישראל בסטעטן-
אייל נד, זכה לקבל לרב ומרא דאתרא את תלמידי היקר
והחביב הרה"ג ר׳ משה מאיר וייס שליט"א – הריני בטוח
שאנשי הקהלה יהנו מאוד מרבנותו של הרה"ג הנ"ל מחמת
מדותיו והנהגותיו הישרים ומחמת ידיעותיו הגדולות
בש"ס ובהלכה, שיועילו לו ליעץ ולעזור אנשי קהלתו בכל
אפשרות שיהיה לו.

ובאתי בזה לברך לתלמידי הרה"ג ר׳ משה מאיר וייס
שליט"א וגם לכל הנהלת וגבאי בית הכנסת וגם לכל חברי
ביהכנ"ס הנ"ל שינהל רבנותו בהצלחה גדולה לתפארת ה׳ ולתורתו
ויזכה ללכת בראש אנשי קהלתו לקבל פני משיח צדקנו בקרוב.

בידידות משה פיינשטיין

*HaRav Moshe Feinstein, ל'צז, wrote this letter on 26 Shevat 5744, in praise of the
author, Rav Moshe Meir Weiss, upon his assumption of the position of Rav of Agudas
Yisroel of Staten Island.*

אברהם פאם
RABBI ABRAHAM PAM
582 EAST SEVENTH STREET
BROOKLYN, NEW YORK 11218

ב"ה אור ליום ...

הנה יב"צ הרב מו/הר"ר מאיר ... שליט"א, חתן ... הגאון
ובנוגע רבינו ... ברכות, עם קבוץ ... לכבוד ... של אבירית וכזומה,
... חיזוק והתאמצות בתורה והעבודה כ'ב ... ...
... ... לשון ... מאמת ... ...
... שהזאי'רים דו יקחו ... ... כי כבר
... לעמוד ... הטבות וכבוד... ... בשלים ... ...
ונבשים לב.
ולו/ ... ... חן ... ...
חולצם, ...
אברהם יצחק הכהן פאם

It is with great pleasure that I write this haskama for HaRav Moshe Meir Weiss ני׳, a distinguished talmid of our yeshiva.

In the Yeshiva HaRav Weiss was זוכה to be משמש my father the Rosh HaYeshiva, the Gadol HaDor HaRav HaGaon Rav Moshe Feinstein זצ"ל, from whom he gained many insights. These insights coupled with his growth during his years as a talmid enabled HaRav Weiss to develop the ideas and principles that he personifies, and that he teaches to his many talmidim.

HaRav Weiss's abilities in the oral medium of lectures, shiurim, and tapes are legendary. His famed ability to articulate is extraordinary. He now desires to utilize the written word to inspire and elevate as well. There is no doubt in my mind that HaRav Weiss will be equally successful in this endeavor.

May Hashem grant him and his wife Miriam Libby שתחי׳ continued hatzlacha in disseminating Torah to all of Klal Yisroel.

13 Menachem Av 5758
HaRav Reuven Feinstein

Rabbi Ephraim Greenblatt
5556 Barfield Rd.
Memphis, TN 38120

בס"ד

הרב אפרים גרינבלאט

רב ושו"ב במעמפיס

מח"ס שו"ת רבבות אפרים ח"א

וזכות אבותינו

הנה ידידי החשוב הרב ד' אשר אבוב ואום שלום, שלאנו אלי אותי וכמו אותנו וכמו

הרב האלוף ד' אשר פייטוב צעי, כאשר שנים, ולאות הכתב הנוף אתי צעי,

פלא לי יצוף ממט בהילאנת שמירה לה... ביעני והדות, הקטות ויוטני

ואדבות עי הטבוף, ואלוני בצוף מדברים לטוב... אלא בזה שבכפה ברוט... טוב

טאבטאת הפלות, והדברים של שום אשרת בוף חוקל, ולן אני עוני ליוטן

הרב שלום... הטטו עי טטו, וכאטני טאטו בני ושטאטי, וטטט טבו האטט טוטט

ובבב וויטאטי ידויי בט שלום, כאטטו דא אטרת עטי טם טי וויטו תטטם בכטוף

אבטוט עטטאות כאטעטים, ותעלום לכבד אטות פב כטי שטם שפטט

וטטו כיטי ביטטף בטטא כטטאא טטטי כטטט בטטטטט אטטפ טטט וכט טטט עטטטן

ונטני טטן טן טיכב והטדף טיאטות רב כיטטאטי הטטסות, וטטטי וטכב טטט

ואאטטטי דוד כטטו טאטים כטטפ טטיאט דב טטי וטטיב עטטות טטטטם טטטטן

וכבב כטאו טה עי טי טטאטף דבאטכאו טטי.

הטף אטטף טטטטט, כה, טטט, אטט, בטט שטטטם טטטי.

טטט שטט... וטטטטט טף שטטע תטט ה טטטט שט ט יטקיף.

Telephone: (901) 682-3291 :טל׳   Fax: (901) 685-0258 :פקס

DEDICATED BY

Rabbi Dr. Menachem Yurowitz, *shlit"a*
grandfather of the author

━━ • ━━ • ━━

In memory of his very special brother

R' Yehuda Aryeh ben Yitzchok Yurowitz, z"l

* *A wonderful husband for over 59 years,*
a father, grandfather and great-grandfather.
* *Supported his family with integrity.*
and dedication, toiling for them for over 60 years.
* *Sacrificed much to care for many relatives.*
* *Dedicated president of the Chuster shul*
for over a quarter of a century.
* *Actively involved in chevra kadisha.*
* *Had a great love for Eretz Yisroel and*
settled there in the last years of his life.
* *Displayed greatness during the terrible war years.*

━━ • ━━ • ━━

And in memory of his beloved wife of nearly 50 years

Chana bas R' Moshe
חנה בת ר׳ משה

━━ • ━━ • ━━

Also in memory of a wonderful daughter

Rachel, *a"h,* bas R' Menachem, *shlit"a*
רחל ע״ה בת ר׳ מנחם שליט״א

לזכרון עולם בהיכל ה׳

* ⋅ *

ר׳ יוסף יצחק אייזק בן בן ציון Kohn ע״ה

* ⋅ *

נתן יצחק בן אלימלך זאב
Schiffer שיפפער

* ⋅ *

ת.נ.צ.ב.ה.

נר זכרון

לעילוי נשמת האשה החשובה
מרת רייזל ע״ה בת ה״ר אלטר יעקב דוד ז״ל
נפטרה ט״ו אלול תשנ״ה
אשת חיל עטרת בעלה ה״ר אליעזר זאכטער תחי׳ לאוי״ט

לעילוי נשמת האשה החשובה
מרת רחל ע״ה בת ה״ר יהודה ז״ל
נפטרה ו׳ שבט תשנ״ח
אשת חיל עטרת בעלה ה״ר משה זיטצער הלוי תחי׳ לאוי״ט

In loving memory of our beloved
mothers, grandmothers and great-grandmothers
Rose Zachter, a"h
and **Ruth Sitzer, a"h**

Phyllis and Mel Zachter
Cindy, Elie and Ephraim Becker
Yaakov and Yehuda Zachter

THIS BOOK IS ALSO DEDICATED
IN LOVING MEMORY OF

my wonderful father

ר׳ אהרן צבי בן ר׳ מאיר ווייס ז״ל

Mr. Herman Weiss, z"l

.ת.נ.צ.ב.ה.

*who gave me a superb upbringing
and the yeshiva education
that made this sefer possible!*

———•—•———

And in memory of his parents

ר׳ מאיר בן ר׳ יוסף וזוגתו אסתר גיטל

and four of his younger siblings

יוסף, ישראל, חיי שרה, מרים גאלדא

.ת.נ.צ.ב.ה.

*all of whom perished at the hands of
the wicked Nazis—*ימח שמם וזכרם.
*May Hashem bring the
techiyas hameisim speedily in our days!*

With deep appreciation

to Hashem Yisborach

Passionate Judaism

Table Of Contents

About The Title: Passionate Judaism

My parents named me Moshe Meir. Meir is after my paternal grandfather, a devout Spinka chosid and a talmid chochom. Moshe was in memory of my maternal grandmother's father, Reb Moshe Weinstock, z"l. I asked my grandfather, Rabbi Dr. Menachem Yurowitz, (may he live to greet the Mashiach) to tell me something about the man whose name I am privileged to bear. He told me, "He was a real *Chassideshe Yid!*" I asked what he meant, and he illustrated it with the following story:

Every year, the saintly Baal Shem Tov chose an outstandingly beautiful esrog for Succos. We are taught that *"Esrog domeh l'leiv—An esrog bears a similarity to one's heart"* [*Vayikra Rabbah* 30:14]. Given this, it is understandable that the Baal Shem Tov would look far and wide for an esrog reflective of his sensitive soul. Each year he discovered an esrog which he was sure was especially slated for him.

One year, the Baal Shem Tov searched and searched but

could not find "his" esrog. As Yom Tov approached, he dreamt that 'his' esrog belonged to a certain Jewish man in Constantinople. Having no choice, the *tzadik* packed his bags and traveled to Constantinople. Upon arriving, the Baal Shem Tov located the esrog's owner and requested to see his precious esrog. As soon as he saw the esrog, the Baal Shem Tov sensed a powerful connection, and he knew that this esrog was the one with which he was meant to fulfill the mitzvah. He asked the owner if he would part with his treasure for a large sum of money. The owner, who was also looking forward to fulfilling the mitzvah with it, declined. However, he invited the *tzadik* to join him for Yom Tov and share it with him. Thus, in order to be able to use this particular esrog, the Baal Shem Tov readily agreed and stayed with his host for the holiday.

After the festival, the Baal Shem Tov profusely thanked his host and, in parting, asked if he could think why he had been *zocheh* (deserving) to be given the esrog "slated" for the Baal Shem Tov. The host asked the Holy Baal Shem Tov specifically when his attention had turned to the purchase of his esrog. The Baal Shem Tov said that he had begun his search several weeks before Succos.

"Ah yes!" said the man, nodding knowingly. "Immediately after Simchas Torah, I take a big jar and each day I deposit coins in it devoted towards next year's esrog. This way I perform the mitzvah of esrog throughout the winter, spring, and summer!"

When the Baal Shem Tov heard this, he acknowledged with appreciation, "Now I know why you merited having 'my' esrog!"

This, my grandfather concluded, is the meaning of a *Chassideshe Yid*! And *this* is what I mean when I say *Passionate Judaism*. It is the feeling behind the mitzvos:

• The wife who sheds a tear for her husband's happiness, and her children's success while lighting the Shabbos candles.

• The meaningful kiss one gives to his tefillin, realizing that tefillin lengthens one's life (as the verse states *"Hashem aleihem yichyu*—If Hashem is upon you, you will live," [*Yeshaya* 38:16] which the Gemara in *Menochos* [44b] says refers to tefillin).

• Not leaning one's elbows on the Gemara while learning, out of respect for its sanctity (cf. *Reb Yaakov, a* biography of Rabbi Yaakov Kaminetsky [ArtScroll]).

• Sharpening the knives and tasting the food before Shabbos begins to give it special honor.

• Having a special section in your wallet for tzedakah money, and a special pen to write Torah, sign tzedakah checks, and assist with your children's Torah homework.

• Handing the Chumash to your child's rebbe, making him your *shaliach* (agent) to fulfill the mitzvah of *"v'sheenantom l'vanecha*—to teach one's child Torah." (This is similar to when a father gives the knife to the mohel, making him the *shaliach* to circumcise his son.)

• Leaving notes of affection and small gifts for your spouse so that the *Shechina's* presence can be increased in your home.

• The yeshiva bochur who sends a telegram to parents in order to tell them in one more way how much he loves and appreciates them.

• Hanging up a bottle of oil on the *schach* of the Succah to use for the Chanukah menorah.

• Checking the bungalow for chometz before departing for the city at the end of the summer, knowing that you won't be back before Pesach (in addition to including it in the Rov's sale of your chometz).

• Jotting down some notes before davening to remember

what today's special requests are to the *Ribbono shel Olam*.

 • Sitting on the floor of your home, once or twice a year, with your family, after returning home after midnight from a late wedding, and tearfully reciting some prayers for the rebuilding of the Beis HaMikdash (better known as *tikkun chatzos*).

 • Standing up while talking on the telephone with an *Adam Gadol* (cf. *Reb Moshe,* a biography on Rabbi Moshe Feinstein, zt"l [ArtScroll]).

 • Smiling while *bentching*, for after all, we are talking to Hashem!

 These and countless other deeds, small and large, make up the definition of *Passionate Judaism*. It is my prayer to Hashem that this *sefer* should help us to come closer to this ideal!

Passionate
Expressions

I. Gratitude to Hashem

As I write this preface, an onslaught of thoughts and emotions clamor for first mention. Like everything else, for this too, the Torah provides direction. We are taught that before we do anything, first and foremost, we should thank and bless Hashem. The great Malchitzedek (better known to us as Sheim ben Noach) was severely punished for blessing Avraham before he gave the Almighty homage [*Bereishis* 14:19].

The importance of showing gratitude and expressing thanks is obvious from the fact that every Jew begins each day of his or her life with a declaration of thanks to Hashem— "*Modeh ani l'fanecha*—I give thanks before You." Furthermore, we exist solely to be able to show appreciation, as it says, "*Am zu yatzarti li t'hilasi y'sapeiru*—I created this nation for Me, to relate My praise" [*Yeshaya* 43:21]. This is why the Jews are called Yehudim, signifying those who give thanks. The source of this is the name of one of Leah's sons, Yehuda, which Leah explained to mean, *"Hapa'am odeh es Hashem—*This time I will give thanks to Hashem" [*Bereishis* 29:35].

A good Jew's day is chock full of thanks since we are expected to say a minimum of one hundred *brachos* every day! This means we say a minimum of one hundred thank-yous to Hashem daily! This one-hundred-*brachos* formula was enacted by Dovid HaMelech to stem the tide of a troubling rash of Jewish casualties! We are taught that the deaths ceased when all the Jews got into the habit of saying one hundred *brachos* a day [*Bamidbar Rabbah* 18:21].

It is therefore with intense emotion that I give my thanks and praise to Hashem *"Hachonein l'adam daas—*He, Who gives wisdom to man," for granting me the thoughts contained in this *sefer*, and for the health and ability to focus on presenting this modest work to the public.

Rav Yaakov Kaminetsky, zt"l, wittingly comments that rabbis, while saying *Boreich Aleinu* in the *Shemoneh Esrei*, should have in mind to thank Hashem for their Torah knowledge. As this benediction is dedicated to one's livelihood, this is particularly appropriate since for rabbeim, Torah knowledge is a tool of the trade.

II. The Opportunity to be Marbitz Torah

Indeed, it is a privileged milestone in one's life to be able to share with the "Olam HaTorah" some Torah thoughts. The *Pele Yoetz*, on the word *zechiya* (meritorious) writes, "If one helps even a single person out of a thousand during any future generation with his words, it is worthwhile for the writer to have been born—just for that accomplishment." In his preface to *Yoreh Deiah*, the Har Tzvi writes that one's primary duty in this world is to attempt to write, according to one's ability, something worthwhile so that one's name and memory will always be remembered. The enormity of such an achievement can be demonstrated by the amazing words of Rav Hirsch Melech of Dinnova, the author of *Derech Pikudecha*, on the mitzvah of *pirya v'rivya* (to be fruitful and multiply), who states that presenting a *sefer* to the public is the fulfillment of spiritual *pirya v'rivya*. We can conjecture that the reasoning behind this is that our Torah novellae are the "fruit" of our spiritual thinking.

In the preface to his first volume in the *sefer Mevaser Tov*, Rav Issacson writes a fascinating anecdote relating how Rav Hirsch Melech of Dinnova, began his career writing *seforim*. When he was poor, a guest visited him and left him two *agurot* (pennies). His Rebbitzen gave one of the coins to a neighbor to buy her bread. This neighbor was hard of hearing and misunderstood, purchasing some writing parchment instead. In response, the Rebbitzen gave her the other coin and again instructed her to buy some bread. This time the neighbor brought back some ink with a quill. When the Rebbitzen told her saintly husband the strange sequence of events, he responded, "Obviously, in Heaven, they want me to write," and he commenced to produce *seforim*.

The Chazon Ish goes one step further. He states that when one publishes a *sefer*, it is like leading a son to the chupah. This is probably because one is taking the "offspring" of his mind and sending it out to the world, as a father does when marrying off a son. Bearing this awesome comparison in mind, it behooves the writer to express even more heartfelt thanks to Hashem realizing that this milestone is tantamount to marrying off a child! Just like the marriage of a child is the beginning of many more simchos such as grandchildren, etc., so, too, it is my hope that this *sefer* will be a springboard to generate further speculation and Torah discussions on these topics, and lead to yet more *kavod Shamayim*!

III. Is a *Shechiyanu* warranted?

When we see the kinds of accomplishments that publishing a *sefer* is compared to, it is no wonder that poskim debate the propriety of making a *shechiyanu* to thank Hashem for this accomplishment. In the *hakdamah* to the *sefer Chayei Moshe* [cheilek 1], the author cites the Mor Uktzia and the Minchos Yitzchok, who indeed hold that a *shechiyanu* should be made. The Machane Chaim believed that one should say, "*Boruch atah Hashem, lamdeini chukecha Shechiyanu v'kiyamonu,*" etc. The *Chemdas Shlomo* and the *Ginzei Yosef* [responsa] write that one should eat a new fruit or put on a new garment, and then make the *bracha* keeping the *sefer* in mind as well.

(As an aside, this method of combining several subjects in the same *bracha* should be regularly incorporated when we make a standard *bracha* of "*Shehakol nihye bid'varo*—That everything comes about through His word." Thus, whether one is sitting under the umbrella at a favorite outdoor table, or around the pool in the summer basking in the sun and delighting in one's vacation time, one should have in mind the umbrella, the table and the sunshine, when making a *bracha* on the lemonade or the ice cream. Likewise, after finishing an invigorating game of tennis or basketball while grabbing a much-needed drink, one should incorporate one's thanks for the ball game and good friends into the *shehakol bracha* before drinking the beverage!)

IV. Long-term Investing

Another wonderful aspect of publishing a *sefer* is the long term investment it provides to the writer. On the word *chiddush*, the *Pele Yoetz* writes *"V'limtei lei hanaah, sheyihyu sifsosav dov'vos b'kever*—It provides him (the writer) benefit, so that his lips will move even in the grave!" How marvelous! In an age replete with financial planners and investment advisers, this is long term investing at its best!

V. Encouragement for those who want to write a sefer

I would like to offer a word of encouragement to the many aspiring *mechabrim* (authors) in the *olam haTorah* (Torah academia) intimidated by the massive task of sifting the material, researching the facts, and getting one's thoughts down on paper, so that something which does not "feel" like *emes* (truth), the signature of Hashem, can be weeded out. (The Rambam says that when something is printed, a review of even a thousand times is a small number!) This feeling of intimidation, which overwhelms us when we contemplate writing a *sefer* for the public's benefit, is understandable! The intensity of the *yetzer hara*'s efforts to thwart one from one's designs is in direct proportion to the importance of the mitzvah he's engaged with. Thus, we find that the Satan did not confront Avraham in open warfare while he was engaged in chesed. Nor did he oppose Yitzchok while he was occupied in prayer. But when Yaakov adopted a career of Torah, Samael (the angel of death) came down from heaven to wrestle with him barehanded and face to face!

The Chofetz Chaim, zt"l, explains that the Satan can tolerate chesed and even tefillah, but when someone attempts to study Torah, he declares all out war! This is also the reason why *shalom bayis* (peaceful relationships in the home) is so challenging and demands constant vigilance. Since the presence of the *Shechina* in one's home depends upon marital harmony (*"Ish v'isha—Shalom beineihem, Shechina shruya beineihem*

—For husband and wife—when they have peace between them, the Divine Presence dwells in their midst" [*Sotah* 17a]), the evil inclination diligently plants a veritable minefield to frustrate us from achieving this lofty goal.

Similarly, this also explains why parental respect, the commandment of *kibud av v'eim*, is sometimes so difficult. The thinking person might even figuratively scratch his or her head in wonderment as to why greater pains aren't taken to give attention to aging parents. Additionally, many a good yeshiva bochur or Bais Yaakov maidel are often disgusted at themselves for yelling or causing pain to a parent—something they know is wrong and so harmful to their spiritual lives! Once again, the reason for the difficulty of this mitzvah is that the evil inclination's goal is to frustrate us. The Gemara in *Masechtas Kiddushin* [31a] teaches us that if one doesn't give parents respect, Hashem declares, "It is well that I don't dwell with them!" So, as previously explained, when Hashem's presence is at stake, the *yetzer hara* presents himself in full force!

This further explains why people covet mitzvos which they have no responsibility to do. Some women, for example, might want to learn Gemara or put on tefillin. The simple reason for this is that, since they have no obligation to do so, the *yetzer hara* does not combat their pursuit. To the contrary, he is happy to distract them from the more valuable mitzvos which *they* should be doing!

This also explains the puzzling behavior of people dashing out of shul, as if in a great rush, as soon as the last amen is heard. Oddly enough many of these same people linger and find time to shmooze right in front of the shul! Consider also the habit of leaving the bathroom and touching the tap with one's hands instead of opening the faucet and rinsing them properly. These puzzling habits can more easily be understood when we uncover the *yetzer hara* lurking in the background who attempts to make activities that are mitzvos into burdensome tasks and yokes around our necks!

Keeping this in mind, it should be obvious why writing a *sefer* is so difficult to accomplish. The potential *harbotzas Torah* (Torah dissemination) is vast—with a possibility of reaching people across the globe and throughout the generations. In addition, the power of a *sefer* to encourage masses of people towards stronger *yiras* Hashem (fear of G-d) and stimulate finer behavior is so great, that the *yetzer hara* challenges us to fail from beginning to end! Indeed, in the preface to his great work, the *Meam Loez,* Rav Yaakov Culi writes that he girded himself to persevere in the writing of his (spectacular!) *sefer*, since everyone has an enemy, namely, the *yetzer hara*.

I personally can testify concerning the many setbacks I had in writing this *sefer*. There were many distractions which pulled me from this work (primarily worked on during summer months). These included technical complications such as computer malfunctions, power surges, etc., the difficulty of getting back into it after a long hiatus, and the naturally hard time I had in getting myself to sit down and write. I am sharing this with you to encourage you to be persistent in your desire to write a *sefer*. The rewards are great—and, as the Gemara says, in the way that a man wants to go, Hashem will help him [*Makos* 10b]. Rav Avigdor Miller, *shlit"a,* once instructed me that *seforim* are (usually) not written by people who lock themselves in a room for a few weeks. Instead, *seforim* are completed over time—after work or before work. He advised me to fix a time to write consistently every day, and after a while this would add up and bear fruit!

VI. Gratitude to One's Parents

After thanking Hashem, I would like to express warm

and intense thanks to my wonderful mother (the Gemara in *Kiddushin* [30b] equates the honor of one's parents to the honor of Hashem!), Mrs. Agnes (Esther Fradyl) Weiss-Goldman, may she live a healthy and happy 120 years. In *Mishlei* it states "*Yitzpon l'yesharim sushiya*—Hidden for the upright is *sushiya*" [2:7]. The Medrash [*Mishlei* 2:4] relates that Rabbi Elazar asked Rabbi Yehoshua the meaning of this verse. Rabbi Yehoshua explained that as soon as an embryo is formed in a mother's womb, all the Torah that he or she will learn is taught to him or her. This posuk teaches us that Torah (*sushiya*) is stored (*yitzpon*) for the upright. Similarly, the Chasam Sofer asks a question concerning the song at the end of the Haggadah, *Echad Mi Yodeah*: Why, when we get to the stanza who knows nine, do we answer, "The nine months of gestation"?! Is nine months of morning sickness, nausea, shortness of breath, heartburn, etc. on the same level as "One is Hashem, Two are the *Luchos*, Three are the *Avos*, Four are the *Imahos*, Five are the Chumashim etc.?!" Furthermore, since nine months of gestation is common to all humans it would seem that the explanation for the number nine is the only one that is not reserved exclusively for the Jewish nation. (This is odd since the thrust of the seder is a discussion regarding the anniversary of the birth of the Jewish people.) The Chasam Sofer answers that nine months are special since it is then that the *Malach* (Angel) teaches a Jewish child the entire Torah! Thus, we are taught "*Mayim amukim eitzah b'lev ish*—Deep waters are the council in the heart of man!" [*Mishlei* 20:5]. Thus, I have my wonderful mother to thank for all the insights I now share with you, for it was within her womb that the *Malach* first taught me these *chiddushim*!

In the finest tradition of Rochel Imeinu's credo "*Im ayin, meisah anochi*—If you don't award me (children), I am like one who is dead" [*Bereishis* 30:1], my mother's entire life

revolves around her children! We are her ambition and fulfillment. Thank you Mom for all the years of devotion and love!
May Hashem bless you together with your very, very special
husband, "Saba" Yaakov Goldman, to a long life of great health,
happiness, and everything wonderful.

My father, Heshy (Herman, Aaron Tzvi) Weiss, zt"l,
was a survivor of Auschwitz. I vividly remember Rav Moshe
Feinstein, zt"l, according him great honor. When I questioned
Rav Moshe concerning this, he told me not to take lightly the
fact that my father went through such horrors and still raised
a dynasty so devoted to Torah. (My younger brother, R. Yosef
Asher, subsequently married Rav Moshe's granddaughter.) My
father (together with my mother) gave us a great upbringing.
My career in *harbotzas* Torah was jump-started when my
father took us to hotels on Pesach and Succos, and convinced
the management to allow us to give the major *drashas* and
shiurim. This strengthened our confidence and gave us
remarkable experiences.

My father, of blessed memory, gave us another great gift.
He demonstrated unabashed and unbridled pride at all our
accomplishments. This made us strive to please him! I remember the many times I looked to him after concluding a shiur.
How I felt a surge of joy when I saw his beaming face! As parents and grandparents, this teaches us a great lesson—how
powerful a motivation it is for children when you show them
how thrilled you are at their accomplishments. This is a far cry
from the sad behavior of many parents nowadays who are either
too busy or simply disinterested in their children's development.
How I must thank my father (again with my mom's instigation)
for putting me through ten years in the Yeshiva of Staten Island,
where I gained most of my spiritual development! May his
neshama have a great aliyah in Gan Eden, and may he continue to intercede on our behalf to Hashem *Yisborach*!

VII. Gratitude to Rav Moshe, zt"l

The Gemara teaches us that everyone has two fathers: a biological father who brings him into the world, and his Rebbe who brings him into the World-to-Come. (In my case, my biological father fits in both categories since he paid for my tuition throughout my formative years allowing me the opportunity for *Olam Habah* as well!) *Boruch Hashem*, I had the great *zechus* of studying under the great Gaon and posek Hador, Harav Moshe Feinstein, zt"l. For ten years, I had the further advantage to be *meshamesh* (attend) him at yeshiva and at Camp Yeshiva Staten Island. Unfortunately, during my adolescence, I was too young to realize the encyclopedic scope or the amazing Torah abilities of my mentor to fully benefit from them on an intellectual plane. (I remember one day when Rav Moshe was especially jubilant, having just received a package from Russia containing some of his *chiddushim* (Torah novellae) on *Yerushalmi D'mai*. In my seventeen year old naiveté, I asked him if he only studied the Gemara *Yerushalmi* on those tractates that didn't have a Gemara *Bavli* (like *D'mai*). He mentioned that, when he was my age, he had already written on the *Yerushalmi Bava Kamma*, *Bava Metzia*, and *Bava Basra*!

I feel, however, that I gained immensely from my rebbe's enormous personal warmth. When he shook any man's hand, he used both his hands and embraced the man with care and warmth. His smile was genuine and he freely bestowed it on everyone. I drank from his love of shalom and his extraordinary concern for all people! Furthermore, he gave all of us who had the great privilege of observing him, a model of what true Torah *hasmada* (diligence) really means. The words of the *Navi* "*Lo yamush sefer Torah hazeh m'picha*—Let not the words of Torah be removed from your mouth" [*Yehoshua* 1:8] were brought to life when watching him. I can personally testify that he was never idle—he was always either learning or doing mitzvos! His students learned to utilize every second when we watched him learning Mishnayos while wrapping his tefillin, glancing at the parshah between aliyahs (on Shabbos), or reviewing Tanach while waiting for his car to arrive, etc. We understood, whenever we watched his total concentration while immersed in tefillah, that Torah is studied with the goal of serving Hashem. I hope and pray that I, as one of the least of his talmidim, bring him some *nachas* in Gan Eden. May he be a *meilitz yosher* for us and for all of Klal Yisroel, to whom he dedicated his life!

One of my main intentions in writing this *sefer* is to fulfill the mitzvah of *kibud av v'eim* and *kavod rabbo* (honoring one's parents and rebbe). The *Kitzur Shulchan Aruch* writes "One who wants to fulfill the mitzvah of honoring one's parents should study Torah and do good deeds—for the real honor to parents is when people say, 'Fortunate are the parents who have a son/daughter like this!'" [143:21]. The *Yesod V'shoresh Havodah* thus writes that a portion of one's intent, when doing any mitzvah, should be to fulfill the command of *kibud av v'eim* since, when doing the mitzvah, one brings honor to his parents, as the *Kitzur Shulchan Aruch* mentions. This remains true, both for one's parents and one's rebbe, even after their passing. Thus, it is my hope and wish that this *sefer*, if the reader finds it inspirational and helpful, should bring honor to both my parents and my rebbeim.

VIII. Special *HaKoras HaTov*

When discussing my rebbeim, it is fitting to show *hakoras hatov* (appreciation) to the spectacular yeshiva in which I studied all of my youth, the Yeshiva of Staten Island. The triumvirate of Rav Reuven Feinstein (present Rosh Yeshiva), Rav

Gershon Weiss (*menahel*), and Rav Chaim Mintz (*mashgiach*), created a superb environment conducive to Torah greatness and character development. By personal example and incredible devotion, they taught us the priorities of life and the Torah way to succeed. May Hashem *Yisborach* reward them with good health and *nachas* from all their talmidim.

Lovingly, I remember my wonderful in-laws. Reb Aaron Gelbtuch, zt"l, my *shver* (Reb Aaron ben Moshe), was a Kapishnitz and Boyana chosid. During his last years, we had the *zechus* to have him live with us. His devotion to our children, and his zealousness when it came to any area of shalom, was remarkable. I hope that when my daughters get married, *bezras Hashem*, I will treat my sons-in-law the way he treated me. He worked hard all his life and saved his money for his family. It is only due to his foresight and generosity that we were able to make a down payment on the house we live in today!

My mother-in-law, Mrs. Devora Gelbtuch (Devora bas Aryeh Leib), was an extraordinary woman. As a volunteer for many years in Ezras Torah, she ran many an errand for the great Rav Henkin, zt"l. Her devotion to chesed was her life. My wife, Miriam Libby, *tichya*, recounts how, as a little girl, she would go with her mother to drop off bags of clothing at poor peoples' homes. They would ring the bell and dash away so as not to embarrass the poor recipients. As a role model for her children, she has succeeded marvelously—all of them are vested with this passion of helping people. How important it is for us to exhibit good traits to our progeny! May Hashem *Yisborach* help my in-laws climb higher and higher in Gan Eden, and may they be *melitzei yosher* for our entire family!

As was already mentioned, when it comes to the mitzvah of learning Torah, the *yetzer hara* girds himself with all his strength to do battle. One of the chief strategies to combat this force is to create a *hischayvoos* (obligation) for ourselves. This is a situation which forces us to learn in order to be prepared to say a drosha, a shiur, answer a halachic query, etc. This insures that when the evil one whispers in your ear, "You're not really in the mood to learn now," you have a ready rejoinder. "Yes, but I must prepare shiur!" In yeshiva, an older bochur might make a seder with a younger colleague, for this "forces" him to prepare the material ahead in order to present it to his younger learning partner. Or one might commit oneself to saying a Mishna Yomis shiur, for this will insure that one will eventually finish Mishnayos. I owe a great amount of gratitude to the Agudas Yisroel of Staten Island Beis Eliezer. As a Rav of the shul for the past fifteen years, the *hischayvoos* that the shul has created to allow me to speak on the parshah, teach Gemara, halachah, *Navi*, discuss *Pirkei Avos*, Moadim, and literally all areas of Jewish life, has been priceless!

Although my appreciation goes out to everyone in the shul, I would like to single out several extraordinary individuals. Mr. Eliezer Furer, zt"l, (together with, *tibadel l'chaim*, Chana), who gave us, rent free, the oversized basement of their own home for fifteen years, sacrificing their personal privacy to jump-start our shul's existence. I extend my thanks also to Rabbi Moshe Frederwitzer who had the vision to start our special minyan, and who initially brought me to the shul as Rav. Thanks also to Rabbi Shmuel Leifer who, as president of our shul during the critical transition years as the shul went from a basement to a beautiful new Beis HaMedrash, demonstrated selfless dedication, Torah, *yashrus* (uprightness), and true friendship. I extend my thanks also to Mr. David Ceder and Mr. Lenny Lowenthal, who, as President and Vice-President, continue to bring our shul to new heights of *harbotzas haTorah* and all kinds of community involvement. A particularly special word of heartfelt thanks to R. Mendy and Miriam Profesorske. Mendy has literally been my right-hand man, not only in shul matters, but also in many other aspects of my family's life. May Hashem *Yisborach* bless all of us at the Agudah of Staten Island with long life, good health, much *nachas* from our children and great Torah accomplishments. May we be *zocheh* (meritorious) to go together with our distinguished Beis HaMedrash to Yerushalayim, speedily in our days!

Another wonderful *hischayvoos* which Hashem blessed me with, *bli ayin horah*, is the nightly *daf yomi* shiur which I give in the Agudah of 14th Avenue in Boro Park, Brooklyn. I wish to warmly thank all the wonderful people who have supported the shiur for the last nine years. I'd also like to particularly thank some outstanding individuals without whom the shiur would not run smoothly: Reb Aaron Finkelstein, who is the soul of operations for all my Boro Park shiurim, Yaakov Ganjian, Moshe Chaim Hutner, Moshe Metzger, Aaron Green, and Mr. Isaacs. Recently, with the help of new technologies, we have added four new 'sites' to the shiur via live video hook-up. I'd like to warmly mention Don Levitt of Fresno, California; Rabbi Berel Rothman and his congregation in Cherry Hill, New Jersey; Shmuel Rothman in Monsey, New York; and Dov Herman in Flatbush, New York. May we all be *zocheh* to finish Shas together, many times over!

Thanks also to Congregation Beis Yisroel, and my good friends Mr. Lobel and Mr. Einhorn, for supporting my weekly Chumash shiur given there for the past eight years. And warm thanks to all the marvelous people that support that shiur as well!

In the secular world there are locations well known to everyone. Most people, for instance, recognize such landmarks as the Empire State Building, the Eiffel Tower, Buckingham Palace, etc. *Lehavdil* (in distinction), there are certain places that have gained world fame in the spiritual arena for themselves. One such place is the Torah-communications-nerve-cen-

ter controlled by that great *marbitz* Torah, Rabbi Eli
Teitelbaum. Knowing that Hashem rewards us not only for what
we learn ourselves, but also for what we cause others to learn,
it is mind-boggling to consider the amount of *zechusim* that R.
Teitelbaum has collected with his worldwide Dial-a-Daf and
Dial-a-Shiur. I owe an immense debt of gratitude to him for
including me in the Dial-a-Shiur lineup, thus enabling me to be
a part of one of the most important vehicles for *harbotzas* Torah
since the giving of the Torah at Sinai. May Hashem *Yisborach*
bless him with longevity to continue his vital work for
Yiddishkeit!

Similarly, I'd like to thank Yossi Toiv for giving me the
opportunity to be *marbitz* Torah in the written media for the
last ten years. Most recently, he has also enriched me by allowing me to broadcast a Torah vort to thousands of listeners on his
exciting radio program on 1430 AM. How wonderful it is for me
to know that when I write a Torah article for him, (he has just
celebrated his 75th magazine issue), it is made available to
20,000 people and, when I speak on his various radio shows, literally tens of thousands of listeners are tuned in! Yossi, I wish
you long life to utilize your many special talents for the sake of
Klal Yisroel!

Thanks is due also to *The Jewish Press* for giving me the
opportunity to write on a weekly basis in their international
publication.

Looking back over the years, I would like to thank the
people who set in motion my start in disseminating Torah on
the radio—Dov Shurin first suggested the idea of *daf yomi* on
WNYM radio. Yitzchok Reinitz financed the first eight weeks to
get me started. Paul Trenk paid for a full season of "on the air"
Chumash; an anonymous, mysterious donor from Meadway
Avenue, somewhere in the tri-state area, mailed us envelopes
filled with traveler's checks which paid for the radio time for a

long time. Whoever you are and wherever you are, know that you helped many people learn Torah! Lastly, I'd like to thank Zev Brenner who freely aired my Torah thoughts on super-station WLIR.

Both my devotion to *daf Hayomi* and my career in Staten Island are due to a great extent to Harav Tzvi Pollack, *shlit"a*, of Staten Island, who offered me the opportunity to give the *daf yomi* in his wonderful Beis HaMedrash while I was still a bochur. In this way, I was introduced to the Staten Island community which eventually led to my position as Rav of the Agudah. Over the years, I've treasured Rav Pollack as a close friend and an experienced Rav, from whom I've learned much. May we share many years of friendship together, and may he succeed in all of his wonderful endeavors!

Speaking of good friends, I would like to take a moment to show appreciation to my wonderful *chaver* (friend), Rabbi Dr. Yitzchok Kurtzer. The Mishna advises us *"K'nei l'cha chaver*—Purchase for yourself a friend"* [*Pirkei Avos* 1:6]. If I paid millions of dollars, I couldn't encounter a better friend. Thank you, Yitzy, for all the medical advice you've given us over the years, for the joy of discussing Torah with you, and for the continual sharing in each other's happiness! May we continue to share good things with each other until the coming of Mashiach!

A special word of thanks to Yeshiva Sara Schnierer (Rabbi Meisels), (Tiferes) Kesser Bais Yaakov (Rabbi Balkany), Machon Bais Yaakov Seminary (Rebbitzen Wolpin), and most recently Bais Yaakov L'Banos of Manhattan (Rebbitzen Assaf) for giving me the experience and opportunity for over a decade to prepare young women for marriage and motherhood.

My ability to devote myself to the study of Hashem's Torah is largely due to all the wonderful families who have been subscribing to my weekly tapes (some for over a dozen years now). Those who have bought my tapes have enabled me to live a life of Torah dedication. My appreciation to these loyal listeners is boundless! May we continue to share Torah together in good health until the coming of Mashiach speedily in our days!

As this *sefer* becomes reality, I offer my warm thanks and appreciation to my good friend and talmid, Shelley Zeitlin. Without his continual encouragement and editorial help, this work would never be enjoyed by the public. I also thank him for setting up video hook-ups, disseminating tapes, etc. May Hashem bless him with a great shidduch and everything wonderful!

I'd like to thank Abie Sprei and his family for helping me substantially fund the editing costs of this *sefer*. He also helped by purchasing another tape duplicating machine as well as numerous other benefits he's so generously given to us over the years!

A warm expression of thanks to Aryeh Mezei of Judaica Press for warmly embracing me into his world of publishing, and handling me with incredible friendliness and dedication. A special thanks also to Bonnie Goldman for her editorial expertise and Zisi Berkowitz for designing and formatting this project with unusual alacrity. Thanks also to Barbara Weinblatt, Yehudis Friedman and Moshe Ibsen for their proofreading. I fondly remember Aryeh's father-in-law, Yaakov Dovid (Jack) Goldman, zt"l, of Otzar Hasefarim and Judaica Press. May his memory be uplifted through this work.

It is fitting to voice appreciation last to my life's mate, Miriam Libby, *tichya*, not only because of the Talmudic adage *achron achron chaviv* (loosely translated as "save the best for last"), but, also, because my dear wife is literally associated with, in one way or another, all of these acknowledgments. It was my wife who accompanied me, during our newlywed years to WNYM when I gave the *daf yomi* on the air—at the inhumane hour of 1 A.M. It is she who is constantly quieting the household, telling them that Totty is taping for Dial-a-Shiur. It is she who allows me to give a shiur in Brooklyn every night, which means that I never get home before midnight! Living in Staten Island was a great sacrifice for her initially, since it was a dramatic change from the busy city bustle she was accustomed to growing up on Manhattan's Lower East Side. The life of a shul Rebbitzen is one of self sacrifice—living in the "fish-bowl" of the Rabbinate can be exceptionally trying. Furthermore, it tends to make normal social interaction with one's neighbors awkward.

I am deeply grateful to Miriam Libby, *tichya*, for putting up with such a lifestyle! Much of our recreation time together has been spent duplicating tapes, writing, labeling, stamping and sealing our Torah Tapes envelopes. Over the fifteen years that we have been, *boruch Hashem*, married she has helped me mail out more than a quarter of a million tapes to people all over the globe. She has orchestrated shiurim for me in hotels, bungalow colonies, camps, and shuls and schools around the country. Warm thanks are due to her as well for always being home for our children, from the early morning bus stops to the late night homework and bath times, and for revolving her life around my frantic schedule and crazy hours!

May Hashem *Yisborach* bless us together, that we should have good health, prosperity, and happiness to raise our wonderful children in the *derech* Hashem, and may we together celebrate the weddings of our grandchildren, *bezras* Hashem *Yisborach*!

Moshe Meir Weiss

3 Av 5758 (on the *yartzheit* of my beloved father,

R' Ahron Tzvi ben R' Meir, zt"l, of blessed memory)

To Write...Or Not To Write

I. Humility

Before any *mechaber seforim* even sits down to write they have to first grapple with the warnings of the saintly Chasam Sofer, zt"l. He forcefully cautioned any would-be writer [*Orach Chaim* 208] that if self-aggrandizement is among the motives for his writing, he renders himself vulnerable to the curse in *Pirkei Avos* [1:13], *"N'gid shmei avad shmei*—One who attempts to enlarge his name, his name will perish."* Furthermore, the Chasam Sofer says, an author with fame as the objective transgresses the biblical prohibition against writing down the oral law. This prohibition was waived only because, *"Eis la'asos L'Hashem heifeiru Sorosecha*— When it is the time to do for the Lord, we may 'annul' the Torah" [*Tehillim* 119]. Obviously this allowance was given only if it satisfies the demands of the verse, namely: To do for the Lord. Thus, the Chasam Sofer concludes, if there are selfish motivations, the biblical prohibition of not recording the oral law returns in full force!

In the preface to *Moadim Uzemanim*, Reb Moshe Shternbuch writes that aspiring authors are filled with fear when they hear these words. It seems to slam the door on any-one who is considering writing anything. However, writers of English books are spared one of the aforementioned problems since the Rama states that the prohibition of recording the oral law does not apply to any language other than Hebrew [respon-sa 34]. To address even the appearance that they were seeking glory, many saintly authors chose to have their works published only after they died, in order to avoid any hint of such possible motivation.

However, the great Chida writes that having your book or books published post mortem can lead to problems. It's bet-ter for authors to supervise their publication to guarantee that everything reflects the opinion of the author.

The writer of an anthology avoids these problems. In his preface to the Tur on Chumash, R' Yaakov ben R' Asher points out (with incredible humility), "Let no one judge me with disfa-vor by thinking that I wrote this to magnify my name, for all I have done was to anthologize...." In fact, the Shelah HaKodosh praises the *melakeit* (writer of an anthology) comparing an anthologist to a bee who collects material from everywhere in order to produce scrumptious honey. To this, he contrasts the spider, who weaves his web all from himself and produces a flimsy and fleeting product!) Thus, those who publish an origi-nal work—not an anthology—still must come to grips with the Chasam Sofer's dire warnings.

II. Anonymity?

One might justifiably wonder, "Why not publish a *sefer*

anonymously and avoid any hint of self-aggrandizement?!" Indeed, the *Yeitev Lev*, written by the saintly Sigiter Rav, zt"l, was published anonymously. In his book *Sefer Chasidism*, Rav Yehuda HaChasid writes that the early sages wrote their *seforim* anonymously [367]. As examples, he cites the *Mechilta, Toras Kohanim* and *Seder Olam* (the latter attributed to the Tanna, Rabbi Yose ben Chalafta) all "published" without their author's names. The simple answer would seem to be that the reader should be apprised of an author's identity in order to determine if he is a G-d-fearing Jew whose writings are worthwhile and proper to study. My good friend, Mr. Hy Goldcrantz, rejected this answer, suggesting that prefacing a reliable *haskama* (approbation) to the *sefer* would negate this fear without forcing the author to reveal his identity.

The probable reason for publicizing one's authorship is to enable people to fulfill the dictum of, *"Kol haomer davar b'sheim omroe meivi geulah l'olam—*Whoever repeats something in the name of the author, brings redemption to the world" [*Avos* 6:6]. In the preface to his monumental work, *Ben Yehoyada*, the Ben Ish Chai, zt"l, writes that he is *mevatel* (cancels) any reason for writing his *sefer* other than doing so for the sake of Heaven. Yet he then requests that everyone pay particular attention, when repeating his thoughts, to quote them in his name! At first this sounds contradictory! If he has no selfish motivation, why insist that his name be mentioned whenever his work is quoted? But now we understand from the verse in *Avos* that one reason for this is to ensure the speedy arrival of the redemption.

Still we may counter—couldn't we satisfy the dictum in *Avos* merely by mentioning the title of the work without the author's name? To answer this I'd like to suggest that to bring the redemption, I think one must actually mention the person's name. To hasten our redemption, our deeds must resemble the initial incident that teaches us this concept. This decisive event took place in the Megillah, where Esther, in the name of Mordechai, told about Bigsan and Seresh. This action brought about the salvation of the Jewish people.

In his preface to *Masechtas Megillah*, the *Sifsei Chachomim* writes that the Megillah was named *Megillas Esther* in order to automatically generate our fulfillment of this dictum concerning redemption, since every time we mention that something is stated in *Megillas Esther*, the title includes the author's name. Thus it is clear that the *Sifsei Chachomim* believes that the **author's** name must be mentioned to fulfill this obligation.

III. Bringing Honor to Others

Another reason for proclaiming authorship may be to bring deserved honor to one's wife, who most certainly has sacrificed, and more likely greatly assisted, in the writing of the *sefer*. That this is a worthy motivation can be deduced from the following story. Once Rav Yaakov Kaminetsky, zt"l, and Rav Shneur Kotler, zt"l, were entering a huge gathering of people. Rav Kotler suggested they sneak in through a door near the dais to avoid the necessity that everyone stand up for them (based on a Gemara in *Kiddushin* [33a]: "*D'ee makif chayai*—A sage who takes a circuitous route will prolong his life"). Rav Kaminetsky surprised him by insisting on entering in full view, explaining, "Our wives are present, let them have the pleasure of seeing everyone stand up for us."

My wonderful friend and benefactor, Rav Shmuel Dovid Friedman (author of the *Sedei Bracha, Metzuveh Veoseh*, and other *seforim*) suggests a practical reason for not publishing a *sefer* anonymously. He relates, through his experience as a writer, that even if one tries to publish anonymously, many people will already know the author's true identity—such as the publisher, typesetter, and distributor of the book. Thus, it's inevitable that the author's name will ultimately be revealed. Therefore, attempting to remain anonymous is an exercise of false modesty best to be avoided.

Returning to the Chasam Sofer's warning (that one who writes a *sefer* with the intent to magnify his name endangers himself), I once had the privilege of speaking privately with Rav Shimon Schwab, zt"l, at an Agudah Convention. He asked me, "How is it possible for a Rav, or a maggid shiur, to give a brilliant shiur totally *l'sheim Shamayim* (for the sake of Heaven)? Doesn't he bask in the admiration of his disciples and colleagues at his wisdom and cleverness?!" He answered that the teachers have to hope that, among the students, there are some who are learning Torah *lishma* (for its own sake) and we will then share in their merit, since we are generating their pure learning. (Perhaps this is a novel interpretation of the Gemara in *Taanis* [7a], *"Um'talmidei yoser m'ku'elom*—I derive more benefit from my disciples than from anyone else!") Similarly, I'd like to apply the words of Rav Schwab here. The writer of a *sefer* hopes that his words will generate, over the ages and across the oceans, many hours of pure learning. This is his license and saving grace for the allowance to print his *sefer*!

Furthermore, we find in the *Even Shlomo* on the Ramban [siman 42] and the *Afraksta D'anya* [siman 2] that there is no prohibition concerning writing a *sefer*, even if done with ulterior motives. To the author, we apply the Talmudic adage, *"M'toch shelo lishma ba lishma*—Learning of Torah even without pure intent eventually leads to pure learning!" [*Pesachim* 50b]. This, of course, is with the proviso that it is not done *lekanteir* (to show-up someone and to belittle others). If this were case, the Medrash states, *"Noach lo shenehefcha shilyoso al panav vlo yatza lavir haolam*—It would have been better for his fetus to have been overturned in his mother's womb and not exit into the world!" [*Vayikra Rabba* 35:8]. The unusual terminology might allude to the learning taught by the Malach in the womb. In this person's case, he did not benefit from entering the world and corrupting that pure learning. It would have been best for him never to have left the womb! It is noteworthy that the Ohr HaChaim HaKodosh wrote a *sefer* on *Masechtas Brachos* called *Cheifetz Hashem*. In his preface, he asks those who learn his *sefer* to do so for the sake of heaven. He then requests that if one learns it *lekanteir* (to be contentious with others) he should remove his hands from it and desist from studying the *sefer*!

Most authors have, as part of their motivation, the lofty ideals of *harbotzas haTorah* and sanctifying Hashem's name by showing the beauty of His Torah. Therefore, even though these motives may be adulterated with selfish causes, there is a saving grace. In his *Sichos Mussar* [5633, pg. 90], Rav Chaim Shmulevitz, zt"l, cites the Talmudic teaching, *"Hadan es chaveiro l'kaf zechus, danin oso l'kaf zechus*—One who judges his fellow man favorably, Heaven will judge him favorably." Rav Shmulevitz asks, "How is it possible that Heaven should judge someone on the side of merit, allowing him the benefit of the doubt, when there is, of course, no such thing as doubt by the Almighty?" He explains that, if one does something for a variety of reasons—some praiseworthy and some selfish, Hashem will zoom in on the proper reasons—and judge him favorably. Therefore, an aspiring author who judges people favorably can hope that Hashem will focus only on the appropriate reasons for why he wrote his *sefer*!

There is yet another hurdle for a Torah educator to overcome. In *Moed Katan* [17a] and *Chagiga*, the Gemara gives the following demanding directive to students, "Rav Yochanan says, '*Im domeh harav l'malach Hashem—y'vakshu Torah m'piv; v'im lav, al y'vakshu Torah m'piv*—If your teacher is similar to an angel of G-d—seek Torah from his mouth; if he is not like an angel of G-d, do not seek Torah from his mouth.'" This is mystifying! Who could live up to such a requirement—to be a veritable angel?! Furthermore, how are we to gauge if a Rebbe is like an angel when we've never met an angel and have no idea of an angel's mindset or characteristics?

The latter question troubled the *Mishna Halachos Tinyana* in the preface of his *sefer*. The simplest approach, he said, is that the Torah teacher should manifest known angelic qualities. We know, for example, that angels live for the sake of heaven, for we say in *birchos Shema* on Shabbos morning, *"Osim beima rtzon konam*—They do with awe the will of their Creator." We also know angels embrace peace, as it goes on to say, *"V'nosnim r'shus zeh l'zeh*—They gladly give permission one to another." Torah educators, like angels who are wholly spiritual, should also avoid materialism and physical pleasures. This, however, is a tall order for any rebbe to live up to.

In the preface to his *sefer M'yam Hahalcha* [volume 1], Rav Yonah Metzger cites a Torah leader who said that the Malach mentioned by Rav Yochanan in the above Gemara is the same Malach who visited Yehoshua and berated him concerning the neglect of Torah study. You should seek Torah then from a rebbe who shows attention and diligence to the learning of Torah, as seen in this Malach's message to Yehoshua.

We can also explain this dictum in a novel manner. As mentioned, while we are in our mother's womb, a Malach teaches us the entire Torah. If we sense that the Torah our rebbe is espousing (through his pursuit of the truth, sincere dedication, and practicing what he preaches) could have come from his prenatal angel, we should seek Torah from him! One further important point: Rav Yochanan only determines who we should or should not seek Torah from. He never bans the study of Torah from one who is not angelic!

IV. Do we really need another *sefer?*

One might ask a contemporary writer, "Why clog up the system with another new *sefer*? Let people spend more time on the timeless classics of the giants of old, works written by saintly authors whose encyclopedic knowledge, depth of grasp, clarity of expression and piety of spirit astound us! After all, there isn't enough time in one lifetime to study even a portion of these important works!" True enough. Yet, contemporary responsa are needed to deal with modern-day questions not dealt with in older *seforim*. Such questions arise: Can you converse with someone on the Internet when it's Friday afternoon for you and already Shabbos for him (and he's a gentile)? Or the reliability of DNA testing in Torah halachah. These are examples of subjects which must be written about (contemporarily). Indeed, such *seforim* are the quintessential examples of *"Halomed al m'nas la'asos*—Learning to fulfill," and are a veritable kiddush Hashem (sanctification of G-d's Name). They demonstrate how eternal the Torah is! However, other *seforim* seem to be superfluous, or worse, an exercise in arrogance!

Reish Lakish relates that Hashem revealed to Moshe Rabbeinu, *"dor dor v'dorshav*—every generation and its Torah disseminators" [*Masechtas Sanhedrin* 38b]. The novelty of showing Moshe each generation's leaders (although we ascribe to the belief that *niskatnu hadoros*—every successive generation gets intellectually weaker), was the fact that each leader was knowledgeable and suited to the needs of his time, and understood the challenges, vulnerabilities, and strengths unique to his day and age. Thus, a modern writer speaks more directly to a twentieth-century audience, understanding the new challenges such as television, video, Internet, and cinema, etc. This is more direct than discussions about idolatry and sorcery, which were great challenges for Jews during other eras in history. A modern writer can help steer people to use their unique opportunities and technologies such as Dial-A-Daf and Speed Daf, tapes from Rabbi Frand and Rabbi Reisman's *Navi* shiurim, etc. So, too, a present day writer can observe the weaknesses around him—such as lack of marital happiness, pressures from the economy, ostentatious celebrations and dress—and then address them directly through the lenses of our timeless Torah!

Furthermore, each individual author has the ability to connect with people on their own wavelength! As the Gemara states, *"She'ain daatam domeh zeh lzeh vain pirtzufaihen domim zeh lzeh—No* two people think alike and no two people have the same exact facial characteristics" [*Brachos* 58a]. An American-born rabbi raised in our hedonistic society has a better chance of connecting with other American Jews. Similarly, a passionate chosid will identify more easily with works written by Chassidic masters! This, therefore, is another reason to seize the mantle of authorship: In order to reach the people who think the way we do!

The Chasam Sofer addresses this issue in *Masechtas Shabbos* [150]. He notes that, nowadays, there are a plethora of *seforim*, with everyone attempting to build an "altar" to himself! He justifies the trend though, suggesting that it was an institution of the Gaonim who observed a tendency in the populous towards forgetting the Torah. They therefore applauded the explosion of writing *seforim* as a means to promote Torah recall!

It is well known that the Maharsha explains the Talmudic dictum of *"Ashrei me'e shebah l'kaan v'talmudo b'yado—*Fortunate is he who arrives here (in *Olam Habah*) with his Talmud in his hand" [*Pesachim* 50a], to refer to one who literally wrote the Talmud with his own hand. The *Kav Hayashar* [53] homiletically explains the mishna in *Pirkei Avos* [1:6] which states, *"Knei l'cha chaver—*Acquire for yourself a friend," to be read, "Let the quill be your friend!" (The Hebrew word *knei* has two meanings: it means acquire and it also refers to a reed quill.)

In the preface to his first volume *Mevaser Tov*, Rabbi Meyer Isaacson, *shlit"a*, cites the words of Shlomo HaMelech at the end of *Koheles* (which, he adds was, according to many opinions, Shlomo HaMelech's last *sefer*). "*Asos seforim harbeh ein keitz* —Create many *seforim* beyond number." Rabbi Isaacson suggests that this statement may be interpreted as a directive to publish numerous new works and never to desist, even if we reach the point that there are more writers than readers! After all, he reminds us, we are known as the *am hasefer* (the nation of the book).

Yet another justification for today's Torah author is a revealing Gemara in which Rebbi says, "*Makom hanichu avosai l'hisgader bo*—My ancestors left me room for personal greatness" [*Chulin* 7a]. This teaches us that although we are preceded by generations of awesome Torah giants, Hashem, in His boundless Torah, left us room for personal achievement too! So when we pray, "*V'sein chelkeinu B'sorosecha*—Give us our portion in your Torah," we are asking to merit the discovery of our own unique contribution to the Torah.

The concept that Hashem gives each individual his "place" in the Torah, can explain another writer's custom. The Rokeach firmly established the custom for an author to somehow allude to his name in the naming of his *sefer*. Thus, in gematria, Rokeach is the equivalent of Elazar, which was the Rokeach's first name. This custom is probably based on something found in the Gemara, "*Maay shem 'olam etein lo'? Zeh sefer Daniel, shenikra al sh'mo*—What is the meaning (of the verse) 'a perpetual name was given to him'? This is the *sefer Daniel*—which bears his name" [*Sanhedrin* 93b]. Thus we see, it is a perpetual memory to have a *sefer* in one's own name. Furthermore, we already mentioned (from the *Sifsei Chacho-*

mim) that when a *sefer* bears the author's name, when one quotes from the *sefer* and mentions the name of the *sefer*, he fulfills the dictum of repeating something in the author's name.

However, this custom can be explained in yet another way. In his preface, the *Likutei Mariach* says there are two functions for the title of a *sefer*. The first explains the content and direction of the *sefer*. The second hints at the name of the author. I believe, therefore, if a name which describes the objective of the *sefer* also alludes to the author's name, this indicates that the Torah written within is the author's unique portion to share with the world.

On an individual level, many authors grapple with a series of gnawing doubts, such as: Do I really have anything worthwhile to offer to the public? Has the material been researched thoroughly enough? Have I covered enough angles of the subject matter? Finally, is it worth the painstaking, tedious and time consuming efforts required in order to write a *sefer*?

Let's try to deal with each of these issues. Since the Torah is *ein chaiker* (boundless), one can never really finish researching any topic completely! We should view ourselves as a building block—not a building! How many times, when preparing a chabura or shiur, have you looked in tens of *seforim* to crystallize a subject from a variety of angles?! Each of the classic works dealt with only one or two aspects of the subject! Authors can only hope that readers of their *seforim* will perhaps discover an additional kernel within, to help in their understanding of the whole Torah subject!

In the preface to his brilliant work, *Tzlach*, the saintly Rav Yechezkel Landau writes that if nothing else, by writing his book he will save readers' time. This is because he has spent many hours collecting, putting together and organizing the information which is then appealingly presented for a reader. This is encouraging (besides being incredibly humble)! If authors just locate the proper sources and present them in an orderly fashion, there is already justification for their efforts!

Rav Moshe, zt"l, writes in his preface to the *Dibros Moshe on Bava Kamma*, that each individual will be held accountable for the Torah he could have disseminated, yet did not. Thus, when one writes a *sefer*, one can reach people in Bnei Brak and Tzfas, Johannesburg and Sydney, Stamford Hill and Denver, Memphis and Miami, etc.—many places where his words would otherwise not reach. Furthermore, his *sefer* continues to be *marbitz Torah* for future generations and in, as yet, unbuilt Torah communities as well! So the tremendous effort a book takes to put together is well worth it.

Let's contrast preparing a lecture for a hundred people and toiling on a *sefer*. Even if the effort for a book is greater, an author should be enthusiastically encouraged because his efforts are for thousands of people—many of whom may cherish the author's efforts and have an opportunity to review his writings more than once!

The Chofetz Chaim, zt"l, presented this theme in a powerful way. In the third volume of the *Kol Kisvei* [*Dugma Midarchei Avi* 48], the Chofetz Chaim's son recalls the efforts he expended to help out the Jews of a certain hamlet. His saintly father explained to him that writing *seforim* produces even greater results. The Chofetz Chaim elaborated that while his son expended all his efforts on fifty families, he wrote *seforim* about the *middos* of chesed and kindliness and spread this behavior to thousands of our brethren that would be read over many generations!

We must not let the *yetzer hara* talk us out of this holy pursuit! Indeed, Rav Yehuda HaChasid in *Sefer Chasidim* cautions us that one who has Torah novellae and does not publish them is guilty of a grave sin—tantamount to withholding prophecy! Similarly, the Chida writes, one who possesses revealed Torah secrets and abstains from sharing them with others is destined to be held accountable for such an omission!

I feel a special responsibility to write because my father (of blessed memory) survived Auschwitz and the ensuing death march out of that terrifying place. My mother (may she have long years) escaped from Budapest on the last boat in 1939! I therefore qualify as a real *"ood mutzal mei'eish*—an ember saved from the fire" [*Zecharya* 3:2]. May this *sefer* be a small token of thanks to Hashem for my family's survival, and may it also serve as a memory to all our beloved ancestors who perished in the inferno of the Nazis, *yemach shemam v'zichram* (may their names be obliterated).

I would like to commit, *bli neder*, to use part of the proceeds of this *sefer* towards tzedakah, in emulation of the sage advice of the *Meam Loez* whose *sefer* met with such phenomenal success and popularity. In his preface, to the *Meam Loez*, the saintly Rav Yaakov Culi, zt"l, wrote that the proceeds of the sale of the *sefer* would be given to charity. This notified all those who bought the book that they would be fulfilling, through their purchase of the *sefer*, not only the great pursuit of learning Torah, but the holy mitzvah of tzedakah as well! Perhaps this is one of the reasons (besides the obvious excellence of the *Meam Loez*) why the *sefer* has been a perpetual hit!

Finally, I'd like to conclude with heartfelt thanks to Hashem for, *bli ayin horah*, the wonderful life He is giving me! I pray and hope (I think that's the proper order to say them!) that just as I have finished this *sefer*, I will be able to share many other *seforim* with the public and that, together with my dear wife, Miriam Libby, *tichya*, we should have only good health and be able to lovingly guide our generations to grow up in the ways of *Yirah* and Torah!

Passionate Tefillah

One of the greatest challenges of our time is our ability to pray properly. Life in urban America is not simple. There is limited time and a multitude of distractions. In our search to learn how to pray with increased intensity and meaning, we should focus on a critical verse, cited by the Gemara, *"U'lavdo b'chol l'vavchem*—Serve Hashem with all your heart" [*Devarim* 11:13]. The Gemara then asks, "What constitutes the service of the heart?" It answers, *"Hevei omer zu tefillah*—Service of the heart is prayer" [*Masechtas Taanis* 2a].

To me, this was a novelty. If I had been asked what constitutes service of the heart in Judaism, I would have answered working on one's feelings or sensitivities. The Talmud informs us otherwise. When it comes to the heart, working on our prayers is front and center!

Perhaps we can begin to understand why tefillah is so crucial from an extraordinary statement cited by Rebbe Elazar, *"Gedola tefillah m'maasim tovim*—Prayer is greater than good deeds" [*Brachos* 32b]. This is perplexing. How can you compare apples to oranges? It would be like someone exclaiming that a vacuum is better than a crock-pot, or the washing machine in more important than the refrigerator. How can you make this comparison?

Rebbe Elazar is possibly pointing out that while good deeds can be done for a vast array of ulterior motives (i.e., *quid pro quo* benefits, such as receiving a plaque at a dinner, accolades from friends and relatives, or prompting a good shidduch for your children), when one is standing in prayer, sincerely concentrating on talking to Hashem, only you and your Creator know this. Thus, in this area, prayer is a much greater barometer of one's *yiras Shamayim* (which is the essence of life) than good deeds.

Let's not kid ourselves. Proper prayer is hard work. It is aptly described as the labor of the heart, for it takes effort and discipline to focus on Hashem, Whom we cannot see in front of us. We are further challenged because we must clear from our minds a vast array of distractions when we attempt to pray.

How many times have you observed people in the synagogue reciting their prayers in bullet-like incomprehensible mumbling and mutterings while, simultaneously, their eyes are roving, taking in the goings-on in the synagogue. You wonder, "Is this what our worship is all about?" If you saw someone in the street talking to his dog in this kind of gibberish, you may think of notifying the nearest psychiatric hotline! Yet, when people talk to G-d, this type of communication seems to be the norm.

In addition to the style of the prayer, people will say their prayers, day-in and day-out for decades, without ever understanding the meaning of these prayers! If you guessed that this phenomenon must be a modern problem, you'd be wrong. It's not another example of *niskatnu hadoros*—a decline in the quality of Jews as we proceed farther away from Mt. Sinai. In fact, Dovid HaMelech addressed this same problem. He said, *"Krum zolus l'bnei adom"* [*Tehillim* 12:9], which the Gemara homiletically interprets as, *"Eilu devarim she'omdim b'rumo shel olam, u'vnei adom m'zalzalin bahen*—these [prayers] are matters that reach the very heavens, yet people neglect them" [*Masechtas Brachos* 6b].

So, too, the *Sefer Chasidim* [#315] cautions us (in advice written more than 850 years ago by Rabbi Yehuda HaChasid), to say our prayers slowly and not hastily. As an example, Rabbi Yehuda HaChasid cites the Leviim, who in their service in the Beis HaMikdash, always chanted the hymns in a slow tempo.

Perhaps I've convinced you that there may be room for improvement in the way many people pray. To figure out how to change something it helps to first dissect the problem. First there is the crucial issue of being cognizant that **when you pray you are talking to G-d**. While this may seem like a childish lesson, Rabbi Eliezer HaGadol actually teaches us this exact sentiment. *"K'she'atah mispallel, da lifnei mi atah omeid*—When you pray, know before Whom you are standing" [*Orchos Chaim*, Rabbi Eliezer HaGadol 18].

I often tell groups of children and young adults that for too many of them *bentching* is similar to eating a bowl of Cheerios. Just as when they eat their cereal there is a relationship between them and the bowl, and they are sure to eat each and every Cheerio in the bowl, so, too, in their *bentching* there is a relationship between themselves and the *bentcher* and they scrupulously should make sure to say each and every word in the *bentcher*. While I'm explaining this, groups often wait expectantly for a punch line. I don't disappoint them when I inform them that when their *bentching* is simply a relationship between themselves and their *bentcher*, they've missed out on the main point—*bentching* is not a chore to complete. It is davening and an expression of gratitude to Hashem.

One who prays *to* the siddur or *bentcher* is like an airline pilot who circles the airport runway and never takes off. The first drill for proper prayer is to work on focusing specifically on Whom you're praising, thanking, beseeching and petitioning the Almight-y while you are davening.

Our external physical actions, such as the three steps we take forward before we say our prayers, help stimulate the feeling that we are approaching Hashem. So, too, the kneeling and bowing we perform in our prayers should help foster the awareness that we are standing in front of our Maker.

You would be surprised at how your davening will improve if you simply habitually concentrate on actually talking to Hashem while you are praying.

This leads to the next issue—understanding the meaning of your prayers. Once you authentically feel that you are, in fact, talking to G-d, you may then become self-conscious or embarrassed at addressing Him with words that you simply don't understand. My wonderful uncle, Mr. Motti (Robert) Miller taught me a lesson more than 30 years ago which I still value and use. He told me, "Moshe Meir! You'll be davening three times a day every day of your life. You might as well learn all of its meaning once. This will enhance your prayers for the rest of your existence!" A simple example of this is learning the meaning of the *shir shel yom* (a different psalm for each day found in the morning services). Learn the meaning once and you will understand it each time—instead of repeating it without meaning every week for decades. My uncle also used to tell me that whatever I did, I should try to do as well as possible. Why should our standards for davening be any different?

Many times I advise mechanchim or rabbonim just out of school to focus as much of their lessons as possible on tefillah.

This is for two reasons. First, if they teach something about tefillah that makes an impression on their students, this will be incorporated every day into someone's life. Secondly, much of what we teach is forgotten because of a student's lack of review time. But when a lesson about prayer hits home, this will automatically be reviewed repeatedly in students' daily prayers, which will ensure that the lesson is cemented in their minds.

Then there's the issue of combating distractions. In the frenetic pace of our lives, the interlude of prayer sometimes affords a tempting turn-off time—an intermission when so many people can recuperate and turn their minds off and put their mouths on auto-pilot. Others use the oasis of prayer time to mull over their next presentation or sales pitch. It takes proper preparation and considerable discipline to clear one's mind of the mundane and redirect our thoughts to the One above while we talk to Hashem. This is why the *chasidim harishonim* (the ancient pious ones) used to spend a full hour in preparation before each prayer. One great tactic in the pursuit to pray properly is to work on our belief that if we succeed in proper prayer this will help us more than nearly anything else to achieve all of our daily goals. When we do something which we believe will help us reach our aims, it is easier to make sure we concentrate.

Rav Shimon advises that, *"U'kshe'atah mispallel, al taas tefilascha keva, ela rachamim v'sachanunim lifenei HaMakom* —When you pray, don't make your tefillah a mere routine" [*Pirkei Avos* 2:13] (e.g., "Oy, I didn't daven *Minchah* yet!"—or, "When will we take care of *Maariv*?"). Rather let it be with a sense of asking for mercy and beseeching the Almight-y." It is no wonder that Reb Yochanan ben Zakkai describes Rebbi Shimon [ibid. 2:8] as a *yarei cheit* (a sin-fearing person). Meaningful prayer develops in a person who has a heightened awareness of G-d's presence—which, of course, is connected to someone who also fears sin.

Human beings tend to be reactive. Typically, we seek Hashem's help only when we have a problem. However, this is the wrong approach. When Iyov's friends observed his suffering, they asked him, *"Haya'aroch shuacha shelo batzor*—Did you arrange your prayers before the troubles started?" [*Iyov* 36:19].

The ideal way to pray is in *anticipation* of troubles. Dovid HaMelech advises, *"Al zos yispallel kol chosid l'eis metzo*—For this every pious person should pray towards the time of finding" [*Tehillim* 32:6]. Dovid is teaching us to pray ahead to avoid difficulties in such areas as finding a mate or a Torah teacher and even to pray for the privilege of a proper burial. Indeed, in a critical Gemara (which, if we can emulate, already makes this *sefer* worthwhile) we are advised, *"Laolam yispallel adom shelo yechele*—A person should always pray not to become sick" [*Masechtas Shabbos* 32a]. Unfortunately, we usually take what we have for granted. Most of us only focus on what we want and what we think is missing. Proper prayer, however, trains us to ask Hashem for things that we already have—we ask Hashem to allow us to continue to live, that our kidneys will continue to function, our lungs will still operate, our bosses will continue to appreciate our work, our children will listen to us, and our spouses will love us, etc.

As the *Chovos Halevovos* so beautifully expresses it, *"Devarim she'rotze l'hasmid bah, al tiftach bah*—Things that we want to continue, let us not be sure of them." Rather, we should pray to the One above Who makes all final decisions that the basics in our life will improve and not diminish.

It's helpful to remember that while any prayer is valuable, there is no comparison between someone who prays under duress and someone who prays out of appreciation and knowledge that his or her continued success lies solely in the Hands of the One above. We proclaim this sentiment three times a day in *Ashrei*, when we say, *"Karov Hashem l'chol karov, l'kol*

asher y'kriu'hu b'emes—Hashem is close to all those that call
to Him, to all who call to Him *in truth"* [*Tehillim* 145:18].

Thus there is a special intimacy between Hashem and
those who call to Him—*not* because of trouble or duress—but
rather because they desire the closeness of spending time with
Hashem, thanking Him for their past gifts and asking Him to
give them greater happiness in the future.

There is no question that much of the passion in Judaism
finds its place in suitable prayer. However, as the Gemara
describes it, it is difficult to train our heart to communicate with
our Creator properly. Still, we should always strive to improve in
this service. It's important, however, to realize that those who
attempt a rapid, cold-turkey change in prayer habits are often
doomed to disappointment. As with anything else, gradual
change is the way to go. Before you begin to pray, direct your
focus and slowly train yourself to acknowledge that Hashem is
in front of you. Condition yourself to concentrate completely
and filter out distractions while you are talking to Him.

Don't underestimate the value of investing in prayer!
This habit can literally save your life! Dovid HaMelech states,
*"Mah betza b'domi brid'ti el shachas. Hayodcha afar?
Hayagid amitecha?*—What profit is there from my blood if I go
down to the pit. Will the earth thank You? Will it proclaim Your
truth?" [*Tehillim* 30:10]. He also states, *"Lo hameisim yaha-
lelu Y-ah, v'lo kol yordei duma. Va'anachnu nevarech Y-ah*—
The dead will not praise You, nor those that descend to silence
(the angel appointed over the dead). But we will bless You!"
[*Tehillim* 115:17-18]. Likewise, in the *tachanun* prayer, we say,
"Ki ein bamaves zechrecha bishol mi yodeh lach—There is no
mention of You by the dead. Who thanks You from the grave?"
[*Tehillim* 6:6].

Over and over, we see Dovid HaMelech asking for continued life entirely for the sake of being able to thank and praise

Hashem. We, in turn, voice the same sentiments in our prayers, in *modim d'rabonom*, when we beseech Hashem, *"Kein t'chai'einu us'kaimeinu..., al she'anachnu modim lach*—So (Hashem) please give us life and establish us..., because we give thanks to You."

And, as is wholly appropriate, let us end this essay with a sincere prayer to Hashem that He help us to learn to communicate with Him more deeply and sincerely and, in this merit, may He fulfill all of our requests for good.

Prescription
For Ruchnius

Every now and again something stops us while we are in the rush of life and we suddenly seriously begin to consider upgrading our ruchnius, i.e., our spirituality. A newly married person may desire to inaugurate his or her new life with a heightened spiritual awareness. Yet another may resolve to embark on the new year with a commitment to do better. A bochur in yeshiva may decide to *shteig* (climb) to a higher level. Middle-age may spur another person to make an improvement. Anytime someone has a stirring of *hisorerus* (an energizing feeling) to elevate him or herself spiritually, it's useful to have some guidelines.

A perfect starting point for a spiritual campaign is the first dictum of the *Kitzur Shulchan Aruch*: "*Shivisi Hashem l'negdi tamid*—We must train ourselves to realize that Hashem is always watching our every move!" This is the great talent of *yiras* Hashem, of which the *Navi* promises, "*Yiras Hashem yoseif yomim*—Awareness of Hashem will cause long life!"

[*Mishlei* 1:28].

On Shabbos night, in the song of *Aishes Chayil* we sing heartily, *"yiras Hashem hi tis'hallal*—[The woman of valor] is to be extolled for her realization of G-d" [*Mishlei* 31]. This signifies that *yiras* Hashem is the most important virtue for a Jewish wife. In fact, Moshe Rabbeinu teaches us that this is the entire purpose of our existence: *"Mah Hashem Elokecha shoel me'imcha—ki im l'yirah*—What does Hashem ask from you, but that you must fear Him" [*Devarim* 10:12]. Indeed the saintly Rabbeinu HaKodosh, writer of the Mishna, teaches in *Pirkei Avos* [2:1] that, "to avoid sin one should realize what is above him, namely, *Ayin roeh*, (an Eye that sees all)!"

How is it possible to train oneself to become more aware of this twenty-four-hour surveillance? Indeed, it is a learned art and entails plenty of conditioning. *Tehillim* teaches us, *"Reishis chochma yiras Hashem*—the beginning of wisdom is knowledge of Hashem" [111:10]. This teaches us that, like all branches of wisdom, it takes considerable study and training to master this important objective!

It is interesting to note that awareness that we are constantly being observed has parallels in our daily lives. When we drive on the thruway, for instance, we are conscious that, at any moment, our speed can be clocked by radar. The President of the United States, similarly, knows that he is being followed by cameras and that—at any given moment—his actions can be photographed or videotaped for the front pages of newspapers around the world. Surgeons in operating rooms (in many hospitals), airline pilots, stockbrokers and others are also vividly mindful that every word they utter while at work is being recorded and may be reviewed. This is the mindset that we, too, must cultivate to attain our ultimate goal of life—to realize that Hashem is watching and listening and recording for all eternity our each and every move!

Because Hashem realizes that attaining this awareness is not easy, He gave us a multitude of tools to help us attain this state of mind. In centuries past, Jewish men would wear their tefillin the entire day to remind themselves of their being "tied" to Hashem. Even nowadays, the wearing of tzitzis, reminds males that they are servants of Hashem and are expected to comply with His 613 mitzvos. The yarmulke also continually reminds us that Hashem is above us. Women do not have these handy reminders, so they should make good use of the mitzvah of mezuzah, which reminds us of Hashem day and night as we enter and depart every room.

Shabbos is also of vital help in cultivating *yiras* Hashem. Each and every week, Shabbos demonstrates that we have a boss who can ask us to completely desist from all creative labor. Indeed, Shabbos is a once-a-week refresher course that we must obey Hashem!

The Gemara cites the great Rabbi Meir who taught that the recitation of 100 blessings a day is a critical step towards acquiring awareness of Hashem [*Menochos* 43b]. Thus, it is logical if every time we take a drink or eat something, we pay particular attention to recite with sincere intent and devotion that everything in the world exists because of Hashem's command (*shehakol nihye bidvaro!*), this will cause us to think about Hashem—a huge step in the right direction.

During our prayers, we should train ourselves to retain the image in our minds that we are **really** bowing to Hashem, and not simply engaging in a regimen of exercise. Prayer is *communication* with Hashem—we are actually talking to G-d and not simply "doing" *Minchah*!

Even while in the bathroom—a room devoid even of a mezuzah—and thus a place where direct thoughts of Hashem are forbidden, there exists opportunities to sharpen our skills in *yiras* Hashem! One who is cognizant that Hashem is always looking will be careful to adhere to the laws of personal modesty even while behind the locked lavatory doors. He'll be vigilant to avoid using his right hand in his hygienic activities since that is the hand he uses to put on his tefillin. While using his left hand, he will try to avoid the middle finger since the tefillin strap is wrapped on the middle finger. One will also be careful to properly wash one's hands and not just touch the tap with them. When leaving the bathroom, in full awareness that Hashem is watching, we crown these activities with a sincere recitation of the *bracha Asher yotzar*—thanking Hashem for the marvels of our excretory system, saying the *bracha* while standing in one place instead of mumbling it while running from the bathroom!

Yiras Hashem should set the tone of our lives each day. As soon as we open our eyes, our first daily waking act should be the fervent saying of *Modeh Ani*, sincerely thanking Hashem for returning our *neshamos* to us completely invigorated and ready to go. Our final act, ending each day, should be the saying of *Shema* Yisroel in our beds—testifying to our love of Hashem and our dedication to His commands.

In addition, thrice daily, we say the prayer of *Ashrei*, which starts off with the important statement "*Ashrei yoshvei veisecha*—Fortunate is he who dwells in Your house." On one level, this means, fortunate indeed is the one who realizes that Hashem is in his or her house and that they are always under Hashem's scrutiny and observation!

The goal of attaining *yiras* Hashem is ambitious. Since it is our prime fulfillment of life, as mentioned in the *Kitzur Shulchan Aruch* and other places, we can understand that the *yetzer hara* dedicates himself full time to thwarting us from succeeding in this important art. Indeed, the *Navi* tells us, "*Im t'vakshenu kakesef...*—If we pursue *yiras* Hashem as we toil for money..." (and we know how much time and effort we invest in that)! Only then the *Navi* concludes, *"Tavin yiras Hashem*—Will we understand the fear of Hashem!" [*Mishlei* 2:4]. We must learn to make the chief inhibiting influence in our life the fact that Hashem is watching. The *Navi* Nechemia relates that he did not choose to behave like the governors before him, who heavily taxed the people. Rather, he refrained from burdening them, *"mipnay Elokim*—because he feared G-d" [*Nechemia* 5:15]. In other words, his motivation was not to gain the popularity of the people. Rather it was because he knew that Hashem was watching. Similarly, the Gemara relates that when the great Rabbi Yochanan Ben Zakkai was on his deathbed, his disciples asked him for a final blessing. He honored their request with the blessing, *"Y'hei morah Shamayim aleichem k'mora basar v'dam*—May the fear of heaven be as real to you as the fear of another human being!" [*Brachos* 38b]. As previously stated, here again we see the principle stressed that the greatest accomplishment in our life is to attain awareness of Hashem. Of all the blessings that Rabbi Yochanan could have bestowed to his beloved talmidim, he chose as his last wish that they should excel so greatly in *yiras* Hashem that they should sense Hashem's nearness in the same way they feel the proximity of their human counterparts!

On a practical level this means that, just like one might refrain from screaming at a spouse in a two-unit bungalow (bungalow walls are so thin that one may be embarrassed that the neighbors might, G-d forbid! hear the outburst), then surely one should always refrain from such behavior since Hashem is always right alongside us!

Similarly, Dovid HaMelech teaches us, *"L'chu vanim shimu li, yiras Hashem alamed'chem... n'tzor lishon'cha mei'ra ...*—Go, oh sons, listen to me, the fear of Hashem will I teach you...guard your tongue from evil...." [*Tehillim* 34:12]. We see vividly from here that the first manifestation of *yiras*

Hashem is an ability to guard one's tongue. For if one is aware that G-d is all around us listening, one will surely refrain from talking deprecatingly about others. If we find ourselves habitually discussing the other people's failings, we will know that we are sadly lacking in the single most important pursuit of our lives! In Lithuania, in the mid-nineteenth century, Rabbi Yisroel Salanter created the new entity known as the Batei Mussar, which was a place where a man would go to sharpen his awareness of Hashem. Indeed Rav Avigdor Miller, *shlit"a*, has told that he has sat for an hour just contemplating that Hashem is watching him in order to hone his awareness that there is an *Ayin roeh*—an Eye that is always watching. We, too, could utilize the quiet of the mountains, a deserted baseball field or a silent meadow and devote ourselves, single-mindedly, to focus on the fact that Hashem is always before us!

However, as in everything else in life, we should begin slowly. Perhaps we can begin by just really focusing our attention on thinking of Hashem each and every time we mention His name! [This is one of the reasons we do not *shuckle* (shake) the lulav when we say Hashem's name during Hallel. We make sure to desist from any activity which might distract us from concentrating on His holy name.] Instead of mumbling *Boruch atah Hashem* blindly and without any authentic glimmer of recognition regarding the meaning behind the words, let us pause for a moment and acknowledge Hashem in each individual word. After a while, we could work on thinking of Hashem throughout *Shemoneh Esrei* and during *Krias Shema*. Then gradually, we can devote more of our attention to concentrating on Hashem while we do His mitzvos (namely, to do them *lishma!*). This is particularly true whenever we sit in shul and with respect to the mitzvah of Torah learning. Soon, perhaps, we could also condition ourselves to reflect on Hashem whenever we see a mezuzah, or someone's tefillin or tzitzis. Progressively, with Hashem's help, we will think of Him more and more often until we achieve the ultimate achievement of, *"B'chol drachecha dei'eihu—*to acknowledge Him in all our ways" [*Mishlei* 3:7]!

The reward for such great efforts is chanted by everyone who says *Birchas HaMazon*, namely, *"yiru es Hashem k'doshav, ki ein machsor liyrei'av—*Fear Hashem, oh holy ones, for those that fear Him will not lack anything," and again we reiterate, *"V'dorshei Hashem lo yach's'ru kol tov—*And those that seek Hashem will have everything which is good!"

May it be Hashem's will that we acquire this finest of all traits, and all of the wonderful blessings that come along with it—both in this world and in the next!

Making Our Marriages Sweeter

Domestic harmony and tranquillity are without doubt one of life's deepest and most precious gifts. Imagine returning home to the warm greetings of a spouse and starting off each day with words of endearing encouragement. Imagine having someone to share in your successes, and cheer you up when you are feeling down. Imagine a partner who will exalt at your triumphs and fortify you during your losses. It's a universal desire to be married to someone who will put your needs before everyone else's and have eyes brimming with love reserved only for you. To be able to share life with such a partner is indeed an enormous blessing!

Wait, you exclaim. Why is Rabbi Weiss penning such farfetched romantic clichés and naive fantasies! Isn't it wrong to give people unrealistic expectations? Wouldn't it be better to let young couples know that it's normal to have screaming matches and disappointments? That they should expect that living together will have its ups and downs?

The truth is the latter advice is also sound. Indeed in *Tehillim* [68:8] we find *"motzee aseerim bakoshorous"* which is interpreted by the Gemara in *Sanhedrin* [22a] to refer to marriage. The Gemara elaborates that the word *bakoshorous* is a corruption of two words *bchee vsheeros* (crying and singing). I have heard from Rav Avigdor Miller, *shlit"a*, that this is a commentary on a typical marriage. *Tehillim* is teaching us that in a marriage, couples share moments both of crying and singing which is completely normal and to be expected during any long marriage. However, *Bereishis* [2:18] teaches us that Hashem created the institution of marriage to bestow upon man goodness *"lo tov heyos hadam lvado eeseh lo aizer knegdo*—it is not *good* for man to be alone. I will make him a partner."

Let's examine for a moment the term *tov* (good). This word is often used to refer to Torah, as we are taught in *Brachos* [5a], *"ain tov ela Torah*—there is no goodness but Torah". So, too, *tov* is a word often used to refer to closeness to Hashem as it states, *"ani kirvas Elokim lee tov*—to me being close to Hashem is good" [*Tehillim* 73:28]. We may conclude that just like the goodness of Torah and Hashem are indeed absolutely good, so, too, the marriage bond, referred to as *"tov,"* can also contain absolute goodness and thus be fully enjoyable. All one needs to learn is how to create and build the proper relationship. Similarly, the Gemara teaches us that a wife brings her husband goodness and blessings [*Yevamos* 63a].

So my introductory paragraph was not merely a wishful pipe dream. It can be a reality; however, it necessitates hard work and dedication from both husband and wife. To make our marriages work we have to overcome many challenges. There is, for instance, the great challenge of familiarity which dulls many marital unions.

Forty days before our creation Hashem hand-picked our spouse just for us. He knew what would make us happy. So His involvement in this relationship signifies that it is clearly feasible to achieve an existence of happiness with our life partner. This should be heartening news! Many people feel they have made a wrong choice or could have done better or got stuck with a "lemon". In today's throw-away generation when we don't fix watches and toasters but just dump them and buy a newer and better model, this mentality has rubbed off on our attitude towards marriage. Too many people react to discontent in marriage with the attitude—it's just not working so I have to find someone finer, kinder, nicer, etc. Jewish *hashkafah* teaches us that the person we have married was preordained. If we behave properly this person has the potential to be the best spouse imaginable for us. This should serve as a powerful incentive for us to figuratively roll up our sleeves and learn some nifty marriage skills which will astronomically uplift the quality of our unions!

First, I would like to offer a heartfelt prayer to Hashem that He grant me the wisdom to write ideas which can help people sweeten their marriages and improve their relationships. At the same time I would like to ask the reader to use this essay as a guide for improvement but never, never as a weapon. *Please* do not use my humble words as a spear to attack your spouse! Please don't say, "You see, Rabbi Weiss says this!" or "Why can't you be more like the person Rabbi Weiss says you should be!"

It is important to understand before you read this that no two marriages are alike. Personalities vary drastically from one couple to the next. This makes the giving of marital advice inordinately tricky. While one husband should be advised to pay more attention to his wife, another man may be counseled to give his wife more space and to stop stifling her. Similarly one spouse may crave receiving gifts while another one may prefer buying things on their own. Indeed, Rav Yaakov Kaminetsky, zt"l, [as noted in a recent biography(ArtScroll)] compared each marriage to a ship out at sea. Every ship has to cut its own path through the water and no two paths are ever exactly the same. So, too, each marital union has its own needs and trials and no two are ever quite the same. Chazal, however, have given us some general rules for successful relationships which pertain to all couples. It is these ideas which we will try to elaborate upon in this chapter.

Before we discuss helpful marital techniques and ideas I will present an array of real life problems—ones that tend to erode the magic of many marriages. Then we will attempt to outline some tips which, with Hashem's help, should help solve some of these frustrations and disturbances.

Following are a few samples of the most common complaints made by husbands and wives.

1. A wife complains that all her husband ever talks about is his business—the deals he closed, the clients he has wooed. Even when they go out to dinner, he always brings the subject around to his *parnasa.*

2. A wife complains that her husband comes home, gulps down his supper, sits down to read the newspaper, and promptly falls asleep. Although she knows he works hard, all she asks is for her husband to stay awake a little longer so that she can talk to him.

3. A husband complains that his wife is never home. She is supposed to be creating a proper home environment, yet she's always at a tzedakah tea or luncheon. He and the children eat take-out food the entire week and rarely seem to see her.

4. A husband complains that his wife does not seem to appreciate how very hard he is working to support them. All his wife seems to do is complain about why he doesn't see his children more. As soon as he comes home, the children go to sleep. Doesn't she see that he has no choice but to work so hard to bring home what they need?

5. A wife complains that after a day of diapers, car pools, dishes, doctors, etc. all she hears from her husband is how nice Mrs. Goldfarb looked at the wedding or how clean Mrs. Steingarten keeps her house.

6. A wife complains that she is afraid of her husband. He's never hit her or anything like that, but when he gets angry, he storms through the house, he bangs his fist on the table, he yells at the top of his lungs. How can she ever feel loved or return love to a person who behaves in this way?

7. A husband complains that his wife spends all of her time screaming and yelling. The house, he says, always feels tense. The children are suffering debilitating effects from all her ranting and raving.

8. A husband complains that he cannot relate to his wife. He wants to talk politics, sports and stocks, yet she is not interested in any of these topics. She would rather discuss fashion and children.

9. Often either the wife or the husband have bitterly complained that their partner is always criticizing them and finding fault. Their spouse, they say, constantly complains and never has a good word to say about them.

10. Both the husband and wife complain that they are always fighting. No matter how the conversation begins it always end up in an argument. To their great sadness nothing they do seems to stop their constant bickering and quarreling.

11. A wife complains that her husband does not give her enough money to buy decent clothing for herself and the children. Even when it comes to normal household expenses he begrudgingly gives her only the bare minimum and then demands an accounting to the very last penny.

12. A husband complains that his wife pays no attention to how hard he is working and how tight the budget is. All she does is ask for more and more.

13. A husband complains that his wife is too concerned about how she looks for others. They always miss the chupah because she goes to such great lengths to prepare. Yet at home she doesn't care about her appearance. She wears the same old unattractive robe and *tichel* for weeks on end. The wife similarly complains that the husband is dirty and pays no attention to his personal hygiene.

14. They both complain that their partner never wants to socialize or is devoid of any social skills. Also quite common is the protest that their spouse is simply not polite to or even tolerant of their friends.

15. They both complain that their partner is invariably negative, always spreading doom and gloom. The only time they can be heard giggling or laughing is when they are on the phone with others or meeting with friends.

16. One of the most bitter disappointments in a marriage is when one partner complains of the lack of affection and warmth they receive from their spouse. Comments such as "she's as cold as ice" or "he's as unfeeling as a stone" underscore deep sadness in their union.

17. Then there are the in-law problems: The wife says that he's always siding with his parents, while the husband says that she constantly puts her parents before him.

If you looked at this list and found things you could relate to, it's because these complaints are astonishingly common. But they're all solvable! With advice from the Torah and from chachomim, let's now attempt to solve these problems and discuss ways we can add greater joy and happiness to our marriages.

Having the *Will* to Change Ourselves

The first step to improving any relationship is perhaps the most difficult. It's the task of acknowledging that we are also at fault and so in order we, too—not just our partner—will have to change some of our behavior to improve our marriage. This is not easy to admit! The Gemara teaches us, "*Ain adam roeh nig'ay atzmo*—A person does not see his own faults" [*Sifri, Behaloscha* 12:12]. It's much easier to see other people's short-comings and failings. However, when it comes to our own blemishes we seem to have a blind spot. Perhaps Hashem made it this way as a safety mechanism. Our blindness to our own faults allows us to avoid walking around in a state of depression and insecurity. But, from time to time it is incumbent upon us to take a blunt look at ourselves and pierce this veil of self-protection so that we can examine our flaws and deficiencies. It is only then that we can really embark on a program of self improvement. To ferret out our vices it helps immensely to have a rebbe or a wise friend who will lovingly and gently tell us what we may be doing wrong.

How easy and painless it is to blame everything on our spouse! And how unfair and unrealistic it is! Do we really think that we are perfect and blameless? The Gemara informs us, "*kol haposail, b'mumo posail*—whoever criticizes does so with their own deficiencies!" [*Masechtas Derech Eretz* 1]. So if we take an honest look at ourselves, we may discover that the very faults we are assigning to our partners can be found within ourselves!

In general, in order to succeed in life we must be prepared to continually change and improve. This is one of the reasons why the oral law is called the Mishna. For the Hebrew letters that spell *Mishna* also spell the word *meshaneh*, which means "to change". This is because one of the major focuses of the oral law is to guide us regarding how to better ourselves.

It's important to remember that we will not be rewarded and credited much for the raw materials that Hashem gave us. If Hashem caused us to be born into an observant family and allowed us to have a fine Jewish education it's almost automatic that we will grow up keeping Shabbos and kosher, etc. Our challenge is what we do with these raw materials—how we overcome adversity and meet life's hurdles.

Sefer Chinuch [on the mitzvah of *milah*] asks why Hashem made the foreskin if we have to cut it off anyway (by circumcision). If it is considered loathsome then why would Hashem create it in the first place? He answers that this foreskin exists to make us realize that just like each man was created with a physical imperfection which needs to be removed, so too do we all have character imperfections as well. And just like we cut away this physical flaw, so, too, we must cut away our character vices. Thus this is another reminder that we are imperfect and should continually strive to refine our behavior.

Take a good look in the mirror. Ask yourself if you've improved your marriage this year compared to last year. How about over the last five years? If your answer is "there's not much that needs fixing," then you are fooling yourself. You are becoming complacent. Cruise control is not an option in the special bond of marriage. Each partner must be committed to continually work towards introducing fresh vitality and new skills into their relationship.

Try this illuminating exercise. If you are middle-aged, imagine that you've been granted the opportunity to go back in time and have a lunch date with the twenty-year younger you. How would your more idealistic younger self view who you are now? Would it be with disappointment? Embarrassment? Pride? This can be a telling barometer of how you are living up to your life's expectations.

The Gemara teaches us, *"ain davar omaid bifnai haratzon*—nothing stands in the way of a firm resolve." In English we have a similar expression, "if there's a will there's a way!" The Vilna Gaon reveals that the first word in the Torah, *"Bereishis"*, is an abbreviation for life's most important goals. Thus the "bais" stands for *bituchon*—trust in Hashem. The "raish" stands for *ratzon*—to have the correct will and resolve. The "alef" stands for *ahava*—love. The "shin" stands for *shtika*—the knowledge of when to keep silent. The "yud" stands for *yirah*—fear and awareness of Hashem. And the "tauf" stands for Torah. We see from this fundamental teaching how supremely important is the development of a sincere resolve to improve and become better.

The Sfas Emes teaches that what Hashem wants from us is that we have the will to do good. Once we've achieved this Hashem helps us do the rest. In the *sefer Sharai Moadim* [Elul] he quotes from his son-in-law that we can prove this from a famous Talmudic lesson. The Gemara teaches us, *"bederech sheadam rotzeh laleches molichin oso*—in the way a person wants to go Hashem leads him" [*Makkos* 10b]. The Sfas Emes points out that the Gemara doesn't say, "in the way a person **goes**," rather it says, "in a way a person **wants** to go!" Thus we see that mere wanting is already enough to give us Divine help to achieve our goals!

In Hebrew the word describing one's will and desire is *"ratzon"*. The letters of this word also spell the Hebrew word *"tzinor"*—which means a pipeline or conduit. This is because one who has the correct will creates for himself a pipeline which brings him help from heaven. Another anagram of *ratzon* is *notzair*—meaning, to keep, for if a person has a sincere will to improve, Hashem will keep him around and give him time to turn his life around for the better.

In marriage many of us focus on what is missing in our spouses and how we would love to have our mate do this or do that. Let's force ourselves to look at the relationship from a different angle. A man should consider that after a hundred and twenty years he will be asked by Hashem—did you fulfill the directive of *"v'simach es ishto*—to make your wifc happy"? Hashem entrusted you with a wife to care for and fulfill. Did you succeed at this? A woman should ask herself if she is living up to the Torah expectations of being an *aizer*—**a helper par excellence to her husband.** When we start viewing our marriage from this perspective and we resolve to become better at these challenges we are well on the way to tremendously upgrading our marriages!

We have to be ready to honestly analyze ourselves to ascertain if we are quick to anger, if we are ungenerous with our money or habitually curt with our responses. We have to be willing to investigate if we are affectionate enough, attentive enough, clean enough, and nice enough. We must also determine if we spend enough time with our spouses and take their needs into consideration and help them when they are down. Once we are ready to do all this, then we are demonstrating a positive and truly wonderful attitude towards making our marital bond something very special!

When we talk about introducing change in our marriage, it's important to realize a common mistake many couples make. When we try to fix something and it fails we do not attempt to fix it the same way again. Thus, for example, if a doctor gives an antibiotic and it doesn't help, he switches to a different one. Similarly, if a car mechanic attempts to fix a vehicle a certain way and he doesn't succeed, he does not try the same repair twice but looks for another way to solve the problem. Yet quite often in marriages couples argue about the same issues repeatedly for years. And then they try the same unsuccessful methods which have never worked—sometimes they repeat this for decades—trying to repair their differences and satisfy their needs. So change in the marriage can introduce refreshing vitality and remove much unhappiness even if it existed in the marriage for many many years!

The Reciprocal Nature of Marriage

Shlomo HaMelech wrote, *"Kmayim hapanim lapan-im kain laiv ha'adam l'adam*—As the face of man is reflected in a pond of water so, too, is the heart of man to man" [*Mishlei* 27:19]. The *Metzudas Dovid* on *Mishlei* explains that Shlomo is pointing out that just as when a person glances into a pond of water and sees his reflection, so too our treatment of people is reflected back at us by their behavior. *Metzudas Dovid* elaborates that if we smile at someone, they will smile back. If we show them wrath, they will respond with an angry expression.

Let's use a more contemporary analogy. When we look in the mirror we see only what we present to the mirror! We will similarly find that people's hearts respond in kind to how we treat them. This is one of the greatest lessons of marriage! How we treat our spouses will come back to us in how they treat us! Imagine for a moment how we look in the morning right after we wake up—usually we are all disheveled. If we were to look in the mirror we would probably see a frightful reflection. It would be foolish of us to shake the mirror and lament that it is a lousy mirror! It's not the mirror's fault! The mirror simply reflects what we have presented to it. So, too, although we have the tendency to blame our mates when things go wrong, let's remember it's a little like blaming the mirror! Usually our spouses are simply responding in kind to how we have been treating them.

So the golden rule is *the best way to get something is to give it!* If we feel that we are lacking affection, we should try showering our partner with affection. If we crave more attention, let's make sure we are attentive. If we pine for laughter, let's make sure we are cheerful and in good humor.

Of course, this is all much easier said than done. For

even if you've been neglected and not treated properly, you'll have to relinquish your anger to change the relationship. Although you might feel justified in not smiling at your mate or giving him or her your affection or sympathy, understand that whether you are right or wrong—what you don't give, you will not get back. Therefore, one of the great challenges of marriage is the ability to smile even when you don't feel like doing so and even when you feel your mate has behaved poorly! This is the remarkable trait mentioned by Shlomo HaMelech in *Aishes Chayil*—"*gmalashue tov vlo rah kol ymay chaiyeha*—she repays good but never bad all the days of her life!"

We may think we want to resolve all the hurt we've felt from the other person. Keep it on the back burner. Once you've built a new line of communication you'll be able to talk about it.

This is a formidable talent. To be able to give warmth to someone who is being callous to you, or to be caring to a spouse who has been neglecting you is not a natural way of reacting. This is, however, the way to succeed in ensuring that you will get a more loving response from your mate. After all, isn't that what we really want out of our marriages?

This lesson in human relationships explains why a spouse might laugh with a friend but never crack a smile with their spouse. They are merely responding to the relative moods of the person they are relating with. This can get viciously cyclical. A husband may complain that his wife is always gloomy with him. She, in turn, will respond that he's always so serious with her. It is up to us to take the initiative to jump-start the mood in a positive direction and we will then see that we will be rewarded greatly by a reciprocal change in our spouse's entire demeanor.

However, reciprocity takes time! Old habits take time to change. But once you begin to warm up, you will see a gradual thaw in your partner and the kindling of a new glow in your relationship. In the meantime, you will delight in the knowledge that with your efforts you are renewing your relationship and creating brand new magic!

Here are a few practical ways to implement this important technique:

• Ask your spouse on a Sunday, "Honey, is there anything you would really like to do today?" Such concern for your mate's happiness will be infectious and eventually reciprocated.

• Without waiting to be asked, start inquiring if your partner needs help in the kitchen or with some paper work. Such blatant consideration when done repeatedly cannot fail to elicit similar treatment from your mate.

• Find little ways to pamper your spouse. It might consist of occasionally buying her a favorite snack on the way home, or preparing a hot bath for him if he has had an especially hard day. Such special attention and considerate affection is sure to be rewarded with similar acts of tenderness by your mate!

The Bad Habit of Too Much Criticism

One of the most common complaints and sources of dissatisfaction in marriages today is the destructive tendency of partners to criticize too often and about too many things. How often does a Rav or a therapist hear from an unhappy person: "He's always criticizing me," or "She's always finding fault." Now many unwitting perpetrators of this "crime" downplay the whole issue. They exclaim, "Oh, he's just being so sensitive," or "She also tells me I'm doing things wrong" or "Stop being so thin-skinned about everything!"

Yet others aren't even aware anymore how many times each day they've been criticizing their spouse!

It is imperative to realize that this destructive habit

makes the criticized spouse's life incredibly unpleasant. A spouse who is continually chastised will feel awful. Eventually their self-esteem will be destroyed. Imagine being condemned to a life of constantly being told in detail all that you are doing wrong and having to face new complaints and a litany of all the attributes you are missing daily! This is not a pleasant prospect for anyone to have to look forward to! It can cause a mate to view his or her partner with unhappiness, edginess, and sometimes even dread. It is easy to become bitter towards your partner if you are always the brunt of reprimands and recriminations.

Let's study a hypothetical situation. Chaim returns home from work. He rings the doorbell and waits seven minutes before Sara his wife buzzes him inside. Upon entering the house he trips over toys and clothing scattered right at the entrance. He looks around him and notices that the house is littered with dirty diapers and has an unpleasant odor. While he's assimilating all this he hears his wife's voice shrilly proclaiming—"Will you come in and help me with the kids already!" He's hungry but sees no sign of supper at all. When he gets to the children his wife scowls at him and comments, "Well, it's about time you showed up!"

Chaim deals with his frustrations the only way he knows how. He begins to berate his wife for not keeping a clean house. He points out that she is never attentive to him. He reprimands her for failing at the domestic duties of cooking for her husband. He complains that she spends too much time yelling and is never soft and gentle!

Constantly being the source of her husband's scolding and derision takes a toll on hardworking Sara. She dreads her husband's next tirade. Gone is the happiness she feels from his presence. It seems to her she can never do enough to please him. She doesn't see an end in sight to this almost nightly barrage of chastisement from her mate.

When Chaim is confronted with this, his immediate response is, "Well it's all her fault! She simply isn't doing what a wife is supposed to do!" While he might be accurate in his diagnosis of his wife's marital prowess, he has handled the situation terribly. He will surely cause his wife to slowly begin to dislike him. She will find reasons to be away from the home to avoid his onslaught of insults and will prefer the company of friends over her spouse in order to be spared from his barrage of criticism. She may even begin to always invite guests to the house since her husband is too embarrassed to scold her in front of them. In the meantime, Chaim is indignant. He believes that it is his wife's behavior and not his that has instigated this entire cycle of dissatisfaction!

Now while this may be a somewhat extreme example, this scenario is not rare. Sometimes the situation is reversed and it's the husband who is not bringing home enough money, not spending time with the children, and is completely inattentive to his wife. In this case, the wife becomes the rebuker and she is the one who mounts a steady volley of complaints and recriminations. Either way, the result is a home that is a dodgeball field filled with unhappiness instead of marital tranquillity and support!

The posuk says, *"Yaish boteh kmadkoros charev oolshon chachomim marpay*—There are those who speak and it is like the piercing of a sword while the tongue of the wise is therapeutic" [*Mishlei* 12:18]. If we look at the above case of Chaim and Sara we can illustrate the meaning of this verse. Sara begins to feel stomach cramps. She goes to her internist who sends her to a gastroenterologist. He scopes her and finds that the lining of her stomach is penetrated by ulcers and lesions. How did this happen? Over the years her husband had been continuously stabbing her! Not *chas v'shalom* literally, but his constant criticism gnawed at her until it wreaked its toll. This is what is meant by the posuk when it states that there are people who speak and it's like the piercing of a sword.

We must absorb this potent lesson. Often the rebuking spouse isn't aware of how miserable he or she is making their partner. Their goal is simply to improve the relationship. Unfortunately in the process they are making their spouse's life miserable!

So here are some guidelines and ideas to break the criticism addiction:

• Limit yourself to a certain amount of criticism per week. If possible make a quota for each day. I once heard Rav Keller say at an Agudah Convention that a spouse should ask himself before issuing another remonstration—Did I already criticize today? (Remember, it's preferable if you don't fill your quota!)

• Conditioning yourself to criticize sparingly will make you more selective about the issues you choose to bring up. You will begin asking yourself, "Is this really worth making a fuss about and upsetting my partner? Is it weighty enough of an issue to mar the evening's mood?"

• Before you criticize, thoroughly think through the issue. Don't waste a criticism on something where your spouse may be unconvinced and show you that you have no complaint at all. In this area the mitzvah of *"b'tzedek tishpot amisecha—* judge your friend righteously" [*Vayikra* 19:14] and the rule of *"hevay dan es chaveiro lkaf zechus—*give your friend the benefit of the doubt" [*Pirkei Avos* 1:7] are very important!

• Rav Keller has also counseled that we should weigh a criticism before expressing it and judge its eventual success or failure. For if there's little chance for it to be heeded, there's no reason to bring it up.

• Be careful about *what* you criticize. Remember—if you rebuke your partner over something, you are setting a standard for yourself that you yourself will never act that way! Thus, before chastising your spouse about making a promise to the children that he might not keep, make sure that you never do that yourself. Otherwise you are being hypocritical, and hypocrisy and criticism make for a nasty combination!

• *Never* ever criticize your partner in front of the children, his or her parents, your parents, or in the presence of other relatives or friends!

• When criticizing don't ever compare your spouse to someone else. Such declarations like, "Why can't you be more like your sister," or "Now you're acting just like your father!" are counterproductive! This includes even such comments as, "why can't you be as nice to me as you are to your friend!" or "I wish you would get as excited to talk with me as you are with so and so." Although you may think these comments are accurate assessments of reality, they are usually unsuccessful at improving the situation. More likely they will infuriate your spouse and generate a biting retort such as, "you're always watching the way I am with other people!"

• When a criticism is warranted, present it gently. When Hashem rebuked Aharon and Miriam concerning their discussion about Moshe, He said to them, "*Shimue nah dvaray—*Please listen to My words" [*Bamidbar* 12:6]. The *Sifsei Chachomim* explains that although it is clear that Hashem was "angry" with them, He still addressed them gently and used the term "please". *Sifsei Chachomim* says, "*She'eeilue hayue dvarav b'kaas lo hayue dvarv nishmaim v'lilmod kal vchomer lbasar vdam sheyihyue devarav b'nachas—*If Hashem would have spoken to them angrily His words wouldn't have been heard." And utilizing *a fortiori* we'll find that this is definitely the case when humans are doing the rebuking. In order for criticism to be absorbed they must be said with gentleness.

• Criticism and anger do not mix! If you are angry,

chances are you'll forget to be gentle! Anger can also cause your criticism to be unfair. And if your spouse is angry then it is inappropriate for you to bring up any criticism since it will have no chance to be digested in a positive manner and will probably just fuel the fires of dissent and hard feelings!

• When criticizing, it's more constructive to avoid labeling your partner! If your husband is sloppy don't call him a slob. Rather remind him to keep things neater. If the food is burnt don't call your wife a rotten cook. Instead point out that you prefer food a little less well-done!

• Avoid the terms "always" and "never!" It's deflating, disheartening and not constructive to hear from your partner that you're *never* on time or you're *always* moody!

• Make your criticism palatable. Coat it with compliments. Instead of curtly saying, "You should dress the children better," add some sweetness to your criticism and instead say, "You're always so fantastic with the kids, I'm surprised they are not dressed better."

Perhaps your spouse has criticized you repeatedly about something. Even if you feel it was handled badly, consider the message and write it down. Consider what you could do to correct it. Try purging from your behavior any repetitive habit that irritates your mate. Constantly clicking your pen, picking your nose, etc., are little habits that can be infuriating to someone who will be with you for the next seventy-five years. Remember if you make an effort to change things that annoy your partner you're sure to get reciprocal treatment! And it helps to keep in mind your goal—which is to do what you can to have a good relationship.

The Great Trait of Giving Compliments

Many of us have someone—whether it's a favorite aunt

or uncle or close friend—who we enjoy being with. Invariably it's partly because they always have nice things to say about us. It's such a pleasure to hear words of praise and be around someone who appreciates us. Wise marriage partners please their spouse with frequent words of praise and admiration.

Why is it that we tend to be so stingy with our compliments? It doesn't cost us anything to praise a well-cooked meal, a clean house, or a pretty spouse, so why are we so lethargic at giving this easy pleasure to our mate? Why do we criticize so much more naturally than we compliment?

I'd like to suggest the following psychological dynamic. When we are lacking something—the laundry isn't being taken care of, we aren't being given enough money, we feel neglected—then these problems prompt us and propel us to criticize and try to do something about the situation. If everything is functioning properly, then nothing urges us to make a comment. After all, when everything is the way it's supposed to be, nothing needs to be said!

Thus we need to train ourselves to take note when things are operating smoothly. We need to notice whether things are going well because of our mate's prowess, skill, patience, tolerance, diligence, calmness, resourcefulness, etc., and find time to frequently praise these virtues with sincerity and thankfulness. A positive reaction rewards our spouse for their efforts, pleases them and also lets them know that you appreciate all their effort and hard work!

It is because spouses tend not to recognize and appreciate all the things their partner does for them every day that husbands and wives often are more eager to do things for others than for their mates. While this seems unfair, it is often due to the fact that people crave appreciation and while they regularly can receive it from others, invariably they do not get it from their partners! Recognizing this fact of life will help us repair the situation and lavish our spouses with well-deserved recognition. Once we regularly communicate our appreciation we will quickly see that they are gladly willing to do for us above and beyond what they are willing to do for others!

It is a human failing that we take things for granted. One of the reasons we say a hundred blessings every day is to force us to recognize all the many things that Hashem does for us. Similarly, it's easy to overlook a husband's hard work to meet the family budget or a wife's unending devotion to the children. So once we've committed to improving our marriage, a good first positive step is to train ourselves to regularly mention our spouse's accomplishments. This tiny step will make a home a much happier and more enjoyable place to be.

Don't forget, your mate doesn't have to *do* anything to deserve praise. You can sometimes compliment your partner for not getting angry or not rushing you or for not fretting at your tardiness. Noticing your spouse's tolerance or self-control and saying something nice will give your spouse an incentive to continue such behavior.

The Right Way to Say I'm Sorry

If we were honest and realistic with ourselves we would acknowledge that we make plenty of mistakes. In fact, there are times when we are even inconsiderate and unfair. Occasionally we are also selfish or waspish, irritable or moody. It is important for us to learn how to fix our mistakes. The last thing we want to do is compound any errors we've made with a faulty apology.

This is true for all human relationships, but when it comes to marriage the skill of apology is critical and can improve the quality of the relationship. Couples that have not mastered this talent find that insignificant actions can mushroom into lingering bitterness. Small disagreements can erode the mood of a whole evening and sometimes can "kill" an entire weekend. When partners have not learned to make up with each other (this is the kind of "make up" which is important for men as well as women!) their mistakes can result in a cold war between them lasting sometimes for days. Not only is this destructive for their relationship, but the children can discern the uneasiness between them and it can undermine the entire serenity of the home. And unfortunately, when a couple is experiencing such animosity the *Shechina* moves a distance from the home—something we want to avoid at all costs.

Of course, the first step is to acknowledge to ourselves that we slipped up. Remember, *"V'ahavta leraiahcha kamocha* —Love others like yourself" [*Vayikra* 18:19]. Just like you want people to apologize when they have wronged you, we have to make sure that we live up to this responsibility as well. Such thoughts as, "she'll get over it," or "that was no big deal" are merely excuses! It takes strength to apologize! But it shows integrity and consideration for the other person's feelings.

However, many apologies make matters *worse*: If a spouse indignantly exclaims in a huff, "OK, I'm sorry. Now does that satisfy you?" this doesn't help diffuse the tension. Similarly, such declarations as "I said I'm sorry already. How many times do you want me to say it!" or "All you want are apologies!" or *"I'm sorry, I'm sorry, I'm sorry.* There, does that make you happy?" usually add more fuel to the fire and are generally ineffective at correcting any wrong.

So let's turn to the Torah for advice on how to wisely repair our mistakes. Fortunately it is easy to learn the correct recipe for an apology. All we have to do is to study the proper procedure for doing teshuva (repentance). Teshuva is the act of repairing the mistakes we've made in life. It is therefore a terrific model for us to utilize to correct the wrongs we perpetrate in our marriage.

The Rambam teaches that there are four steps to a proper teshuva. They are: 1) regret for what we did wrong; 2) forsaking the sin; 3) verbal confession; 4) a commitment not to do it again in the future.

Let's study the first step: regret. Often a spouse apologizes and it doesn't seem to be helping. The other spouse repeatedly brings up the issue. This is often done when someone still feels injured and doesn't feel as if the regret was sufficiently exhibited. This is critical. When we do something wrong it's important that we *show* contrition! Just saying I'm sorry and expecting it to be the magic formula to undo the harm is unrealistic and unfair! It's imperative that we take the time to truly empathize with the hurt that we have caused our spouse. Such statements as, "I can imagine how you feel. If that happened to me I know that I'd be *very* upset" are good ways to convey that you understand the pain you've inflicted.

The next step is forsaking the sin. If your mate is upset at you for being uncaring and your apology itself is without feeling then you are not departing from your mistake. Instead you are adding insult to injury!

Similarly, the fourth step of committing not to do "it" again is vital. If you apologize for screaming at your spouse in front of people, but continue do it, your apology will quickly ring hollow! For this reason, discussing with your spouse steps you plan to take to ensure that you won't let this mistake happen again is an effective way to pacify a hurt mate.

The third step is verbal confession. It is critical that when we say I'm sorry we truly *mean* it. It should *not* be said flippantly. Nor should it be said simply to get our spouse "out of our hair". On Yom Kippur we confess, "*Al chait shechataunue b'vidduy hapeh*—For the sins which we've sinned through verbal confession." This refers to the transgression of insincere confession. Apologies are absolutely not the right time for lip service!

Let's study an example. Reuvain and Chavi are sitting with several couples. Reuvain is regaling the crowd with anecdotes of what Chavi did when they were first married. Everyone roars with laughter except Chavi who fantasizes being swallowed into the ground. Of course, she pastes on an obligatory smile and forces a chuckle here and there. Inside, however, besides dying of embarrassment, she is seething at her husband for both his insensitivity and "traitorous" revelations.

On the way home Reuvain turns to Chavi and says, "Wasn't that a swell party?!" Her murderous expression hits him with shock as he realizes his blunder. It is at this moment that he can make or break the rest of the evening. If he says, "Oh, don't be such a spoil sport! You're always ruining my fun. Stop being so sensitive!" then he has blown it big time!

However, if Reuvain cherishes his wife and has mastered the art of apology he would behave as follows: "Uh, oh! I made a huge mistake! I got so carried away telling stories that I forgot to consider how you might feel about it! Ugh! I know if you did that to me I'd be upset! I'm *so* sorry! I'm sorry if I hurt and embarrassed you! *Please* forgive me! From now on, before I say anything about our personal lives to anyone else, I'll run it by you first! This way I'll be sure not to embarrass you in the future!"

Using this approach Reuvain would have successfully incorporated all four steps of teshuva. And he would acknowledge Chavi's feelings—even if he may disagree with them he would show that his intention is never to hurt her. Behaving considerately and keeping to his part of the bargain (to run it by her first) he would have a very good chance of succeeding in appeasing Chavi!

At the same time it is important that when Reuvain is sincerely apologetic Chavi soften and be forgiving . If you want your spouse to work on an honest apology then you have to make it worthwhile by accepting the apology and putting the matter behind you. If your spouse's apology is honest and caring, there is no point in holding onto the anger. After all, both partners are aiming for the same goal—a restoration of peace and harmony!

Strong relationships often have phrases used to achieve closure on a certain incident or disagreement. Such lines as, "Can we start fresh?" or "Are we friends again?" can help to close the door and get a couple past an unpleasant episode!

The Warmth Factor

A common complaint of husbands and wives is that they aren't receiving sufficient warmth from their partners. A wife will say with frustration, "He's so cold." A husband might exclaim, "I married an iceberg!" Human beings crave affection and tenderness, warmth and attention. We wither and begin to die a little inside when we lack these benefits. Therefore, wise spouses who want to create a fulfilling life for their partner will try hard to relate to their mate with cultivated caring and warmth.

Of course this is not easy! It is easy to be friendly with someone whom we see occasionally. It is effortless to greet them warmly and cheerfully. It's much harder to manufacture such emotions for someone you see all the time! It's a real challenge to be friendly and warm immediately after you wake up or after a long hard day! It's also not easy to muster up the energy to be warm on a frenetic Friday afternoon or on a long Sunday when you are bickering about what to do. And, of course, it's naive and foolish to expect a warm attitude at all times! However, if we aim to create a special relationship in our marriage we should constantly try to remind ourselves, "don't forget, this is not just anybody you are talking to! It's your life partner!"

The Torah is often compared to fire. Thus it says, "*Miymeeno aish das lamo*—from Hashem's right hand a fiery law to his people" [*Devarim* 33:2] and "*halo koh dvaraiy k'aish*—behold my words are like fire" [*Yirmiyahu* 23:27]. The Torah is analogous to fire for a mulitude of reasons. Just as fire illuminates a path, so too does the Torah show us the way to live. And just as fire burns and consumes, so too does the Torah aid us in burning out and purging the evil within us. And just as fire creates warmth and heat, so too one who absorbs the Torah will develop a character infused with warmth. It is for this reason we find that our Gedolei Torah are invariably people who have great personal warmth and caring.

So let's resolve to focus on being more caring. Let's discover and be alert to our partner's insecurities and fears—not to use it against them in a fight—but to lovingly bolster their confidence at just the right moment. Let's make sure to warmly notice and congratulate them on their successes and to be there to commiserate with them on their setbacks!

Let's be on the lookout for little things we can do to display our affection: A small note left on a hat with a wish for a wonderful day, a chocolate inserted in a coat pocket with a message that she or he is as sweet as the chocolate. Indeed, the Rambam teaches us [*Hilchos Ishus* 15:19] that we should give gifts to our wives (and in today's society where many women are earning large incomes the same responsibility applies to them as well)! He elaborates that we should give according to our financial abilities. But the giving is not enough. The Gemara teaches us in *Masechtas Kiddushin* [31a], "*Yaish maachil aviv phisyonai vyoresh Gehinnom*—There are those who give their fathers pheasant and yet inherit Gehinnom." The Gemara explains that if a son says to his father, "Eat up already old man," he has ruined the magnanimous meal with his rough tongue! So, too, if we give our spouse a gift but deliver it with a caustic comment such as, "Don't say I never give you anything!" or "Here—this is much more than you've ever done for me!" we have forfeited any loving benefit we may have been able to accomplish with the present. To emphasize the importance of the *way* we give gifts, let's turn to *Avos d'Rabbi Nosson* [13:4], where we are taught that if one bestows on someone all the presents in the world, but does so with a downcast look, it is considered as if he didn't give anything at all.

There is a huge difference between being asked to do something and offering your assistance even before anyone has asked for your help. Thus a loving husband who anticipates his wife's fatigue and offers a hand in the kitchen is displaying caring and consideration. So too a wife who proffers a helping hand at attacking some paperwork is exhibiting loving consideration. So *don't wait to be asked*! Take the initiative and offer your help! This is wonderful confirmation that you are a team and are working at being there for each other!

Try to figure out what your mate needs to hear. Some people need encouragement, others need continual appreciation. We will be able to make our spouse happy only when we properly understand what our spouse needs and wants. Again, don't make the mistake of thinking that what you need is the same as what your partner needs. Everyone has different needs and different expectations.

The Huge Importance of Greetings and Goodbyes

In *Avos d'Rabbi Nosson* [13:4] the Tana offers this crucial lesson, "*Aval hamkabail es chavairo bsaiver panim yafos maaleh alav hakasuv keilue nossan lo kol matonos shebolam*—But one who greets his friend with a smiling face is likened to one who gave him all the gifts in the world!" The Tana is pointing out a fundamental principle—a joyous greeting is a major gift to its recipient. A wife who knows how to greet her husband cheerfully and sometimes perhaps with friendly anticipation is setting the tone for a pleasant evening. Similarly a husband who returns home from a nightly lecture and makes sure to greet his wife happily and with warmth is investing in domestic tranquillity.

At least as important is how we send off a spouse in the morning. A wife who screams at her husband before he leaves to work, "Thank G-d you're leaving already! At least now I'll get a few hours of peace and quiet" is probably unaware of the havoc she may cause to her husband's day. While she may forget her comment moments later, he carries it with him throughout the workday. Thus, while he tackles the stressful challenges of irate clients or a demanding boss, in the back of his mind or eating away at his stomach lining, he remembers the morning's tirade and does not look forward to the end of the day when he is in for more abuse. On the other hand, a wife who has mastered the art of a sweet send-off (even when it wasn't necessarily a good morning) and says to her husband, "I hope you have an easy day. We'll be looking forward to seeing you home later!" has created an entirely different scenario. When her husband has a hard day, he can fortify himself with the thought—well, I'll be here only eight hours, but then I can return home to a cozy house with a loving family waiting for me. What a difference a simple good-bye can make in the mental stamina a husband has throughout the entire day. Of course, reverse this scenario if it's the wife who is leaving to work.

Learning to Accept Certain Traits of Our Partner

We tend to want perfection from our mates. We become upset if they are late, if they forget, if they don't anticipate our needs, if they are not immaculate, or if they don't execute all their responsibilities flawlessly. Yet, if we took a second to stop and think about this we would realize how unfair such expectations are! Firstly, we know that we are far from perfect ourselves. Furthermore we must keep in mind that we married a human being, not a machine, and human beings tend to mess up from time to time!

Even after we condition ourselves to give our spouse some slack, there is another important lesson here. And this principle may take time to get used to. Let's try to learn to live with some of our spouse's faults! Just like we can't change all our bad habits, neither can our partner! In strong marriages, partners have learned to live with certain deficiencies in their mates. Thus you might find a wife humorously chuckling to her husband while commenting, "What happened? You're only fifteen minutes late!?" So, too, a husband might wryly comment to his wife, "At least the house looks like everyone had lots of fun." These spouses have wisely decided not to argue or criticize their spouse in certain areas where it would simply be counterproductive! Instead they have adopted acceptance and seek change only in areas they've decided are more important. By learning to accept some relatively minor faults in their partner they will spare themselves many episodes of aggravation and attrition.

Making our Mate Number One

The Torah commands us: *"Vdavak b'ishto vhayue l'basar echad—He* shall cleave to his wife and become one with her" [*Bereishis* 2:24]. This means a man's wife should be his most important concern. So too the posuk says the woman was created to be his *aizer* (helper) throughout life. Each spouse must make it a priority to make the other feel that they are their ***most*** important concern. As mentioned previously, Rav Pam, *shlit"a,* explained that a bride walks around her groom to demonstrate that from that moment on he has become the center of her universe. So, too, in the marriage *kesuvah*, read publicly to emphasize this commitment (among others), a husband pledges to honor his wife above all others.

This attitude demands that we give priority to our partner's needs. It requires that we *never* put a friend's needs before a spouse's. It means greeting a spouse in the warmest way and saving a special phrase of endearment for your partner over all others. It means stopping everything to help a spouse (within reason!).

A great deal of marital friction is caused when a spouse feels that others are getting better treatment than they. A spouse may feel that more attention and warmth is going to a parent, a sibling, or a childhood friend. We must be diligent at showing our spouse that we hold them dearer than all others. (This is one of the primary reasons why spouses sometimes don't get along with their mate's siblings or good friends. They are jealous of the attention and treatment siblings or friends are receiving which they feel—rightly or wrongly—should be lavished more on themselves.)

Thus when being free with money, one should be freest with his wife. When cooking up a storm, one should do the most for one's husband and not forguests. When sharing news one should first share it with one's wife.

Included in this category is absolute loyalty to your partner! This means *never* divulging confidences. It also means rushing quickly and completely to your partner's defense, even if it may be on an issue which you complain about yourself!

Domestic Disputes: How to Differ Wisely

At the very end of *Hilchos Chanukah*, the Rambam teaches us "Great is peace for the entire Torah was given to make peace." Imagine that the goal of the whole Torah is to achieve peace! On the other hand, the Gemara teaches us in *Masechtas Derech Eretz* "A house that has discord is destined to be destroyed (*rachmono litzlon*).

Indeed the Hebrew word for fighting is *machlokes* which is an anagram of two words, *chailek* and *maves*, meaning a portion of death. How true this is! A home with constant fighting is a portion of death and at times can be even worse than death!

Thus our objectives for creating a Torah home should be clear. We should strive to rid our homes of habitual screaming, fighting and bickering. Rather, we should vigorously attempt to create an ambiance of cheerfulness and tranquillity for ourselves and for our children.

The *Yerushalmi* [*Brachos* 9] warns us that earthquakes occur because of *machlokes*. This is because, just like an earthquake, *machlokes* undermines the very foundations of our homes. The Gemara also say, "A house that has constant fighting is the residence of the *yetzer hara*," and according to the Gemara in *Bava Basra* [16a], the *yetzer hara* is none other than the Satan and the *Malach HaMaves* (the Angel of Death). Now, who among us wants the *Malach HaMaves* to take up permanent, or even temporary, residence in our home? We can see there are ample reasons for us to find the strength, devotion and attention to promoting harmony within our homes.

The Torah provides comfort and solutions. The Gemara describes a couple who fought with each other every Erev Shabbos. Pressures had accumulated throughout the week, and the last-minute preparations, and a myriad of mundane matters, all took their toll. The husband and wife were constantly at each other's throats. Rav Meir came and, in an attempt to infuse some *shalom bayis* into their home, he asked if he could temporarily stay with them. For several weeks Rav Meir stayed with this couple, who were both understandably honored to have this *tzadik* in their home. Throughout his visit, peace and harmony reigned. At the end, the *yetzer hara* announced that Rav Meir had evicted him from this home. This is perfect evidence that just a few weeks of peaceful living can make a dramatic difference, setting up a new pattern and transforming a situation punctuated with strife and discord into one of tranquillity.

Now, how does this look in our times and in our homes?

One spouse may view a problem as insurmountable, whereas the other spouse will deem it ridiculous. Also, many of the subjects over which couples fight, even couples married for twenty-five years or more, are repetitive. Arguments over in-laws, managing the children, climate control, economic allocations and allotments, and friendships are among the hot spots that often erupt into major disagreements.

Why are some couples more likely to fight than others? People who are idle for long stretches of time have more time to find fault. Often we find that when a spouse is occupied and feels fulfilled, he or she does not have the time or energy to obsess over problems. If the other spouse is idle, the situation can become complicated and potentially volatile. Also, petty things often cause marital discord. Examples include, clicking a pen incessantly, making an unpleasant face when asked to do something, squeezing a tube of toothpaste from the middle of the tube and other such trivial deeds.

Now, what are some steps to follow when couples finally agree to sit down, discuss a problem, and pursue solutions?

First, see if a matter is worth a dispute! How will you feel about the matter in an hour? Next, ascertain whether the time is right to discuss the matter. As mentioned previously, don't even consider reasoning with an angry spouse! Wait until both are calm and rational. You can achieve mutually beneficial results only if both of you are in a good, receptive frame of mind. Learn to figure out and articulate the real reasons you are arguing. Don't make excuses that have nothing to do with the issues at hand. Learn how to open up and deal with what is truly troubling you.

Don't use halachah as a blank check or hide behind it to suit your needs. If you have a halachic question, don't belittle your spouse or attack him or her for being less frum than you. Consult your Rav or, if you feel uncomfortable about doing so, consult another Rav anonymously.

Never "kitchen sink!" Doing so is totally detrimental and absolutely unconstructive. What does this mean? When a couple argues about one thing, and one (or both) throws in thirty years of complaints or alleged wrongdoing, they are "kitchen sinking." When you are discussing the orthodontist bill and bring in the car accident from three years ago and every other problem involving money that you can think of, you are not sticking to the subject. Resorting to such "kitchen sinking" is lethal. Don't do it!

And the tone and level of our voice does matter. Try to avoid raising your voice! So many couples say, "I am frightened of my spouse. I can't discuss things rationally—we can't have a normal conversation."

Stop and ask yourself, "Am I falling into one of the following seven traps?"

1. Am I selfish? Am I not giving in because it's ruining my plans?

In a marital disagreement, winners are losers! You may have won the argument, but you'll have to live with your spouse's unhappiness for the next few hours, days, or even weeks. Don't be selfish with your spouse.

2. Am I lazy?

The best way to deal with laziness is to ask yourself how infuriated you would be if your spouse refused to do something for you.

3. Am I stingy?

Am I not doing something, or not buying something because I'm waiting for the money market account to reach six digits, or because I want to aim for an early retirement?

4. Am I being spiteful?

Do you ever say things like, "You didn't want to go to my relative's simcha, why should I go to a simcha from your side of the family?"

5. Am I being inconsiderate? Do I care about my spouse's feelings and what is important to her or him?

Ask yourself if you often automatically answer *"no"* to your spouse as soon as a request comes out of their mouth. Correct this by committing yourself to at least ponder for a while your husband's or wife's request before categorically turning him or her down. This is a great habit to get into.

6. Am I being domineering?

This involves being boss and making the other spouse feel inferior and insignificant. This surely is not a technique for a healthy relationship.

7. Am I being articulate? Am I presenting my argument or point of view in a patient, loving way?

Always treat your spouse with understanding whenever articulating your position. Pepper statements that focus on your needs with compliments about the other person. "You look so pretty when you smile!" sounds nicer and more loving than, "I haven't seen you smile since we were dating!" (The latter comment also invites a barrage of predictable retorts such as, "Why should I smile? You never give me any reason to!")

Creating Happy Lives for Our Mate

An acute barometer of success in marriage is whether your spouse considers himself or herself contented and satisfied! Some people evade this responsibility by claiming that their mate is morose or a chronic complainer. While this can be a problem, it is our responsibility to find ways to make our spouse smile as often as possible! In fact, the Torah allows a husband to return from the ranks of war during his first year of marriage simply so he can fulfill the directive of *"v'seemach es ishto*—to make his wife *happy* [*Devarim* 24:5]." Thus we see that the critical first year of marriage sets the tone and establishes the pattern for a lifetime of bringing joy to one's wife.

This should also be a major objective for wives as well. The Gemara teaches us "One who lives without a wife lives without happiness" [*Yevamos* 62b]. This emphasizes how a wife should concentrate on making her husband's life happy. Indeed the Torah's description of a wife as an *aizer knegdo* (a helpmate) underscores how important it is for a wife to know how to give her husband joy. As an accomplished "helper" to her husband a wife should know how to cheer up her husband and create an atmosphere conducive to happiness.

So how do we achieve this goal? I'd like to suggest a drill. Take out a piece of paper and write down ten ways you can make your spouse happy (include only extra-curricular activities, not doing the laundry or paying the mortgage). If you cannot think of ten then I suggest you begin dating your spouse again, since the last time you thought about these things may have been during your courtship. You might find that talking about each other's dreams and wishes is a refreshing, invigorating, and a wonderful exercise of marital sharing. After you've drawn up your list, which might consist of things like fishing and touring, seeing Gedolim and old classmates, etc., make it your business to set out and fulfill some of these items. You will be beautifully fulfilling Hashem's desire to make your partner happy.

I heard another wise piece of advice from Rabbi Paysach

Krohn. He recommended that a couple should draw up a list of twenty things that can be done on Sunday, then each spouse should separately rate each activity according to how important each spouse considers it, numbering it from one to twenty. Thus if a husband rates a solid breakfast as a three, and his wife rates it as a seventeen they will understand that there is a gap to be bridged. Similarly if a wife lists going on day trips with the children as a one and the husband puts it at thirteen, it will be an eye opener for him concerning how important this is to his wife. This method can also be used concerning how they spend their recreational time or a weekday night, a vacation, or about anything else where they want to ascertain each other's feelings.

In general these drills underscore the importance of couples getting to know each other better—a necessary component of a successful relationship! Once a couple learns each other's differences and similarities it becomes easier to manage the relationship.

The Rambam writes that one of the responsibilities of a husband is *"vlo yihyeh atzav—he should not be sad"* [*Hilchos Ishos* 15:19]. This is an eye opener! This means a man's state of mind is not just *his* problem. His melancholy influences his wife's life and makes her life sadder. Couples should be mindful of the damage they can inflict on the quality of their partner's life by being habitually gloomy or despondent. Conversely, a spouse who radiates good cheer and a happy glow will illuminate the life of his or her mate.

With the above objective in mind, we can now view things like buying a dress for our wives from a different perspective. When a man's wife tells him the outfit she needs for several simchos or for Yom Tov is hundreds of dollars, he will visibly cringe. Mentally he may calculate how many hours he has to toil to pay for such a dress. Is this piece of taffeta or velvet worth scores of hours of hard work!? However, if one keeps in mind the long term goal of making his wife happy and having a good marriage he can view it as money well spent. The Gemara informs us that for many women *"ain simcha ela bbgadim,* etc.—one of her great sources of enjoyment is from clothing!" [*Pesachim* 109a]. Thus with his purchase, he fulfills one of his major goals in life to make his wife happy!

Similarly the Gemara [*ibid*] explains that for men *"ain simcha ela bbasar, ain simcha ela byaiyin*—joy comes from meat and wine." It is therefore wise for a wife to sharpen her cooking skills to increase her husband's happiness. Indeed the Torah teaches us that Yitzchok loved Eisav because Eisav was his personal chef. This reveals to us a secret—culinary talents can be a powerful tool to generate love. Furthermore, gastronomic prowess can enable a wife to get her husband to overlook other faults she might possess, as we witnessed in the relationship between Yitzchok and Eisav!

Handling Bad Moods

Let's face it, we all have our bad days. Whether it's a certain time of the month or being cooped up indoors too long, a particularly depressing day at work or just a succession of rainy days, there are a variety of things that can make us feel down in the dumps. How we handle our interaction with our spouse when we go through such a mood is important for the health of our relationship. When we are moody we can become curt, insensitive, snappish, irritable, and sometimes even downright nasty. Obviously this will be no fun for our partner.

Here's a good idea to avoid much of the fallout from such a situation. If you sense you are experiencing a low ebb in your mood, why not alert your spouse about it? Assure your partner (preferably *before* trouble erupts) that you are not acting in this way because of anything they've done! Explain that you are just in a bad mood or are feeling down and you're sure it will pass soon. Ask your spouse to be patient with you until the feeling passes. By handling it this way your partner will know clearly that it's not because of him or her that you're behaving in this way. By being considerate of your spouse you can convert your mate into an ally who may now solicitously try to help you to escape your doldrums!

When your partner has been moody and has said unkind and unfair things to you, this can unfortunately escalate the problem. When this happens the "victimized" partner will often want to even the score. This reaction, although it is the human one, will only prolong the unhappy imbalance that the relationship is experiencing. The correct behavior, albeit an admittedly difficult one, is to try to forget about your spouse's aberrant behavior and unfair remarks by attributing them to the existence of a foul mood. By doing this you can help greatly to restore the normal equilibrium of your marriage!

Silence is Golden

One of the most potent tools to ensure tranquillity in the home is the ability to know when to keep quiet.

When the Vilna Gaon explains how the first word in the Torah is an acronym for six of the most important pursuits of life, he points out that the letter "shin" in the word *Bereishis* stands for *shtika* (silence). What a crucial statement! He also explains that the "bais" stands for *bitachon* (trust) in Hashem and the "tauf" stands for Torah. What's astonishing is that the Gaon places silence on the same plane as these essential traits. Furthermore, he could have chosen shalom or simcha (happiness) which also begin with a "shin." Instead he chose silence!

Indeed this sentiment is voiced in *Pirkei Avos* [1:17]. Shimon the son of Rabban Gamliel relates that all his days he grew up amongst the great sages and found nothing better for the body than silence! Imagine all the lofty things he must have witnessed! Yet he teaches us that the sagacity and diplomacy to know when to remain silent was what most impressed him!

Similarly, the Gemara teaches us that a person's job in this world is to learn how to be mute (when the situation warrants it) [*Masechtas Chulin* 89a]! Equally powerful is the Gemara which teaches us that the silence is the "best medicine" [*Megillah* 18a] .

There's a well-known expression that "it takes two to tango" which means that fights and quarrels have long life only when both spouses continue to fuel them. If one has the wisdom to drop a subject, not always needing to have the last word, the home will become a much more pleasant place. Referring to the talent of silence, the Gemara relates to us that the quality of someone's pedigree would often be determined by evaluating their ability to be silent! They would watch when two people argued. The person who ceased to bicker first would be assumed to have a finer genealogy [*Masechtas Kiddushin* 71b]!

While this advice is easy to give, it sure is tough to follow! It takes a long time to condition ourselves to keep quiet even when we know we are right! However we must try to consider the effect this discipline will have on our lives. We will be much happier in the long run if we aren't constantly sparring and fighting with our life's mate!

Navigating Marital Hotspots

Marriage has its hotspots—moments when we can potentially put the peace and tranquillity of our marriage in danger. Here are some potential hazards that we should be aware of:

• In a single-income family where the husband is the

earner, the wife should be careful not to treat her husband like a cash register! She should try to become aware if she is speaking to her husband only when she needs money. Furthermore, she should search her motivation to make sure that she is not only sweet to her husband when she is trying to get something from him!

• Similarly, a husband should be careful not to treat a wife like his 24-hour maid and butler! He must remember that his wife is his queen. If he treats her like a cleaning lady then he will become the husband of a cleaning lady! Furthermore, while her domestic duties may be part of her responsibility, the greater priority and emphasis should be on her raising the family and creating the proper atmosphere in the home.

• Be careful not to give more importance to someone else's opinion over your spouse's opinion! For instance, if your wife thinks your tie is too loud and you brush it off and then your mother comments similarly and you are moved to promptly discard it, you are in effect insulting your wife's opinion!

• If you have some big news to share, make sure to divulge it to your spouse before anyone else. Much hurt is caused when a mate finds out that someone knew about some big news before they did! There is a dynamic here to be aware of. If we don't show excitement when our partner talks to us about our accomplishments, then they will prefer to share it with their friends who will be suitably impressed with their successes. Thus a wife should learn to be interested in her husband's achievements at work, and a husband should applaud his wife's attainments in the home and with the children!

• Be careful if you tend to do things on impulse. Although surprises are nice, there are times when they are not advisable and can be counterproductive—particularly in a single-income family where a wife is so dependent. If you are thinking of spending money on a trip—particularly if it's a rare occurrence—give your wife some advance notice. Anticipating an event is often as much of the joy as the event. Thus even taking a four-day vacation can have the pleasure of several weeks of anticipation. If a husband has the habit of springing things on his wife at the last minute, he is cheating his wife of the enjoyment of anticipating these outings! Furthermore, many people prefer to mentally prepare themselves for changes in routine.

• Be certain to make time for your spouse's needs. Let's look at the following example: Chaya has been wanting for the longest time for her husband to repair the living room mirror. It's really important to her and she can't lift it herself. He is always postponing it claiming he has no time. One Sunday her husband tells her he would like to go trout fishing. Like a loving spouse she sincerely wishes him to have a great time. So for the next six weeks he goes fishing. On the next available Sunday she asks him nicely if he can help with the mirror and he brusquely replies, "Will you stop with the mirror! Can't you see how busy I am!" It is at this point that Chaya might begin to wonder who's more important, her or the trout!

• A housewife should be wary of being too cavalier about spending money. Let's study another example: Leah is out shopping with her husband Chaim. They are strolling through a mall and decide to go into a Sharper Image store. Suddenly Leah gives an excited shout, "Look, honey, a talking garbage can! How nice! It says 'thank you' to the garbage collector when he picks up the garbage. Imagine the kiddush Hashem! Maybe we should buy a couple!" Chaim looks at the price tag and he sees they are selling for $175 a piece. It is at this juncture that he mentally calculates, "I make fifteen dollars an hour so that garbage can would represent more than ten hours of my life!" On the other hand, a husband should constantly be watchful that he isn't ungracious when he gives his wife money. It is sad when he clucks his tongue at his wife for buying an expensive brand of tissues while during the same shopping trip he unhesitatingly buys himself a new high tech flashlight which he will probably only use once in a blue moon!

In summation, we should all try to convert our *bayis* (home) into a *mikdash me'at* (a mini sanctuary). The gematria of *bayis* is 412 and the gematria of *mikdash* is 444. The difference between the two is 32 which happens to be the numerical value of *leiv* (heart). This is significant. If we put our hearts into making our home special we will succeed in converting it into a veritable *mikdash*! It is my sincere prayer to Hashem that this essay will help in making our marriages sweeter and more meaningful. And may we all merit having peace in our homes together with good health and wonderful happiness!

The Sin That's Too Heavy To Bear

"**H**ey! Do you think the President will dodge this one?" "How about the investments this year? Does the stock market have another good year left, or are you switching to real estate?" "What d'ya say to what happened at the Olympics?" "What's going on with those Mets? Will they ever make a decent trade?"

Does this sound familiar? Unfortunately, I'm not referring to the chatter around the swimming pool or even at the local tavern. These are the common conversation swirls found at your local shul!

Why does this happen? How sinful is it? And how can we get out of the habit? Finding out why shmoozing is prevalent in shuls is easy. The *yetzer hara* concentrates on the crucial mitzvos of life. In fact, many people neglect Torah study simply because the *yetzer hara* works overtime just on this mitzvah. For similar reasons, there is a great deal of marital discord, for the evil one pulls out all the stops to disrupt things when the existence of the *Shechina* in the home is at stake (as is the case when there's *shalom bayis*).

Tefillah is one of the three pillars of the world [*Avos* 1:2], yet the *yetzer hara* has not succeeded in stopping people from going to shul. So how does he attempt to mess up this mitzvah? By throwing in the monkey wrench of talking in shul! And, in this, he has succeeded on a global scale!

How sinful is talking in shul anyway? At first glance, it doesn't appear to be so disastrous. "After all," people say to themselves, "I work hard the whole week and yet I still spend the entire Shabbos morning in shul. I shlep myself out of bed and go for two to three hours of prayer before even eating breakfast. I even 'suffer' through the rabbi's speech and the shul president's message. So what if I chat a little and am friendly with my buddies who I see only once a week! If this is my only crime, I think I can handle it!"

Think again! It's time for some heavy-duty re-evaluating! Let's just read a stitch of halachah from *Shulchan Aruch* [124:7]. Here, by the way, we're not talking in terms of debatable minhagim. "*Lo yasiach sichas chulin b'shaah sheshliach tzibur chozar hatefilah. V'im sach, hu chotei v'gadol avono minesoh...*" In plain English, "Do not talk while the chazon is repeating the *Shemoneh Esrei*. If you do, you are a sinner, and the sin is **too heavy to bear...**" Why does the *Shulchan Aruch* emphasize that if you don't obey, you are a sinner? To dispel the notion that this talking business is just a shtick. Therefore, the *Shulchan Aruch* states bluntly, "You're a sinner!" (Ouch!) Then, the *Shulchan Aruch* borrows the term, *gadol avono minesoh*. This phrase was used by Kayin (Cain) after he murdered Hevel (Abel) and was told of his impending punishment. This phrase is deliberately used so that we will recognize that we shouldn't take the attitude, "If this is my only sin, I'll survive." The *Shulchan Aruch* proclaims, "Wrong again! This sin is too heavy to bear!"

Let's analyze for a moment the analogy to Kayin. Is the *Shulchan Aruch* comparing talking during davening to homicide! How can this be possible? We are well aware that if someone answers, *"Amen, y'hei shmei rabbah..."* with all his concentration, then Hashem tears up any evil decree written about him. (Hmm, Asher Chaim passed away from a massive heart attack..... or Chaim Yankel was in that skiing disaster! *Perhaps* they'd still be around, but their friends were always talking with them during Kaddish!)

"Don't be so melodramatic!" you may be thinking. But clearly, The Gemara teaches us, *"Kol ha'oneh amen—poschin lo sha'arei Gan Eden—Whoever* habitually answers with a meaningful amen, the doors of Paradise will swing open for him" [*Shabbos* 119b]. So when Chatzkel gets to the next world and the doors seem to be jammed, he'll rue the days he let his buddies coax him into a friendly chat during davening! This may be why Rashi [*Brachos* 5b] also equates one's tefillos to one's nefesh (as in the verse "I will pour my soul before Hashem" [*Shmuel* 1:1]). In a very substantive way, when anyone talks in shul and disturbs others, they are committing a type of homicide!

During Krias HaTorah (the Torah reading), it is even more dangerous to act without thinking. The Gemara teaches that if anyone breezes out of shul during Krias HaTorah, one is putting oneself in grave danger. As it says, *"Ozvei Hashem yich'lu—Those* who forsake Hashem will be destroyed" [*Yeshaya* 1:28]. This is interpreted by the Gemara in *Brachos* [8a] to refer to someone who walks out of shul while a Sefer Torah is open upon the bimah!

Now, imagine the fate of someone who opts to talk about the latest government or financial scandal or other such relative triviality during the reading of the parshah. Talking at this time indicates that one is flagrantly fulfilling the dreaded verse of, *"D'var Hashem baza*—Despising the words of Hashem" [*Bamidbar* 15:31], and demonstrating that he or she considers the conversation they are having more important or interesting than the parsha!

About this, the Gemara tells us that the fate is the loss of one's afterlife, G-d forbid [*Masechtas Sanhedrin* 99a]! In the laws of Kaddish [56:1], the *Mishnah Berurah* cites a scary Gemara in *Masechtas Derech Eretz*. Rav Chama once saw Eliyahu leading thousands of donkeys laden with anger and wrath for those who speak during Kaddish and Kedushah! (Anger and wrath can be metaphoric expressions for cancer, divorce, diabetes, poverty, i.e., manifestations of Divine wrath—*lo aleinu*.) Then the Gemara [*ibid.*] declares, "Whoever speaks in these places, the posuk refers to them and says, '*Lo osee karasa Yaakov*'" [*Yeshaya* 43:22], indicating that one who behaves this way does not deserve the ancestry of Yaakov!

As an aside, I believe that the first mention in the *Shulchan Aruch* of the prohibition of talking in shul is in siman 56. It is interesting that in Hebrew, this chapter [56] is "nun-vav," which phonetically can be pronounced, "noo." Oddly this is exactly the way people in shul respond when they hear people talking during davening—by saying, "noo-noo." Perhaps this is the real source of this expression, and hints that people must remember what *Shulchan Aruch* teaches in siman "nun-vav"!

In addition to all of the above issues, there's the problem that all of this conversing about politics, sports, money (not to mention *loshon hara, rechilus, letzonos*, etc.) is taking place in shul—our Mikdash Me'at, the palace of the Almighty. Shouldn't we at least exercise the same respect in the synagogue as we do in public libraries, or the civilized respectful silence one gives while watching movies in public movie houses (so I'm told). Indeed the *Aruch HaShulchan* [*Orach Chaim* 124:12] laments that our behavior in shul is a source of chilul Hashem in the eyes of non-Jews, many of whom are respectfully silent during their saying of prayers. The Ramban teaches us that Sodom was punished so horrifically not so much because of how they acted but because they had done so in Hashem's land. Had they behaved this way elsewhere, the punishment would have been different. So, too, if the Kohen Gadol ever deviated even slightly in the Holy of Holies he would lose his life in a terrifying way—all because his actions were being performed in such a holy place—the Kodesh Kedoshim. Therefore, we must understand that the crime of talking is intensely magnified when it is done in our Sanctuary!

Once we are convinced *not* to talk in shul how do we stop? First, after reviewing all the above, it's easy to acknowledge that we neither desire the title of sinner, nor do we want to lose the right to proudly carry Yaakov's name. We also have no intention of committing a sin too heavy to bear, nor of opening up ourselves to punishments of anger and wrath. We want the protections of *"Amen y'hei shmei rabbah"* and the doors of Gan Eden to swing open for us!

It may be a good idea to change from our habitual seats and sit in shul with those people who share our desire to daven with respect. I once heard from Rabbi Avigdor Miller, *shlit"a*, that this is one of the reasons why Dovid HaMelech opens the book of *Tehillim* with the lesson of *"B'moshav leitzim lo yashav*—Do not sit amongst the scoffers" [*Tehillim* 1:1], instead of with some other lofty concept such as, *"tov l'hodos l'Hashem*—it is good to praise Hashem" [*Tehillim* 92:2]. This demonstrates that the first step in a campaign of praising Hashem is to choose the right company!

We reveal a great deal about ourselves when we talk during davening. When do students talk and whisper during a lecture? Only when it's boring and they're not interested. Or when they do not respect their teacher. Otherwise, they listen with rapt attention and are annoyed by anyone who rudely distracts them. Similarly, when we talk during davening, we disclose that we really aren't interested in our tefillos!

Think about it. Make sure that you really believe that your davening makes a difference. (And if you don't, this could be the root of the problem!) To daven with meaning signifies your conviction that all your amens after *refo'aynu, baruch aleinu, shema koleinu, sim shalom*, etc., will add up and inordinately upgrade the quality of your life. If you believe all of this—then why are you bothering with idle chatter?

Before this inspires anyone to begin a crusade against others, let's remember that, *"Hamalbin p'nei chaveiro b'rabim ein lo cheilek l'Olam Habah*—One who embarrasses someone publicly loses his afterlife!" [*Bava Metzia* 59a]. Yes, the *Shulchan Aruch* does say *"v'goarim bo*—we rebuke him" [*Orach Chaim* 124:7].However, rebuking is a grave issue that should be handled with the experience of the *Moreh D'asra* and with great care. Rebuking is like walking on a tightrope. It requires delicacy and skill. Rather, let's commit ourselves to fulfilling the mitzvah of *tochacha* (admonishment) only on those who will graciously accept it from us and enlist the support of our *Moreh D'asra* for the more difficult individuals.

It is my fervent hope that we will all take a look at this issue from a different perspective. May we overcome temptations and discover ever more profound delights in our davening and increased blessings in all our endeavors!

Fifty-two Ways To Improve Our Lives

The Jewish nation has been compared to the moon which renews itself every month [*Pesikta Zutrasi, Bo* 12]. We, too, are expected to renew and improve ourselves on an ongoing basis.

The Chofetz Chaim stated that Jews should make a *cheshbon hanefesh* (a spiritual accounting) at four distinct times: 1. Every night before going to sleep; 2. Erev Shabbos before kiddush; 3. Erev Rosh Chodesh and 4. Before the New Year [*Kol Kisvei Chofetz Chaim*].

The Gemara teaches us that if you witness a Sage sinning at night, there's no point even giving it a thought the next day, for it is sure that he has already done teshuva [*Masechtas Brachos* 19a]. This is additional evidence that a wise person is someone who continually checks himself or herself and promptly rectifies mistakes.

The Medrash tells us, *"Ein v'atta ela loshon teshuva—* The word 'now' conveys repentance" [*Medrash Tehillim*

100:2]. This signifies that the enemy of self-improvement is pro-crastination. The primary way to ensure success is to train oneself to change *now* rather than later. (For a discussion regarding the urgency of not postponing teshuva, see the chapter "How to Deal with Fear" page 239.)

With Hashem's help, I have composed a short list that can be used as we work on improving ourselves. (You can add to this or put it in your own order.) While this list can be used at any time, I will point out now how a spiritual overhaul is especially appropriate for the Yomim Noraim, for Purim, and for Pesach.

I. During the Yomim Noraim

In the Yom Kippur liturgy, we say, *"Ki lo yachpotz b'mos hameis, ki im beshuv mi'dorkoh v'choya*—Hashem does not desire the death of a sinner, rather a turning from his ways so that he will live." It's interesting to note that a sudden and complete change is *not* expected. What's desired is simply as the phrase states—a "turn" towards the right direction. It's understood that change is a slow painstaking process. During the Yomim Noraim, when Hashem renders a decision on our lives, it is critical to demonstrate that we are making an earnest attempt to look deep within and improve ourselves.

The Hebrew word for year is *shana*. This word can mean *sheina* (to repeat) or *sheena* (to change). This is our challenge. We must ask ourselves: will the coming year just be a repetition of previous years? Or will we transform the next year into one of change so that we will find favor in Hashem's eyes?

Interestingly, other units of time in Hebrew also convey a message of change. *Chodesh* (month) means *l'chadeish* (to renew). *Sha'ah* (hour) can also mean to turn, as it is used in the verse, *"V'el Kayin v'el minchoso lo sha'ah*—And to Kayin and his offering, he did not turn" [*Bereishis* 4:5].

I hope that the list I've created below will help us approach the *Kisei HaKavod* (Heavenly Throne) with the correct preparation necessary to be *zocheh badin* (successful in one's judgment) and earn a year of good health, prosperity and happiness.

II. Another Side To Purim!

Many of us spend Purim creating a joyful atmosphere for our children. This is the stuff of memories, replete with *mishloach manos* for relatives and friends, gifts to the poor, and a sumptuous Purim feast surrounded by our loved ones.

This is an opportune time to introduce our families to the full spiritual meaning of Purim and create a legacy that can have a deep impact on our children.

An overlooked theme of Purim is the renewed commitment made to the Torah on Purim. In *Megillas Esther* [9:27] it states, "*Kiymu v'kiblu Hayehudim.*" This means that from a renewed sense of love the Jews re-committed themselves to the Torah on Purim [*Masechtas Megillah* 7a]. We chant loudly in unison when we read the *Megillah*: "*Layehudim haysa orah v'simcha, v'sason, v'ykar,*" The Jews, the Megillah is saying, had *orah*, which the Gemara says, signifies Torah, *simcha* is Yom Tov, *sason* is milah, and *ykar* is tefillin [*Masechtas Megillah* 16b]. As the Sfas Emes explains, we don't simply say, "*Layehudim haysa Torah...*" Rather, the code words *orah*, *simcha*, *sason*, and *ykar* are used to convey that on Purim Bnei Yisroel adopted a brand-new attitude towards these mitzvos, treating Torah as their guiding light, and tefillin as their splendor, and so on.

In addition, Chazal teach us that the awesome Day of Atonement, the holiest day of our year, is called Yom Kippurim.

This can also be read as Yom Ki-Purim, a day which is like Purim. Imagine comparing Yom Kippur to Purim! On Yom Kippur we make a solemn pledge and commitment to lead a better life and to improve how we follow the Torah and perform mitzvos. This commitment is also the soul of Purim, the spirit of *kiymu v'kiblu*, a renewed commitment to a more spiritual Jewish existence!

With this in mind, take a look at my Purim *kabbalah* (commitment) list which I hope will serve as a springboard to a dramatic renewal in our lives. Perhaps this list will inspire you to discuss specific issues with your family. You may even discover within this list a few areas to jump-start some life-enhancing pledges (*bli neder*) this coming Purim.

III. Pesach: Uprooting the Yetzer Hara

In the weeks before Pesach we begin the gigantic task of cleaning our homes of leaven, earnestly searching every nook and cranny of our possessions for those "soon to be" forbidden crumbs! It behooves us to understand why we pursue bread during this season so feverishly, while, during the rest of the year, it is such a staple in our lives and the subject of which we bless Hashem that He sustains His world with goodness (in *Birchas HaMazon*).

The Gemara refers to the evil inclination as the "yeast in the dough" [*Brachos* 17a]. For just as yeast causes dough to ferment so, too, the evil inclination enflames our passions and tempts us to "rise" and sin. The Radvaz [#976] writes that he found no satisfactory reason why even a minuscule amount of leaven is **Biblically** prohibited on Pesach, when this is *not* the case for all other forbidden foods. He concludes that leaven is a symbolic reminder of the evil inclination and it is thus understandable why it's so absolutely necessary to purge such inclinations even in the slightest of amounts!

The Alshich adds that this is why the gematria of chometz is 138 which is the same numerical value as *"pegima"* (flawed). Chometz represents the flaws in a person caused by the evil inclination.

Similarly, the *Zohar* [*Shemos* 41:1] explains why we distribute ten pieces of bread around our homes before we do *bedika* (the formal search for chometz). The ten morsels of leaven represent the ten human organs that can lead one to sin, namely, one's two hands, two feet, two eyes, two ears, the male organ, and one's mouth (cf. the *Maharsha* who notes that the nose isn't counted since it rarely sins).

Thus, when we search through our homes and worldly possessions for chometz we be should simultaneously searching through our lives for spiritual imperfections. Then, as we get rid of the chometz, so too, we should attempt to purge ourselves of these imperfections. So cleaning kitchen cupboards should prompt us to question our kashrus standards and cleaning the den should cause us to reflect on how our free time is spent, etc. In fact, the *Rama* [433:11] states that we are required to check our pockets for chometz, which the *Shelah* [*Pesachim*, drush 3:27] explains symbolizes the need to confirm that no dishonest money has adhered to our pockets!

Thus you can see that Pesach is a time for both introspection and teshuva. Indeed, the saintly *Agudas Aizov* (may Hashem avenge his blood) quotes from the *seforim kedoshim* (holy writings) that while the High Holy Days is a time of repentance out of fear, Pesach is a time to repent out of love.

Thus, in the spirit of the spiritual cleansing of Pesach, here is a list of fifty-two areas of life which perhaps could use some scrubbing. With these commitments we will be better prepared to celebrate Pesach, the anniversary of the birth of the Jewish people.

Fifty-two Ways to Improve Your Life

1. I will make Hashem my very first thought every morning as I open my eyes with a passionate thank you— *modeh ani l'fanecha* (and not, oy, another day!).

2. I will wash my hands generously not gingerly, removing the *tumah*, rededicating myself to the service of Hashem, and getting ready for prayer. Similarly, I will not just "touch the tap" when coming out of the bathroom or before my prayers but I will always wash my hands correctly (the Chazon Ish said that correct morning *netilas yadayim* can ward off depression!).

3. I will make it a habit to greet my loved ones with a smile in the morning so that they can begin each day with the assurance that they are loved and cared for! (This can sometimes be difficult, but it is, oh, so rewarding!)

4. I will adopt the following mantra—"Do not scream at home, do not scream at home, do not scream at home!"

5. I will say *birchas haTorah* with intense fervor and introduce this habit to my children. Showing them how to say, "*v'haarev na es divray torsecha*—please sweeten your Torah in our mouths" with a heartfelt plea that we should learn to enjoy our Torah studies. I heard from Rav Joseph Scheinberger, *shlit"a*, that this is a great *segulah* to acquire a zest for learning!

6. I will always attempt to attend a minyan recognizing that my prayers at home may be disregarded but at a minyan they never are!

7. I will remember that davening is referred to as service of the heart and if I pray without *kavanah*, I'm forfeiting most of the effectiveness of tefillah! As it says in the *Chovos Halevovos*, a prayer without thought is like a peel without the fruit and a body without a soul!

8. With this in mind I will finally make it my business to learn the meaning of the more complex parts of prayer, such as the daily "yom," recognizing how ridiculous it is if I don't fully understand what I have been repeating for so many years. Studyng it once will mean that I willl understand it for the rest of my life!

9. I will exert a special effort to say the *Shema* meaningfully knowing that on Shabbos (in the Kedusha of the *Mussaf* liturgy) I declare that all Jews say *Shema*—"*pamaiyim b'ahava* (twice with love)," and anything said with love has to be said with feeling! I will remember that Gehinnom is cooled off for one who forces himself to slow down and meticulously say the *Shema* [*Mishna Berura* 62:1].

10. Whenever possible I will try to prepare myself for the *Shemoneh Esrei*, making a quick list of what I want to have in mind when I say *refa-einu* (for those who are sick or depressed), *bareich aleinue* (for those who are unemployed), *slach lanue* (concerning my latest indiscretions), *Shema kola-inu* (my wishes from Hashem) *Sim Shalom* (for those who are having problems with *shalom bayis*, etc.). I will recognize that such preparation is the best aid against the danger of my prayers becoming either a habit or a burden.

11. I will make it a point to always pray for others realizing that this is the best way to have my prayers fulfilled. I will put special emphasis on praying for the success of my spouse and my parents.

12. (*For males:*) I will put on my tzitzis with the awareness that it represents the 613 mitzvahs (its gematria of 600, plus the 8 threads and 5 knots). I will have in mind that although I can't physically fulfill all the mitzvahs (since we don't have the Beis HaMikdash, etc.), but I would wholeheartedly want to do so if possible.

13. (*For males:*) I will put on tefillin with the excitement fueled by the knowledge that Hashem *aleihem yichyu*—one who puts Hashem upon himself will live [*Menochos* 44b].

I will try to bear in mind while wearing them that I'm "tied" to the Torah way of life and will remember how Hashem took us out of slavery from Egypt so that we would be bound to Him.

14. I will make certain to learn Torah at least once a day and once at night! Just like I find time for my bodily needs, I will also find time for the needs of my soul—remembering that *"ain tchilas dino shel Adam eino ela al divray Torah—*a person is first judged in the next world concerning his Torah study" [*Kiddushin* 40b]. I will also realize that I'm obligated to learn Torah whenever I have free time. I will think of the fact that if I throw all the mitzvahs on one side of the scale and put a *sefer* on the other side, the *sefer* will weigh as much as all the other mitzvahs combined. This is the greatness of the mitzvah of Torah study!

15. I will try to learn two Mishnas a day. It is a wonderful insurance, for we are taught that Asher stands by the door of Gehinnom and doesn't let anyone in who habitually learns Mishnayos! [Preface to *Medrash Talpios*]. (We are taught that he who learns two Mishnayos every day will merit the afterlife!)

16. I will try to learn some halachah everyday, e.g., *Kitzur Shulchan Aruch, Mishnah Berurah, Rambam, Hilchos Chofetz Chaim,* etc. knowing that Hashem loves the learning of halachah more than any other gateway of study [*Masechtas Brachos* 8a]!

17. Knowing how scarce my time for Torah study is I will wisely use any time I spend commuting. If I'm driving I will not waste time listening to the weather, or to a talk show host sharing his "wisdom" or insulting other people and embarrassing them in public. (One of the most heinous crimes imaginable and punishable with the loss of one's afterlife if done habitually [*Sanhedrin* 107a].) Instead, I will fortify myself with a healthy dosage of Rabbi Miller, Rabbi Reisman, Rabbi Wein, Rabbi Frand, etc. turning my car into a veritable Beis HaMedrash joyfully fulfilling the directive of *"uv'lectcha vaderech*—learning

Torah while traveling" [*Devarim* 6:7].

18. I will try to review the weekly Torah portion twice, every week knowing that the Gemara promises that one who does this will be blessed with a long and meaningful life [*Brachos* 8a]. The Chofetz Chaim writes that this also helps in the development of *emunah*. I will put special emphasis on the latter Chumashim that I tend to neglect!

19. Dovid HaMelech instituted the saying of 100 *brachos* everyday to stop Jewish casualties. I will attempt to always do this as well because I acknowldege its efficacy.

20. I will say my *brachas* slowly and deliberately with an empty mouth while holding the item in my right hand and putting special emphasis on the saying of Hashem's holy name. I will not swallow the end of the *bracha* together with my food!

21. I will develop an intense hatred for any kind of *machlokes* (fighting) remembering that even infants die because of the sin of *machlokes* (*Rashi*, parshas *Korach*) and that fighting chases away the *Shechina* [cf. *Sota* 17a].

22. I will actively be on guard not to speak *loshon hara*, training myself not to talk about people. I will choose only friends who are willing to adhere to such a practice. Furthermore, every day when I say *"Elokai ntzor l'shonie mairah—My G-d, guard my tongue from evil,"* I will passionately pray to succeed at this.

23. I will purge myself of the bad habit of slightly changing a story, etc. committing myself to being totally truthful, for it is the symbol of our namesake (*"teetein emes l'Yaakov—grant truth to Yaakov"*) [*Micha* 7:20] and it is the seal of Hashem [*Shabbos* 55a].

24. I will develop the habit of thinking about Hashem when looking at a mezuzah. I will stop to take note of a mezuzah each time I see it and I will ponder its message and its promises to bring life to me and my family and to bring protection to my home!

25. I will get in the habit of saying *Tehillim* whenever I have an available moment—praying for the sick, the childless, the unmarried and the impoverished. I will find ways to use the immense power of these words recited by my ancestors during every imaginable horror.

26. I will find time to visit the sick. The Gemara in *Nedarim* [40a] teaches us that this saves us from Gehinnom, protects us from suffering and the wiles of the evil inclination, promises us good friends, and elevates us to a higher status so that people will be honored just to be associated with us!

27. I will learn to happily give my money to charity. I will recognize that Jewish shrouds have no pockets. The only money we can take with us is that which we give to help others!

28. I will take special care in eating kosher, making sure that I don't simply depend on the fact that everyone else is eating it!

29. I will make sure to hope for Mashiach and *techiyas hameisim* (resurrection of the dead) daily, utilizing the many prayers that we say about these wishes (e.g., *Al kein n'kave* in *Aleinu, Es t'zemach* in *Shemoneh Esrei* and the Kaddish prayer to name but a few).

30. I will fiercely pursue *shalom bayis* (marital harmony) knowing that it is the linchpin of insuring the *Shechina* in the home! And as Rav Chaim Vital has said, "A person's *middos* can be evaluated by how they treat their spouse!"

31. I will try to never end a day before I've made up with my spouse because I never want to go to sleep without the *Shechina* in my home [*Sota* 17a].

32. I will acknowledge that humans are reciprocal in nature and so I will try to initiate love, affection, caring and devotion in my marriage knowing full well that the best way to get something is to give it!

33. Knowing that I will be asked in the next world if I made my spouse happy, I will make a list of ten things that I know would thrill my spouse, and I will set out to fulfill as many of these items as I can.

34. I will learn the art of saying "I'm sorry," demonstrating that I empathize with any damage I've done and showing that I'm making concrete corrections so that it won't happen again. (This is very different than the, "I said, I'm sorry already!" attitude!)

35. When under tension, I will pay special attention to how I speak to my spouse, pausing the extra moment to remove the barb (*shtuch*) and sting from something I was about to say!

36. I'll be ever mindful that the best present I can give my children is more of my presence!

37. Acknowledging how busy my life is, I will be constantly mindful that the best way to teach my children is by example. I'll therefore try to be a role model for them. When I'm at home I will demonstrate how I practice restraint, compromise, flexibility, forgiveness, communication, etc.

38. (*For males:*) I will try hard not to eye other women (thinking of what I say twice daily in *Shema, "v'lo sasuru acharei l'vavchem v'acharei eineichem*—and do not follow after your heart and after your eyes"), and (*for females:*) I will try not to mindfully attract other men.

39. I will honor my parents exceedingly, realizing it is a barometer of my respect for Hashem! I will honor them while they are alive and send them packages when they are in the next world!

40. I will likewise show enormous respect to my "in-laws" realizing that I must be grateful to them for what is most precious to me—my spouse and children!

41. I will treat my son-in-law and daughter-in-law like royalty and, in this way, keep my children.

42. I will say the Shabbos kiddush with the thoughts that Hashem created the world and took us out of Egypt to be His special people (and because of this only Bnei Yisroel has Shabbos).

43. When eating the cholent and the liver (or any other special Shabbos foods), I will pause to reflect on my belief in Hashem, the Creator, and my gratitude to Him.

44. I will make sure that my family and I eat all three meals on Shabbos, for it offers many important protections. I will likewise insist on the eating of the Melave Malka (after Shabbos meal) which sustains the indestructible luz bone, from which we will be resurrected.

45. I will be mindful of personal modesty even when I'm alone in the bathroom for it is a barometer of my awareness of Hashem, since only He sees me when I am there.

46. I will often take my family to see Torah sages, for the Torah teaches us this is akin to greeting the *Shechina* [Rashi; *Ki Sisa*].

47. I will *bentch* with intense concentration (taking out time to learn the *bentching* well), for the Chofetz Chaim wrote that one who *bentches* with *kavanah* will be assured a livelihood with dignity and plenty all of one's life. As was the custom of Rav Yehudah Zev Segal of Manchester, zt"l, I will avoid washing if I feel I won't be able to concentrate on the *bentching*.

48. I will learn to pay attention to the great mitzvah of saying amen, having in mind, when I say it, that the blessing is true, and that I hope that what the *bracha* describes will be fulfilled (when applicable).

49. I will try to acquire the talent of silence, developing the habit of not needing to answer back nor have the last word. It is the trait of the righteous [*Masechtas Shabbos* 88b] and will save one from many downfalls [*Masechtas Sanhedrin* 7a].

50. I will try to learn to be humble, since as our sages teach us it's the most important of all traits [cf. *Masechtas Erchin* 16b and the third Tosefos in *Masechtas Yevamos* 103b].

51. I will say *Krias Shema al Hamitta* and the blessing of *Hamapil* nightly (this is so important because it ends off the day in the correct Jewish way and we know that much is determined by the end) [*Brachos* 12a]. In this way, before I go to sleep, I will have in mind that I'm only sleeping to be able to serve Hashem better the next day (this converts the entire night's sleep into a *hechsher* mitzvah).

52. I will never rest on my laurels. Each and every day I will think about how I can change and improve myself. To this end I will make a *cheshbon hanefesh* every night, and if not, at least once a week before Shabbos.

Whew, there's so much to do and, of course, this is only a sample. *Hatzlocha Rabbah!*

Torah's Many
Wonderful Benefits

— • I • —

Torah is the wrestling match between Yaakov Avinu and the angel. It is in parshas *Vayishlach* [*Bereishis* 32:25] that the Torah relates how Yaakov Avinu crossed the ford of Yabbok alone and was accosted by an angel who struggled an entire night to kill him. This fight was so intense that the Torah characterizes it using the term *vayaiavek*, which literally means to kick up dust. What lasting lesson are we to learn from this legendary wrestling match? And why does the Torah depict Yaakov in the role of a fighter when he had previously always been identified as the embodiment of study and prayer? As the Torah teaches, "*Hakol kol Yaakov*—The voice is the strength of Yaakov; *V'hayadayim y'dei Eisav*—While the hands are the tools of Eisav!" [*Bereishis* 27:22]. Why is Yaakov suddenly using Eisav's methodology?

One way to understand the significance of this battle is

to identify Yaakov's opponent. The *Medrash Tanchuma* [8:1] informs us that Yaakov's antagonist was none other than Samael. In Hebrew, Samael is a corruption of two words: *sam* and *keil*, meaning "poison of G-d," hinting that Yaakov had fought none other than the *Malach HaMaves* (the Angel of Death).

When the Torah tells us, *"Vayar ki lo yachul lo*—The Angel saw that he could not prevail over him" [*Bereishis* 32:26], this episode becomes significant. The Torah is instructing us how to turn aside the *Malach HaMaves* and in this way defend our families and ourselves from death.

What was Yaakov's special strength in fighting the *Malach HaMaves*? The powerful ingredient that Yaakov employed as his weapon was his *zechus* (merit of) Torah. Yaakov personified Torah dedication, as the Torah testifies, *"Yaakov, ish tam, yosheiv ohalim*—Yaakov was the complete man, dwelling in tents" [*Toldos* 25:27]. Why does the Torah say *tents*, and not the singular, *tent*? Is it to convey that, in addition to his winter residence, Yaakov had a summer home? Hardly! *Tents* refers to the academies of Sheim and Eiver, the tents of Torah study. In the same vein, Bilaam prophesied, *"Ma tovu ohalecha Yaakov*—How goodly are your tents, oh Yaakov" [*Balak* 24:5]. Bilaam was not complimenting Yaakov's interior decorating. He was referring to the true goodness which is Torah, as we are taught, *"Ein tov ela Torah*—The only authentic goodness is Torah" [*Brachos* 5a].

Indeed, Yaakov's absolute Torah dedication made him invincible to the *Malach HaMaves*. As Chazal teach us, *"Yaakov Avinu lo meis*—Yaakov, our Father, never completely died" [*Taanis* 5a]. We learn of the Torah's power to stave off death in the Gemara [*Masechtas Shabbos* 30b], where Dovid HaMelech's attempt to frustrate the Angel of Death is revealed. Dovid asked Hashem exactly when he would die. The Gemara relates that Hashem told Dovid that he would leave this world on a Shabbos. Henceforth, to avoid death, Dovid spent the entirety of every Shabbos immersed in Torah learning. It was only by resorting to subterfuge and momentarily distracting Dovid HaMelech, that the *Malach HaMaves* was able to breach Dovid's Torah fortress.

Related to this, one of the reasons the book of *Rus* is read on Shavuos is because Dovid was born and passed away on this holiday. Since *Rus* was written by Shmuel to convey to us Dovid's pedigree, it is fitting to include *Rus* in this holiday's liturgy. (People similarly read *Tehillim* on Shavuos, since it was authored by Dovid.) How fitting it is that Dovid HaMelcch would dodge the Angel of Death with Torah on Shavuos—the day the Torah is specially highlighted and appreciated! On the day of his death, Dovid HaMelech taught us that on Shavuos particularly, we should remember the life-saving qualities of our holy Torah!

It is no wonder, after hearing about the amazing protective powers of Torah, that we want our daughters to marry men with strong Torah idealism and we work to inculcate our sons with an intense love and commitment to Torah learning for—more than any other thing—we want to insure the health and longevity of our families.

~•II•~

Another place where the Torah's promise of health and long life is emphasized is in the seventh Mishna in the sixth perek of *Pirkei Avos*. The Mishna teaches, *"Gedolah Torah, shehi nosenes chaim l'oseha b'olam hazeh u'ba'olam Haba*— Great is Torah, for it promises life for one in this world and in the next world."

The Mishna proves this with eight different sources from Tanach—pointing out the one thing no other occupation can guarantee: Health. Thus, although it quotes a posuk that attests to the promise of wealth and honor, it is noteworthy that the Mishna emphasizes the Torah's life-giving aspect and not any other of its many benefits. Although politics may promise fame, and industriousness might have the lure of great wealth, Torah is unique in its capability to promise good health and long life.

— • III • —

In the above mentioned Mishna in *Pirkei Avos*, the Tana cites a posuk in *Mishlei* [4:22], "*U'lchol b'saro marpeh*— and it brings a cure to all flesh.*" This, too, is a unique feature of Torah. In the world of medicine and pharmaceuticals, the more potent the medicine—the more potentially disastrous are its side effects. Indeed, doctors must often prescribe an array of medicines to counterbalance these side effects of the initial medicine prescribed. Not so with the Torah. Although it promises wondrous therapy, the previously mentioned posuk in *Mishlei* emphasizes that it brings health to all flesh with absolutely no side effects!

— • IV• —

A practical and everyday application of Torah's life-giving qualities is found in the Gemara, "*L'olam yashlim adam parshiosav im hatzibur, shnayim mikra v'echod targum... mareechin yamav u'shnosav*—One should always review the weekly Torah portion twice from the text itself and once from the *Targum* (the classic Aramaic translation of *Onkelos*). This practice will reward one with a lengthening of his days and years" [*Masechtas Brachos*, 8b]. The Gemara's quote is odd. If one is rewarded with years, why is it necessary to mention the reward of days! The *Korbon Nesanael* on the Rosh [siman 8, os 5] answers, *days* refers to an aged man who has nothing but days left, while *years* refers to a young man. However, why does

the Gemara mention *days* first; *years* is applicable to most people and thus should have been mentioned first.

Perhaps *days* refers to the quality of our days, productive and fulfilling in nature, and *years* refers to longevity. It is
also possible that since the promise is a lengthening of one's life
span, this means adding to one's *keitz*, i.e., the allotment given
at birth to each of us by G-d. Therefore, it depends what
Hashem had in mind for each one of us at birth. If a person's life
span was meant to be short, this could mean one could gain
years. A person destined to have a long life might just gain extra
days along with the protection of not losing any of the original
allotment. Once again we have a striking example of how a regular dose of Torah provides an expansion of one's years.

━━ •V• ━━

When a serious-minded person considers what should be
the primary focus and ambition in his or her life, one of the
things usually considered is, "Why did Hashem create the world,
and to what purpose were humans put on this planet?" Once
this question is answered, it becomes easier to decide on one's
life goals. The Torah provides the answer to this quest in its first
few words, *"Bereishis bara…*—In the beginning He created...."
Rashi's second comment on this posuk is, *"Bishvil Torah she'-
nikra reishis darko*—The world was created because of Torah."
The *Pe'er Aharon* demonstrates this fact in a brilliant manner
with an incredible gematria. The numerical value of the phrase,
Bereishis bara Elokim, is 1,202, which is the exact gematria of
the words, Torah, Neviim, Kesuvim. This vividly demonstrates
that the world was created for the sake of Tanach. Similarly, at
the end of Creation, the Torah says, *"Yom Ha'sheeshee*—The
sixth day." Rashi, commenting on the extra letter "hei," says that
with the extra letter "hei" Hashem is informing us that all of creation was dependent on Klal Yisroel accepting the five chu-

mashim, symbolized by the letter "hei," which numerically equals five. Rashi further explains that the "hei" (which grammatically denotes "the special") emphasizes that the world's existence hinges upon *the* sixth day, specifically the sixth day of Sivan, which is Shavuos, when the Torah would be given, for this event was the sole purpose of all of creation.

Similarly, the *Medrash Tanchuma* [on parshas *Noach* 3:1] tells us that when the Torah was given, Hashem held Har Sinai over Klal Yisroel and warned that if we didn't accept the Torah, we would be buried on the spot. In *Yirmiya* [33:5], the *Navi* tells us, "*Im lo brisi yomam v'layla, chukos shamayim vaaretz lo samtiv*—If not for my covenant day and night, the statutes of heaven and earth would not have been affixed." The commentators explain that the covenant referred to here is Torah learning, which it is mandatory to study at some time of each day and each night. Indeed, throughout the ages, great Torah luminaries specialized in learning at times when most people do not learn, like the night of bedikas chometz (during which we search for chometz on the eve of Pesach), Motzei Yom Kippur (at the departure of Yom Kippur), and Purim. The Torah greats did this to insure the survival of the world. The father of the legendary *Iglay Tal* is said to have merited having such a great son because he once learned when no one else in the world was learning! It has also been suggested that one of the reasons the world has different time zones is to ensure that there will always be people awake learning Torah. Indeed, the father of the modern-day Yeshiva movement, the Volozhiner Yeshiva, in Lithuania, used to have three shifts of learning spanning the full twenty-four hours of each day to make sure that Torah learning would not cease throughout the world for even a minute!

Rabbi Yochanan Ben Zakkai comments that even if one has studied a lot of Torah, one should not become haughty, "*Ki l'kach no'tzorta*—For it is for this purpose [i.e., to learn Torah] that he was created" [*Pirkei Avos* 2:8]. This clearly affirms that the main reason for our creation was to study Torah. The converse is also taught by the great Hillel (in the first perek), "*Oodlo yalif katala chayav*—One who does not engage in Torah learning is liable to death." Rabbi Irving Bunim, zt"l, explains this beautifully. He reminds us that anything left dormant begins to deteriorate. Muscles unused atrophy. A car left unused in a garage too long begins to fade. So, too, Rabbi Bunim says, man was made for Torah study. If he doesn't engage in it, he will begin to fade as well [*Ethics of Sinai*].

Thus, it is eminently clear that the world was created for the study of Torah. Hence, our life's ambition should be fulfilling the primary goal of our Creator.

⸻ • VI • ⸻

We could arrive at this conclusion by consulting the Torah. In the first chapter of *Yehoshua* [posuk 5], the *Navi* teaches us, "*Lo yamush sefer Torah hazeh mipicha v'hagisa bo yomam v'layla*—One should not allow his mouth to stray from Torah study, and he should meditate on it day and night." In our *Krias Shema* we say, "*V'dibarta bam, b'shiv'tcha b'veisecha uv'lechtcha vaderech, uv'shachb'cha uv'kumecha*—One should speak about it when sitting at home, when traveling on the road, when going to sleep, and when arising." The Torah unmistakably directs us to study Torah during every available moment of one's existence—even while traveling, and all during the day until just before we fall asleep.

⸻ • VII • ⸻

A wise person, when debating how to spend time, looks for the most rewarding enterprise. After enumerating some of the greatest mitzvos, such as honoring one's parents and making peace between one's associates, the first mishna in *Masechtas Peah* emphatically states that learning Torah equals all of these mitzvos put together. Another vivid example of the supremacy of Torah study is found in *Mishlei* 3:15, "*Yekara hi m'peninim*—Torah is more precious than pearls." In *Masechtas Sotah* [4b] and *Masechtas Horyos* [13a], the Gemara homiletically explains the Hebrew word, *peninim*, as a corruption of two words, *lifnei* and *u'lifnim*. The intent of the posuk in *Mishlei*, the Gemara says, is that the mitzvah of Torah study is more precious than the Kohen Gadol entering—*lifnai u'lifnim*—into the Holy of Holies of the Beis HaMikdash. This is a potent statement. The Holy of Holies was the holiest place on earth. The Kohen Gadol was arguably one of the holiest people on earth. Furthermore, the Kohen Gadol was only able to enter the rarefied chamber of the Holy of Holies on the holiest day of the year, Yom Kippur. Yet, the Gemara is declaring that Torah learning is even more precious than that entire enviable endeavor of the Kohen Gadol. It's extraordinary what untold greatness is available at the feet of mankind!

⭢ • VIII • ⭠

The *Shenos Eliyahu* cites the *Yerushalmi* which states that every word of Torah learning is an independent and complete mitzvas *aseh* (fulfillment of a positive commandment). In the second chapter of *Toras Habayis*, the Chofetz Chaim writes that upon watching as the second hand of his watch moved, he ascertained that it's possible to read 200 words of Torah during one minute. Thus in five minutes of Torah study one can fulfill 1,000 mitzvos, and in so doing, can create for himself 1,000 celestial angels of merit.

With this in mind, one should never say, "I only have five minutes. It's just not enough time to sit down and learn Torah." In the course of five minutes, one could fulfill the equivalent of the mitzvah of lulov and esrog one thousand times! In fact, the Vilna Gaon, explains why, if one is busy learning and interrupted by another mitzvah that can be taken care of by others, one should not leave the Torah study. Rather, one should let another person do the mitzvah and continue learning. The Gemara says, *"Gadol hatalmud, she'm'viah liydei ma'aseh*—Great is learning for it brings a person to do mitzvos correctly" [*Bava Kama* 17a]. One might wonder, "If the goal of Torah is to perform mitzvos, shouldn't one jump at the opportunity to put one's theoretical knowledge into practice?!" The Vilna Gaon explained that since one fulfills a positive precept with each and every word of Torah learning, there is simply no mitzvah that can match the mitzvah mileage one receives when one studies Torah. This can be compared to a doctor reluctant to make housecalls because by the time he arrives at the patient's home, creates a sterile environment, examines the patient and returns to his office, he could have seen ten patients in his office.

It is only when no one else is available, that one is required to close the Gemara and perform another mitzvah. About other mitzvos we can say, *"Oseik b'mitzvah, patur min hamitzvah*—One who is engaged in a mitzvah is exempt from other mitzvos" [*Succah* 26a]. This is not the case for Torah study. If a mitzvah comes along which requires one's attention, and there is absolutely no one else available to substitute, one must cease one's study and attend to the mitzvah at hand. Thus, if your wife needs help with the children, you must close the Gemara and put your learning into practice. If not, the Gemara sternly says, *"Haomer ein lo ela Torah, afilu Torah ein lo*— Whoever only learns Torah, but has not absorbed its lessons, is not credited even with his Torah learning" [*Yevamos* 109b]. Rather, such a person is considered by the Gemara as a, *"Chamor noseh seforim*—A donkey merely carrying holy books!" [*Chovos HaLevovos: Shaar Avodas Elokim*].

The Steipler Gaon emphasized the unparalleled rewards for Torah learning [published in the *sefer Kraiyna D'igrasa*, #17]. He attested, that one hour of Torah learning is more precious to Hashem than one thousand fasts!

Another confirmation of the importance of Torah study can be found in the Gemara which relates that in the sefer *Ezra*, Mordechai is listed as number five among the Torah greats of his generation [*Megillah* 15b]. Twenty-four years later [in *sefer Nechemia*], after Mordechai's involvement with Haman and Achashveirosh, he is numbered six. One would have thought that after Mordechai successfully helped to save all of Klal Yisroel from impending doom he would have skyrocketed to number one. Yet, not only does Mordechai not advance, he is demoted. The Gemara continues with an amazing piece of information, *"Gadol talmud Torah m'hatzolas nefoshos—* Greater is the study of Torah, than even the saving of many lives!"* It goes without saying that if someone is busy learning and confronted with an emergency, he must immediately attend to the urgent situation. Similarly, moneys in a charity fund slated to advance Torah study can be diverted to save lives [see the *Taz, Yorah Deah*, 241:5]. But, the Gemara is teaching us here that if Mordechai had not been interrupted, he would have earned an even greater reward from his Torah learning than he had from saving world Jewry!

The Chofetz Chaim goes a step further in *Toras Habayis* [chapter 5]. He says that if someone had the opportunity to save someone's life but failed to act quickly enough, or perhaps did not properly gauge the severity of the situation, he would berate himself and feel guilty for a long time. The Chofetz Chaim remarks that, since Torah learning is even greater than saving a life, if one has an opportunity to learn and neglects to do so, he should feel even worse!

We should also add that just like a wife of a Hatzolah (volunteer ambulance corp in New York) member rightfully feels proud of her husband's accomplishments, considering him to be fulfilling a vital need in the Torah community, so, too, should a woman be even prouder of her husband's Torah accomplishments.

One of the common denominators of all mankind is the pursuit of happiness. It is accurately described as the universal quest. Yet it is mysteriously elusive and many people, to their sorrow, spend a lifetime searching in vain for the answer to what will make them truly happy. However, after we have already arrived at the conclusion that every good Jewish male is supposed to spend every available moment in the learning of Torah, it's obvious that it is in the study of Torah that man can find true happiness. For, in a world founded upon the concept of kindliness, as it states in *Tehillim* [89: 3], *"Olam chesed yibaneh—* The world is built upon kindliness,"* Hashem would not condemn a man to a life of unhappiness. Indeed Dovid HaMelech reveals to us this great secret in *Tehillim*, *"Pekudei Hashem yesharim mesamchei leiv—*The commandments of Hashem are upright causing the heart to be happy" [*Tehillim* 19]. It is for this reason we are forbidden to learn Torah on Tisha b'Av, and during times of personal mourning, for we must avoid any actions that will cause us to rejoice during those sad times.

In one of the songs that grace the end of the Pesach seder, *Echad Mi Yodeah*, we sing "Who knows five? I know five. The five books of the Torah." It is interesting to note that the Hebrew word for five, *chamisha*, has the same letters as the word, *simcha*, the Hebrew word for happiness, for it is through the study

of Torah that one can achieve true joy. This can also be seen from
the famous *payat*, *"Ein simcha k'simchas HaTorah*—There is
no joy like the joy of Torah!" Therefore, when we are regretful
about how many Sundays go wasted, or how we are sometimes
overcome by feelings of unfulfillment or melancholy, the answer
is as nearby as the closest bookshelf or Beis HaMedrash!

The reason so many people are unhappy testifies to how
the evil inclination throws all his might against people engaging
in Torah. Torah is the *yetzer hara's* arch enemy, as the Gemara
testifies, *"Barasi yetzer hara. Barasi Torah tavlin lo*—(Hashem
says) I created the evil inclination. I created the Torah as its
antidote" [*Masechtas Kiddushin* 30b]. The Chofetz Chaim
explains that the angel Samael challenged neither Avraham nor
Yitzchok, but waited to engage Yaakov in open battle because
even though the *yetzer hara* is not one to procrastinate, it was
willing to tolerate Avraham's chesed and Yitzchok's avodah.
But, when it came to the Torah of Yaakov, the evil inclination
had to declare war!

• XI •

We often excuse ourselves for not learning by rationaliz-
ing that we need to relax or to unwind. After all, there is a positive commandment to keep ourselves healthy. There is, however,
a posuk that undermines this defense. It says in *Tehillim* [19:9],
"Toras Hashem t'mimah, m'shivas nafesh—The Torah of Hashem is wholesome, it rejuvenates the soul." Thus if we need to
unwind, we should remember that there is nothing more invigorating or restorative than the study of Hashem's Torah!

• XII •

As a nation, one of our most precious possessions is the
promise that—if we are deserving—we will be resurrected after
death and enjoy eternal life. For this reason, in the second

bracha of our silent devotion, we thank Hashem for *techiyas hameisim*, although one would have thought that it would be more appropriate to thank Hashem first for those things we have *already* received such as health, peace, livelihood, etc., and only then mention promises for the future such as life after death. However, it is precisely the recognition that everything else is of temporary value and that only *techiyas hameisim* is the key to our eternity, that prompts us to mention it directly after the first *bracha*, when we give the password that allows entrance into Hashem's palace (namely, that we are the children of Avraham, Yitzchok, and Yaakov).

It goes without saying that we should do whatever it takes to make sure we will deserve resurrection when the great time of *techiyas hameisim* arrives. The Chofetz Chaim cites *Yeshaya* [26:19], "*Tal oros talecha*—A dew of 'light' is your heavenly dew." He then refers us to the *Medrash* that elucidates this posuk, "*Mi sheyaish b'yado Ohr Torah, ohr Torah m'chay-ihu. V'kol sh'ein b'yado ohr Torah, ein ohr Torah m'chaiye-hu*—Whoever has the light of Torah, it will resurrect him. And whoever does not have the light of Torah, it will not aid in his resurrection." The Chofetz Chaim concludes that the restorative dew of light is referring to the light of Torah which offers an insight into what a powerful investment for the future Torah learning really is!

• XIII •

"*Ma ashiv L'hashem kol tag'm'lohi alai*—With what shall I repay Hashem for all He has bestowed upon me?!" [*Tehillim* 116]. This question is asked by Dovid HaMelech in *Tehillim*. In the liturgical poem known as *Akdamus* (read on Shavuos), Rabbi Meir of Worms relates, "*Tzvi v'chamid v'ragig d'yilun blausa*—Hashem wanted, desired, and longed that we make ourselves weary in Torah." We see that by dwelling in the tents of Torah, we fulfill a great "need" of Hashem's. Similarly, we learn in the *Sifra* [*Vayikra* 26:3], *"Im b'chukosai seile-ichu—m'lamed sh'Hamakom misaveh sh'yihyu Yisroel ameilim BaTorah*—In my statutes shall you go..., which teaches us that Hashem wants us to labor in Torah." What a wonderful way to repay Hashem for all that He does for us!

•XIV•

Another benefit of Torah learning can be seen from the next verse in *Akdamus*, *"Tzloshun b'chein mekabel vehanya bausa*—Through this [Torah learning] our prayers will be accepted and our petitions will succeed." What a wonderful bonus to have "pull" in *Shamayim* because of our Torah commitment! This benefit is actually taught in a Gemara where is says, *"Kol ha'osek BaTorah, Hakodesh baruch hu oseh lo cheftzin*—Whoever is involved in Torah, Hashem takes care of his needs!" [*Avodah Zarah* 19a].

•XV•

Among the secondary benefits of Torah are wealth and honor. There is reference to this in *Mishlei* [3:17], *"Orech yamim b'ymina; b'smola osher v'kavod*—On its right (is) longevity; on its left (is) wealth and honor." One can easily understand the reason behind the reward of wealth: money enables one to learn without distraction and with peace of mind. However, a reward of honor is puzzling! Why give someone something that is spiritually dangerous? As it says in *Pirkei Avos* [4:21], *"V'hakavod motzeein es haadam min haolam*—Honor chases a person out of the world." Perhaps this reward is engineered to help our Torah learning by enabling one to find honor in the eyes of one's wife. If other people honor someone for his Torah learning, his wife will be more motivated to encourage and assist her husband in his efforts to learn.

Likewise, the respect he will garner in the eyes of his children will enable him to direct even more attention to his studies. Indeed, a husband who feels his wife does not have sufficient respect for him should seriously consider devoting more time to Torah study. He will quickly notice that his stock will rise rapidly in his wife's eyes!

⌒ • XVI • ⌒

A strong daily diet of Torah is also effective as a weapon against the *yetzer hara*. Particularly in the spiritually hostile environment in which we live today, it is crucial to make use of the shield of Torah to fortify our defenses. In *Masechtas Kiddushin* [30b], the Gemara teaches us the antidote Hashem gave us against the *yetzer hara*: Torah study. Similarly, the Gemara teaches us that one of the ways to combat the *yetzer hara* is, "*Ya'asok Batorah*—To be engaged in Torah" [*Masechtas Brachos* 5a].

Elsewhere we find the same concept. Yosef was given the title *HaTzadik*, because he was *pitpeit b'yitzro*—a warrior against his passions. The Chofetz Chaim comments that Yosef succeeded in doing this through Torah study. This is proven from *Bereishis* [39:11], "*Vayavo habeisa la'asos m'lachto*— (Yosef) entered the house to do his work." The Chofetz Chaim stresses that Yosef went to do *his* work, and not the work of his master Potiphar. And what was Yosef's real work? The study of Torah. *Bereishis* continues by relating that Yosef evaded the wiles of Potiphar's wife. The secret of his resistance from temptation? Yosef fortified himself with Torah study!

In *Shemiras Halashon* [2:16], the Chofetz Chaim notes that if someone is struggling with a specific mitzvah one should study that subject in depth. This, he says, will aid greatly in overcoming any temptations regarding that specific area. Thus, if one falters in *kibud av v'eim* (honoring parents), the laws of *kibud av v'eim* should be gone over in depth. If one hopelessly flounders in the snares of *loshon hara* (speaking gossip), one should study its intricacies and pitfalls. This will strengthen and empower you with the stamina to overcome these specific temptations.

~•XVII•~

After proving that Yosef fortified himself by learning Torah, the Chofetz Chaim explains that it is easy to understand why Yosef found favor in everyone's eyes. The secret behind Yosef's universal appeal was his devotion to Torah study, and his zealous application of his learning. Even when Yosef arrived as a slave in Potiphar's house he completely won over his master. As the Torah testifies, *"Vayimtza Yosef chain b'einav*—And Yosef found favor in his eyes" [*Bereishis* 39:4]. Later, when Yosef was unjustly thrown into the dungeon, the prison's warden took a liking to Yosef, as it states [39:20], *"Vayeeten cheino b'einai sar Beis Hasohar*—And he charmed even the master of the jail." In fact, this apparent benefit of Torah learning is revealed to us in *Mishlei* [5:19], when the *Navi* refers to Torah as *"v'yaalas chein*—it causes one to be favored." This important lesson is also taught in the Gemara where Reish Lakish informs us, *"Kol ha'osek B'Torah balayla, HaKodash Baruch Hu moshech alav chut shel chesed b'yom*—Whoever dedicates himself to Torah study in the night time, Hashem rewards him with a thread of grace in the day time" [*Masechtas Chagiga*, 12b]. What an incredible advantage this bestows! This will help someone with *shalom bayis*, with relationships at the office, etc. This secondary benefit of Torah is like being granted a divine charm!

~•XVIII•~

It is not surprising that we glean so many crucial lessons from Yosef. The *Medrash Tanchuma* teaches that the numerical value in Hebrew of the name Yosef is 156, which is the same gematria as *tzion*. This demonstrates that what happened to Yosef is a lesson for all Jews. Indeed, the Chofetz Chaim points out that from Yosef we can learn the importance of learning Torah even during the most trying circumstances. Even after Yosef was sold by his family, ripped away from his beloved father, and condemned to slavery in a hostile and contaminated land, Yosef continued his learning.

In *Shir HaShirim Rabbah* [8:16], the Medrash teaches that the *schar* (reward) for learning during stressful times is five times greater than the *schar* for learning in the midst of tranquil times. This is an important incentive to keep in mind—during tough economic times or, *lo aleinu*, any other of life's rougher moments. Indeed, in *Hilchos Talmud Torah* (the laws of learning Torah), the *Shulchan Aruch* explicitly notes that one is obligated to learn Torah even during an illness, or even if one makes one's living by begging from door to door! Neither of these difficult experiences excuse anyone from the duties of Torah study!

⌒ •XIX• ⌒

In our daily *Maariv* (evening) prayers, we say, "*U'vahem nehege yomam v'alayla*—In them (Torah) we meditate day and night." The obvious question is how can we give the impression that we are continually immersed in Torah when, in reality, we may not be able to give Torah much of our time at all? We may wonder the same thing about the command at the beginning of *sefer Yehoshua* [1:8], "*V'hagisa, bah yomam v'layla*—We should concentrate on it day and night." Why does the *Navi* ask something of us that the average person cannot hope to fulfill. Who—while they are occupied most of the day earning a living and other family needs—can even attempt to be engaged in Torah learning or meditation twenty-four hours a day? In *Sefer HaMakneh* on *Masechtas Kiddushin*, Rabbi Pinchas HaLevi

Horowitz sheds light on this issue. I will elaborate on his holy words with a contemporary analogy. Some people relax by watching a baseball game, enjoying immensely the luxury of being able to sit back with a bag of potato chips and a cold beverage while losing themselves between the lines of the baseball diamond. Others unwind after a long hard day by reading a novel before dropping off into sleep. The mere anticipation of these pleasures can carry them through the day and help them cope with the vicissitudes of life. This, says the *Sefer HaMakneh*, is the way a Jew should feel about the Torah. The Torah should be what one looks forward to—the beacon at the end of the day and the light at the end of the tunnel.

Tosefos [*Masechtas Brachos* 116] asks the question: Why don't we have to repeat *birchas* HaTorah again after our lunch break when we sit down to learn again, although we had a whole morning full of interruptions? This is in contrast, for example, to the *bracha* of *leishav basuccah* (sitting in the succah), which we must repeat each and every time we re-enter the Succah. Tosefos comments that Jews never *masiach daas* (remove their thoughts) from Torah. Their minds never wander far from Torah commitments. This is what we mean when we say in our prayers that we think about Torah day and night. Although we might not be able to actually learn continuously, our heart is always looking for an available moment to dwell in the splendor of Torah. Thus, a Jew's thoughts and desires should always be focused constantly on dedication to Torah.

One sign of maturity is the ability to look ahead and not concentrate only on the here and now. As Chazal teach us, "*Eizehu chochom? Haro'eh es hanolad*—Who is a wise person? One who foresees the future" [*Masechtas Meila* 32a]. The wise person makes long-term investments and continuously keeps an eye on the future. The Torah is the ultimate long-term investment and insurance. The Gemara teaches us, in the name of Rav Menachem B'rebbi Yosi, that it is written in *Mishlei* [6:23], *"Ki ner mitzvah V'torah ohr—A mitzvah is compared to a candle, while Torah is compared to light"* [*Masechtas Sotah* 21a]. The Gemara explains the respective analogies. Just as a lit candle is temporary, a mitzvah similarly promises only a temporary reward. However, just like light is permanent, so, too, the Torah is everlasting. The Gemara then cites the posuk said at every siyyum (completion) of a masechta, *"B'hishalech'cha tanche os'cha b'shach'bcha tishmor alecha v'hakitzosa hee s'sichecha —*When you walk, it will guide you, when you sleep it will protect you, and when you awake it will be your conversation"* [*Mishlei* 6:22]. The Gemara interprets this to mean that our Torah learning will benefit us in this world, protect us while we are "sleeping" in the grave, and will be our fulfillment when we "wake up" to the hereafter. Similarly, at the end of *Masechtas Kiddushin* [82a], the Gemara teaches that Torah is the best "social security," giving *achris v'tikva* (security and hope) for one's golden years. Indeed, we find a wonderful phrase in *Tehillim* [92] where it says, referring to Torah scholars, *"Od y'nuvun b'seiva—He will again sprout in hoary old age."* Where else can you find an investment that spans all phases of one's existence; this world, the next world, and even in the grave!

◆ • XXI • ◆

Learning Torah is the most powerful way to endear ourselves to the *Ribbono shel olam* (Master of the universe). The Kotzker Rebbe proves this homiletically by pointing out that in *Shir HaShirim* [1:2], it says, *"Ki tovim dodecha m'yayin—* How much dearer you are to me, more than fine wine." He interprets this to mean that Hashem's best friends are those acquired from the "wine of Torah." In other words, although there are numerous ways to grow close to Hashem—through prayer, chesed, or the pursuit of peace—nothing develops as intimate a relationship with Hashem as the study of Torah!

⌐ • XXII • ¬

Shlomo HaMelech asks us to consider, *"Ma yisron l'adam b'kol amolo she'yamol tachas hashemesh*—What profit is there in all the toil that a person does beneath the sun?"* [*Koheles* 1:3]. Why does Shlomo specify *beneath* the sun? Because Shlomo, the wisest of all men, is advising us not to fritter away our lives on physical pursuits. Rather, he says, we should engage in spiritual activities that are beyond and over the sun.

How does one determine if something is spiritual or physical? For one thing, every physical pleasure has a saturation point, after which it ceases to be enjoyable and may even become loathsome. For example, the Shabbos afternoon cholent can be a high point of physical pleasure. The first two plates are enjoyable, but it's impossible for many of us even to consider a third helping! Similarly, many of us relish the idea of having more than eight hours of sleep. But after we've had our fill of sleep, it's impossible to even look at the pillow anymore. The same can be said about all physical pleasures.

However, spiritual things never cease to satisfy. This is the nature of Torah study. As we say in the Shabbos liturgy, *"Yisb'u v'yisangu mituvecha*—We are satisfied and delighted from Your goodness."* We are taught [*Brachos* 5a] that *tov* refers to Torah, as it says, *"Ki lekach tov nasati lachem, Torasie al tazovu*—For I have given you a goodly portion, my Torah do not forsake"* [*Mishlei* 4:2]. Thus, even after we are full (*yisbu* means to be satiated), we still derive delight from our Torah study. This is the acid test that Torah is a spiritual pleasure.

Indeed, the Gemara in Shabbos [30a] says that Shlomo HaMelech alluded to this [in *Koheles* 1:3] when he said that there is no profit from toil *after* the sun, i.e., with things which were created after Creation. But one who wearies himself in Torah—created before the sun was created—will gain much profit. This concept can also solve a puzzling question. The very first posuk children are taught is, *"Torah tziva lanu Moshe, morasha kehilos Yaakov*—Torah was commanded to us by Moshe, an inheritance of the Community of Jacob"* [*Devarim* 3:4]. This posuk is homiletically interpreted by the Gemara, *"Al tikrei morasha, ela morasah*—Don't read *morasha* as inheritance; rather read it as *morasah*, a betrothed"* [*Brachos* 57a]. The Torah's relationship to Klal Yisroel is like that of a betrothed maiden to her groom.

The difficulty is—why doesn't the Torah consider itself as being wed to us? Why is our relationship only that of an engagement and not of a completed marriage? One answer is that just like a marriage is not possible without an action, and consummation of the bond, so, too, to be wed to the Torah is not automatic. Rather, one must take action and toil in Torah to be deserving of such a wedded status.

This question could also be answered using the theme we considered above. Since the Torah always remains fresh and new, it is compared to an *arusah*, a betrothed maiden, which symbolizes ultimate newness and excitement! It also stands to reason that since Hashem commanded us to occupy ourselves with Torah, through all the days and nights of our life, He has ensured that its study will continually be stimulating, exhilarating, and challenging, for the Creator would never condemn us to a life of boredom or tediousness.

•XXIII•

The study of Torah is also an excellent way to expiate one's sins. With the word *emes*, truth, referring to Torah, the Gemara in *Masechtas Brachos* [5b], cites the posuk, *"B'chesed v'emes y'chupar avon*—With [a synthesis of] kindliness and truth, one achieves forgiveness of his sins." Similarly, Rabbah states [in *Masechtas Yevamos* 105a] that one may attain atonement through learning Torah. What a pleasant way to cleanse oneself of iniquities!

⭐ •XXIV• ⭐

After hearing so much about the magnitude and supremacy of this glorious mitzvah, it behooves us to understand that there is a proper way to study Torah. An overlooked aspect of this mitzvah is the fact that proper study is best fulfilled when we *verbalize* Torah with our mouths—rather than just reading it "mentally" with our eyes. Rav Yaakov Emdin, in his famous siddur (see the section entitled "Learning After Davening"), comments that one does not fulfill the positive commandment of Talmud Torah if one reads the words of the Torah but does not actually enunciate the words. Similarly, the *Shulchan Aruch Horav* [in *Hilchos Talmud Torah* 2:12] states that by just silently reading words of Torah, one has not fulfilled the command of *v'limadtem osam* (learning them). In *Tanya* the forceful point is made that one can meditate in Torah before saying *birchas* HaTorah in the morning. This is proof that mere meditation is not considered formal Torah study. The *Pela Yo'etz* also wonders why one would settle for only $500 profit (by learning without enunciating the words of Torah) when this profit could be doubled by verbalizing the words as well! He adds that the latter method gives much more *nachas* (enjoyment) to Hashem.

A major source for this attitude is in the Gemara in *Eruvin* [54a]. Here, Shmuel advised Rav Yehuda, *"P'sach puma'ich kari p'sach puma'ich tani, ki haichi d'miskayim beich v'turchu chayai*—Open up your mouth wide and learn Chumash and Mishna for in that way you'll remember your studies and live long." The Steipler Rav cites this Gemara as the source for the fact that learning with *dibbur* (speech) is a *segula yekara* (precious vehicle) to lengthen one's life [in the fourth letter of his *Kraiyna D'igrasa* point #2].

The Gemara in *Eruvin* [54a] also relates that Rabbi Eliezer had a disciple who studied silently for three years and he forgot all his learning! The Ran, in *Masechtas Nedarim* [9a], states that the primary source for the command of Torah study are the words *v'dibarta bam* (and say them) in our twice daily *Krias Shema*. Note the emphasis on *dibbur*. Similarly, in the beginning of *Yehoshua* [1:8], it states, "*Lo yamush sefer Ha-Torah hazeh m'picha*—The Torah should not waiver from your mouth." Likewise, the Maharsha, in *Masechtas Shabbos* [104a] states that to retain Torah, one must use one's mouth and enunciate the Torah's words.

This is why a baby does not retain the learning he or she was taught in the mother's womb. In the womb, the baby's mouth is still sealed and hence, there is no lasting retention. In the Sefer *Olas Chodesh* [*maamar* 214], we find a citation of the famous *Zohar* that every word a person utters brings one closer to the grave, for when one uses up one's quota of words, one's soul expires. This coincides nicely with the Targum in *Bereishis* [2:7] that interprets the words *nefesh chaya* (the spirit of life) as *ruach m'malla*, a spirit that speaks. It also gives us a deeper understanding of Chazal's statement, "*Hachayim v'hamaves b'yad haloshon*—Life and death are in the hands of the speaking" [*Tanchuma Metzora* 4]. Likewise, what Rav Shimon meant in *Avos* [1:16] is now perfectly clear. He didn't find anything better for the body than silence. By being stingy with words, one prolongs the life of one's body. On the other hand, every word of Torah uttered restores words lost in vain. So the Torah actually acts as a fountain of youth. In addition, in the Sefer *Shvivai Ohr* [perek 2], the Gaon Horav Pesach Tzvi

Frank, zt"l, advises that when one learns audibly, one's ears are brought into play with the great mitzvah of *limmud HaTorah*. That is the goal, Rav Frank explains—to be *mekadesh* (sanctify) as much of our body as possible with this sublime mitzvah.

After all this is said, there are clearly times when the above is *not* applicable—when *hearing* is desirable, as opposed to speaking words of Torah. These times include listening to a shiur or learning from a tape, etc. Indeed, in our morning prayers we preface *lilmod u'lelamed* (to learn and teach) with the important element of *lishmoa* (to hear) and indeed our first directive is *Shema Yisroel* (Hear, O Yisroel)!

However, when reviewing or studying on our own, we should train ourselves to read aloud. This may take some reconditioning, since we may have a stereotyped notion that reading with our mouths is something done by those who have trouble with comprehension. We especially hesitate to be vocal in public when we are not alone. However, when all the facts are considered, enunciating each word is the proper way of Torah study!

⤙ • XXV • ⤚

Another aspect of the rarefied mitzvah of Torah study is that success is directly linked to the amount of self-sacrifice we invest in our learning. This concept is taught to us quite forcefully in the Gemara which teaches that, *"Ein HaTorah miskayemes ela b'mi shemeimis atzmo alav*—The Torah is retained only by one who kills himself over its study" [*Masechtas Brachos* 63b]. This proclamation is made when we stay up studying Torah the entire night of Shavuos. Not only do we show our profound love for Torah—and that we value it enough to give up a night of sleep—but we also demonstrate the sacrifice we are prepared to make in behalf of Torah!

In *Bava Basra* [10a], Rav Menachem bar Yitzchok

states that as a reward for talmidei chachomim fighting off sleep to pursue their studies, Hashem will grant them the gift of divine splendor in the world to come. The Rambam cautions us that, *"Ein adam lomed rov chochmoso ela b'layla*—A person acquires the majority of his Torah knowledge primarily in nighttime learning" [*Hilchos Talmud Torah* 3:13]. Therefore, the Rambam insists that one should not squander even one night of one's life without Torah study. Although we are usually exhausted after a long arduous day, if we want to succeed in a career of Torah excellence, we must condition ourselves to stretch our limits and make sure that each and every night we learn some Torah.

•XXVI•

In *Hilchos Talmud Torah*, the *Shulchan Aruch* paskins that, *"T'chilas dino shel adam eino elah al talmud Torah, v'achar kach al shar ma'asav*—A person is first judged by the heavenly tribunal concerning his Torah studies, and only then is he judged concerning the rest of his deeds" [*Yorah Deiah* 246:19]. This *psak* should be enough to galvanize us into taking a serious look at how we manage our time. It should serve as a powerful catalyst to ensure that we treat Torah learning as a major part of our day-to-day schedule. The Gemara in *Sanhedrin* [94b] and the *Zohar* [r.m. section 3, 29a] refer to the *ohl* Torah (the yoke of Torah). The analogy to a yoke is that every Jewish male must continually ask himself, "Do I have a good reason why I am not learning right now?" This is similar to the intermediate days of a festival, on *chol hamoed*, when one needs to ask oneself if there exists one of the five *heterim* (allowances because of a contingency) to be able to do work. So, too, at every moment one has to ask oneself, "Do I have a *heter* not to be studying at this time?" Of course, there are a multitude of *heterim*, such as making a livelihood, providing for the needs of our parents, the charge of *v'simach es ishto* (making one's wife happy), catering to the needs of one's body (including getting a sufficient dose of physical exercise), engaging in community responsibilities, relaxing a little, plus a healthy dosage of chesed and praise, and praying to Hashem. However, if one wishes to be properly equipped when we are judged by Hashem (Who knows the inner workings of our hearts) if Torah was our yoke, and whether we lived with the Torah philosophy of *v'hagisa bah yomam v'layla*, then we must train ourselves to think along these lines, and always be vigilant about our Torah-study time.

⟵ • XXVII • ⟶

In *Masechtas Shabbos* [31a] the Gemara informs us that we will be required to answer to the heavenly judge if we were "*Koveia ittim Latorah*—Made fixed times daily and nightly for Torah" [*Masechtas Shabbos* 31a]. These designated periods should be so sacred that we always make sure to reserve time in our busy day for Torah study. This is another facet of our obligation to Torah study. Even if we have iron-clad reasons why we are exempt from full-time Torah study, we still must ensure that no twelve-hour period of our life passes without some Torah study (barring certain special circumstances). The *Orchos Chaim Leharosh* gives an interesting suggestion in number 44, "*K'va ittim Latorah kodem achila, u'sh'chiva v'dibarta bam al shulchonecha*—Fix times for Torah study before eating and sleeping, and speak Torah at your mealtimes." The Rosh understood the hectic pace of daily life. He wisely advised that we make our Torah commitments *before* we either eat or sleep, knowing that we would have to find time every day for these necessities. By connecting our Torah study to these things, we will automatically reserve time for Torah as well!

∼ • XXVIII • ∼

It is my fervent wish to Hashem that after reading this essay and learning how Torah study promises life, health, wealth, honor, charm, success in this world, protection in the grave, an assurance of *techiyas hameisim*, and prominence in the world to come, that readers will be moved to re-evaluate priorities and ambitions and add more Torah dedication to their daily life!

A Suppositional Interview With The Yetzer Hara

[*This essay was originally written before Pesach.*]

In *Masechtas Shabbos* [105b], the Gemara cites the verse in *Tehillim*, "*Lo yihyhe b'cha Ai-l zar*—There should not be within you a foreign G-d" [*Tehillim* 81:10]. The Talmud interprets this to mean that one should eradicate one's evil inclinations. This is all the more urgent since the Gemara in *Bava Basra* [16a] identifies the *Malach HaMaves* as being one and the same with the evil inclination—and we definitely don't want the angel of death lurking in our vicinity. The following dialogue forewarns us of the many temptations and multiple wiles of the *yetzer hara* before Pesach. With the help of Hashem, we will be able to dodge his many bullets when they inevitably confront us.

Reporter (from the Torah Gazette): Reb Yetzer Hara, I know, as a busy Malach Hashem, that your time is precious. I understand you are quite involved insuring that people always have free will and that serving Hashem will be an exercise of "*u'vacharta bachayim*—choosing life" [*Devarim* 30:19].

Therefore, we will not keep you long.

Yetzer Hara: Don't worry, the more you talk, the more the likelihood is that I'll convince you to lie or reveal *loshon hara* about someone.

Torah Gazette: Whew, thanks for the "warning." Once Purim is over, what do you do first?

Yetzer Hara: That's easy! I get the women thinking that this seasonal crumb-hunt for leaven is ridiculous! Should they be chained to the house and work like slaves to find some rotting bread or moldy crumbs? I whisper in their ears that their husbands will be *mevatel* (renouncing ownership) the chometz anyway, and then will sell the chometz so they don't have to be so obsessive about the cleaning!

Torah Gazette: Surely there are many pious women who realize this is a holy occupation—symbolic of ridding the house of any vestige of the *yetzer hara* (sorry!), and that their ancestors have been doing this identical activity for thousands of years.

Yetzer Hara: Of course there will be the tougher cases. With them I try to wreck their *shalom bayis* by getting them to fight over whether a cleaning lady is necessary, and why the husband isn't helping enough, and getting him to say that his wife isn't enough of a balabustah!

Torah Gazette: What about the many families with loads of children who help out doing the chores!

Yetzer Hara: Oh, that's real fertile ground! I get the bochurim and maidelach to trample all over the Fifth Commandment (honoring your parents) by convincing them to fight and scream at their mom and dad that they work hard enough in school and that now that they are on vacation they shouldn't have to work! I even succeed in getting parents to fight about how to utilize the children!

Torah Gazette: How about the men?

Yetzer Hara: First, I get them to procrastinate about preparing the Haggadah. Although it should be ridiculously simple to them that they should be well prepared on the one night they have the mitzvah of *"v'higadta l'bincha—*to teach the children."* I actually convince them to sit back and listen to their children's *vertlach* (Torah nouvelle) and not contribute anything themselves.

Torah Gazette: What about the learned husbands?

Yetzer Hara: These are easy too! I convince them to be stingy about clothing their wives properly for Yom Tov (you know, clothing brings women joy—it's a Gemara!) or I fool them into adopting unnecessary *chumros* (stringencies) causing their wives needless suffering and heartache.

Torah Gazette: What about the newly married?

Yetzer Hara: Ach, that's a piece of cake. I cause them to fight over whose parents they're going to for the Seder. Then I persuade them to quarrel over whose parents have a more meaningful Seder. After that I have the in-laws mix in by having them observe that the young lady doesn't help enough or pay sufficient attention to the proceedings or that the young man really isn't as much of a learning boy as he was supposed to be ("Why, he hasn't said an original *vort* all night!"). The opportunities are just endless!

Torah Gazette: What about outside the home?

Yetzer Hara: I tempt the storekeepers to inflate the prices on everything just because it's Pesach. I work on igniting the frazzled and overworked nerves of both customers and store owners. You wouldn't believe the anger, and *nivul peh* (obscenities) I am able to elicit from people under stressful circumstances! I also tempt shoppers to buy anything that everyone else seems to be buying even if it doesn't appear to have the proper labeling and Kashrus credentials.

Torah Gazette: What about closer to Yom Tov?

Yetzer Hara: Wow! I have a royal time on *bedika* night.

Torah Gazette: What do you mean?

Yetzer Hara: I instigate wives to ask their husbands why they are checking all the places they've spent the last month cleaning. (The women end up thinking their husbands don't trust them!) I also tempt the tired husband into making a speedy fifteen-minute *bedika*. On Erev Pesach, I tempt the children not to take a nap in the afternoon so they'll be sleepy during the Seder. Then I convince everyone to eat and eat throughout the day so they won't have an appetite by the time the Seder arrives.

Torah Gazette: Does it get "better" when Yom Tov finally arrives?

Yetzer Hara: Don't be naive! It's only the beginning! I induce the wives to convince their husbands that they should rush through the Seder since the little ones are hungry. Then the tired fathers proclaim, "Save the *vertlach* for during the meal." (Yeah, right!) Then I instigate another fight by getting the wives to ask their husbands that as an afikomen present their husbands should be nice to them. Or I make the children remind their parents that they didn't even get last year's afikomen yet!

Torah Gazette: But that's only the Seder night.

Yetzer Hara: Right! Then I have them miss half the davening in the morning because they drank too much wine. And, oh boy, is Chol HaMoed a picnic?!

Torah Gazette: How so?

Yetzer Hara: You know halachah dictates that anything not allowed on Yom Tov, you're prohibited to do on Chol HaMoed as well—unless you have a specific *heter* (allowance) such as, it's needed for Yom Tov, or it's a *davar ha'avud* (you'll suffer a loss), and a relatively few other exceptions. Still, I convince people to get oil changes for their car and to do various other unnecessary activities—all of which are grievous sins! Then I get the family embroiled over what to do on Chol

HaMoed with one or the other spouse accusing their partner that they never spend time with the family. To add fuel to the fire, I tempt them to go places where a pious Jew shouldn't ever venture. I also convince the boys that *bein hazemanim* signifies time off, and in this way I persuade them to miss *minyonim* and not to pick up a *sefer*.

Torah Gazette: Before we let you go, do you have any parting words for us?

Yetzer Hara: Well, one of my nastiest 'tricks' is to get men to violate the Tenth Commandment!

Torah Gazette: The Tenth??

Yetzer Hara: Yup! You see, the women get all dressed up in their holiday finery. I entice the men to look—and covet what is forbidden. This after all is the last commandment—not to desire what is not yours!

Torah Gazette: Whew! Well, thank you again for your time. I really do hope we apply ourselves with such diligence to *Avodas* Hashem as you do to your mission in life!

Sharpening Our Chinuch Skills

—— •I• ——

Looking at how Hashem goes about teaching us proper *middos* (character traits) in the Torah gives us powerful insights into the art of teaching. Hashem does not directly say "be merciful," "be compassionate," or "be kind." Instead, He portrays the lives of our *Avos* and *Imahos*—our Patriarchs and Matriarchs—and tells us to emulate them, as we say, *"Maaseh Avos, simon labonim*—The deeds of our Forefathers are lessons for their children" [*Tanchuma* 9].

The *Tana D'bei Eliyahu* similarly espouses [parshah 23, chapter 1] that every Jew must ask himself or herself when their deeds will reach the level of the great Avraham, Yitzchok, and Yaakov. Similarly, the Medrash in *Vayikra Rabbah* [9:3], affirms that *derech eretz* (proper behavior) preceded the Torah, since the ways and deeds of our *Avos* came before the giving of the Torah at Har Sinai.

Hashem also teaches us the proper manner to behave through His actions. As the Torah teaches in *Devarim* [13:5], "*Acharei Hashem Elokim teileichu*—Follow the ways of Hashem.*" In *Masechtas Sotah* [14a], Rebbi Chama explains that this means we must emulate Hashem's ways. In *Masechtas Shabbos* [133b], Abba Shaul similarly states that this is the intent of the posuk, "*Zeh Keili v'anveihu*—This is my G-d and I will glorify Him.*" (The Medrash further elaborates that *v'anveihu* is a composition of two words, *ani* and *v'hu*—*I* and *he*, meaning that the way to glorify Him is to imitate His ways). We see, for instance, from the Torah narrative that Hashem clothed Adom and Chava or that He visited Avraham when he was ill. In this manner, we learn from His example to give to the poor and visit the sick. The way to glorify Hashem is to try to emulate Him. The greatest praise you can give to anyone is to show that they are regarded as your mentor, someone on whom to model your life.

However, "Why did Hashem choose to teach us *middos* so indirectly? He simply could have given us commandments to be merciful, gracious, etc., in the same manner that He gave us the 613 mitzvos.

One answer to this question, I think, is that Hashem is demonstrating to us how we should teach good *middos* to our children: just like He chose to teach by way of example, so, too, the most powerful way to impart good character traits and Yiddishkeit to our children is to make ourselves correct role models. This way our children will learn naturally by imitating our ways.

The following anecdote about Rav Yaakov Kaminetsky, zt"l, confirms this notion. When asked how one should teach children to make *brachos*, he answered simply, "I don't teach my children to make *brachos*. Rather, they hear me and the Rebbitzen continually making *brachos* in the correct manner, and they automatically do it the same way."

〰 • II • 〰

The Chofetz Chaim emphasized this theme when he quoted from *Devarim*, "*V'limaditem osam es b'neichem*—You should teach Torah to your children" [11:19]. He noticed that the word *osam* is written without the letter "vav," and he commented that without the "vav," the word could also be read *atem* (you). This spelling conveys that the best way to teach children Torah is to sit down and study Torah yourself. If children regularly witness their father learning Torah, this is what they will choose to do with their time as well.

The Kotzker Rebbe comments similarly. He predicts that a father who constantly yells at his son, "Why aren't you learning?!" can expect that when his son is grown, he, too, will scream at his children, "Why aren't you learning?!" However, if one truly desires one's child to learn, the only action necessary is to sit down and learn Torah oneself and set a genuine example.

For this reason, it is even important for someone who attends numerous shiurim outside the home or spends an entire day learning in a kollel, that some learning always takes place at home in the presence of children. This is because a man who simply returns home, eats and plops down on the recliner with the daily tabloid and then falls asleep, is not giving a visual chinuch to his children. And as we've seen from the examples in the Torah, visual chinuch may be the most powerful kind of chinuch.

〰 • III • 〰

One might wonder why we expect so much more from our children than we expect from ourselves. Why is it that we are incensed when we catch them lying, and yet we are not as scrupulous about our own honesty? Why are we so intent that they make a *bracha* with *kavanah*, while our *brachos* are often just mumbled gibberish? Why do we berate them for wasting time, when we are masters at this particular art? Perhaps we do this because we are burdened with a violent *yetzer hara* (evil inclination) that always encourages us in the wrong direction while, when it comes to our children, we have no such *yetzer hara*. Therefore, because we want only the altruistic best for our children, it may be wiser to evaluate how to conduct ourselves based upon the high standards that we desire from our children. Thus, we should remember the following axiom: Don't expect more from your children than you expect from yourself!

 • IV •

Just how perceptive are children? Perhaps a personal anecdote will help illustrate the answer. As an afikomen gift, my wife and I bought a set of imitation dishes for our daughter, Devora. During the second days of Yom Tov, there was a torrential downpour and all of our children (ages ranging from 1 to 9) stayed home from shul. They decided to play house, using Devora's dishes. They set up a mock Shabbos table, appointed our oldest son to be Totty (father), while our oldest daughter became Mommy. The rest were "the kids." My wife relates that, for the next hour, she watched mesmerized as the children imitated our every habit and inflection to an exactitude that was astonishing. From the way I tug at my beard, to the way my wife quiets the children while I make kiddush, they imitated our every move. This incident should remind us of the weighty responsibility that lies upon us to insure that we demonstrate to our children the proper way to live because even though we are not always aware of it—they are watching us and emulating us all the time!

• V •

Rav Shamshon Raphael Hirsch, zt"l, explains that the

Hebrew word *eretz* (earth) contains the word *ratz* (to run), since all the inhabitants of the world are on the run from cradle to grave. This is quite evident to us now since we have witnessed the large number of women who have been pushed out of the house to help pay for children's schooling. In addition, many men need to take on second (and even third) jobs to help make ends meet. The consequences of these developments to the chinuch of the next generation are potentially catastrophic. The quality time parents have available to spend with their children has rapidly dwindled. Coupled with this, the stockpile of patience parents have, is sometimes thoroughly drained when it's time to deal with their offspring by the end of the day. One rebbe revealed to me that he refused a homework sheet signed by a family's live-in maid. (To "solve" this knotty problem, the parents bought their Spanish housekeeper a rubber stamp with their signature!)

How does Hashem expect us to live up to the enormous challenge of raising children in the proper Torah manner while we are in the midst of such a hectic and frenetic pace of life? If we fantasize that one day there will be ample time to sit down with them and have long exploratory conversations, I'm afraid we are being unrealistic. (To confirm whether or not I'm correct, count how many times you had such a heart-to-heart chat with your children *this* month!) Rather, I think that being a Toradik role model, is one of the prime solutions to the scarcity of time that we have available to be master teachers and trainers of our children. Each moment that we are near our children must be utilized as an opportunity to demonstrate to them the proper way to live.

◄━ • VI • ━►

An interesting proof of the importance of personal example in the chinuch process can be brought from a famous

Gemara in *Yoma* [47a]. The legendary woman, Kimchis, had seven children who all ministered as Kohanim Gedolim (High Priests in the Temple). We can only imagine how extraordinary this woman was to have such illustrious sons! The great sages of the era even asked her for the secret that had enabled her to raise such outstanding children. We may expect that Kimchis replied with some master-training technique or some powerful insight concerning how she connected and communicated with her children. Ironically though, her response had nothing directly to do with the children. Rather, she mentioned how she lived with an intense awareness that Hashem was watching her. She said, *"L'olam lo ra'u koros beisi kilaiy roshi—*All my life, the beams of my home never saw my uncovered hair!" In other words, she was primarily invested with the knowledge that Hashem was watching her at all times and therefore she made great efforts to be at her best at all times. So, she always radiated *yiras* Hashem. This reinforces our theme: The key to top-notch chinuch is found in the exemplary way we lead our own lives and is passed on to our children through "familial osmosis."

•VII•

The supreme importance of transmitting our heritage to our children can be learned from Avraham Avinu. One might wonder why Avraham was so endeared to Hashem, and why Hashem chose to start the Jewish nation, specifically, with Avraham. Weren't earlier giants such as Mesushelach, Noach, or Sheim also great men from whom the Jewish people could descend? In *Bereishis*, we find an answer to this question. Hashem says about Avraham, *"Ki y'dativ, l'maan asher y'tzaveh es banav v'es bnei beiso acharav—*I love him, for I know he will teach his children and his household after him" [18:19]. Hashem did not choose Avraham because Avraham had entered the burning furnace of the wicked Nimrod. Nor did Hashem choose Avraham because he had proved himself through his famous ten trials. Not even Avraham's lifelong campaign of chesed caused Hashem to select him. Rather the posuk reveals to us that Avraham was chosen by Hashem to be Father of the Jewish People because of his dedication and ability to transmit the mesorah to his progeny. This character trait is what especially endeared Avraham to Hashem.

Horav Moshe Feinstein, zt"l, explains that this is the reason that, although Shaim V'Aiver had a great academy, there are no survivors of that great institution. They did not have sufficient talent to ensure the passage of the Jewish heritage from generation to generation.

This is why on Pesach, which is the anniversary of the birth of the Jewish nation and a legacy of Avraham Avinu, we have the special mitzvah of *v'higadita l'bincha* (to instruct our children), and quite literally "to pass-over" the major tenets of our faith to them. We emphasize this duty on our national anniversary since, as we explained, it is because of our devotion to transmit our heritage that we were chosen by Hashem to be His people. The famous historian Josephus (*Contra Apion*) attests to the fact that there was nothing more important to the Jews than the education of their young.

The next time we look with dismay at skyrocketing tuition bills, bemoaning the fact that we have to work so much harder than the average American because we can't benefit from a free public school system, let us take heart in the realization that the sacrifice is well worth it. We are living up to Hashem's expectations, sacrificing so much to follow in our ancestor's footsteps of insuring that our children receive the full flavor and understanding of Torah M'Sinai.

⤙ • VIII • ⤚

The unwavering priority of educating our children can

be seen in the first parshah of *Krias Shema*, in which every Jew twice a day makes a commitment to, "*V'shinantom l'vanecha, v'dibarta bam... U'kshartom l'os al yodecha...*—You should teach it to your children, speak about it... And bind it to your hand...." Remarkably, the mitzvah of teaching our children is mentioned before the mitzvah to study Torah. Teaching children is a mitzvah that even precedes the mitzvah of tefillin, which the Rosh calls the most important positive precept of the Torah. This once again emphasizes how extremely important it is that we succeed in properly raising our children.

     • IX •

A beautiful instance of teaching by example, and an illustration of the concept just mentioned, can be seen from a wonderful *minhag* related to me by one of the *chashuva baal habatim* (important family men) in our shul, Reb Abe Newman, *tichya*. At the beginning of each year, he told me, his father would take his first pay check and use it toward his children's tuition payments. He would ask the children to sit with him at the table and, in their presence, he would write out the various tuition checks, letting them know that *schar limmud* (educational debts) must always be taken care of first because the children's education was of such paramount importance to him and his wife and to the success of any Jewish home. If more parents adopted this practice, the next generation would feel more of a responsibility to meet their tuition obligations and would not relegate it to the bottom of their priority list as so many people unfortunately do.

     • X •

Another proof of the tremendous significance of educating our young can be learned from the cherubim that were on top of the Aron in the Holy of Holies in the Beis HaMikdash.

In *Masechtas Succah* [5b], Rabbi Avahu informs us that the cherubim were shaped in the form of young children. The *Meam Loez* [*Shemos* pg. 962] explains that the cherubim were situated on top of the *luchos* which were housed inside the Aron Kodesh. Therefore, the cherubim portray the message of children studying Torah. This is considered the most rarefied and lofty scene of Jewish life and hence, the one most fitting to place in the Holy of Holies. The *Medrash Tanchuma* [*Vayakhel* 7:1] notes that the cherubim are as precious to Hashem as heaven and earth, further emphasizing the importance that Hashem places on the tutelage of the children of Yisroel!

~ • XI • ~

The *Zohar* teaches us, *"Istakel B'oraisa, u'bara alma—* Hashem looked in the Torah and fashioned the world from it" [cheilek 2-161:1]. A striking example of this can be found in the Gemara which relates that Hashem gave every person a different appearance so that an impostor could not claim another woman or another house as his own [*Masechtas Sanhedrin* 38a]. In other words, Hashem looked in the Torah and saw the commandments, "Thou shall not commit adultery," and, "Thou shall not steal," and fashioned the world to work within these parameters. With this in mind, let us ask ourselves why Hashem created a formula of genetics so that children would acquire the habits and character traits of their parents.

I think that Hashem looked in the Torah and saw the mitzvah of chinuch. Therefore, He designed the science of genetics in order to offer parents a sharper insight into their own children, and educate them accordingly. Unlike a rebbe who isn't sure what makes a specific child tick, and thus may fail to understand a child's needs, we have a strong advantage in anticipating and fulfilling the needs of our children. Our children are so like us, and often share with us similar or identical strengths and weaknesses. This knowledge is a powerful tool in the hands of a dedicated parent who desires to guide children on the Torah path of life. This should also impress upon us how important it is for parents to work together with rebbeim and teachers in their children's education.

• XII •

When it comes to the mitzvah of chinuch, there is a tendency to procrastinate. When children are small, we excuse ourselves by thinking that they are too young to absorb any meaningful lessons. When they grow a little older, we rationalize that they are already overburdened by schoolwork and we don't want to overload them. Then, the boys may disappear to an out-of-town yeshiva and are basically out of reach.

There are other causes for the temptation to procrastinate. In the winter, we reason that we are just too busy dealing with the crush of earning a living. We assure ourselves that in the summer, when things are slower and we have vacation and more leisure time, we'll focus on giving the children some quality time. But alas, the summer comes around and we say to ourselves that it's just not a good use of the time right now. Summer is the time to relax and recharge our batteries lest we fall apart altogether. Before we know it, we've hardly given our children any attention at all.

It's important to keep in mind that we really don't have all that much time to leave a distinct mark upon our children in the first place. Until they are six years old, they are babies. By thirteen years old many children are already out of the house most of the time. When they finally return home, they are soon packing their bags in anticipation of the next phase of their lives, hurtling toward the chupah, leaving parents shaking their heads with regret and wondering, "Why we didn't spend more time with them while they were our full-time charges?"

Therefore, it is crucial to be aware of the *psak* of the Gadol Hador of the previous generation, Horav Moshe Feinstein, zt"l. In his *Igros Moshe* [*Yoreh Deiah*; cheilek 3, siman 76], Rav Moshe advises that there is no fixed age to begin training children to believe in Hashem. Many times, the obligation starts before the child begins to talk—as soon as the child recognizes its father or mother and other frequently seen family members or friends. This is an eye-opener. It makes us realize that we should begin to feel a responsibility to inject Yiddishkeit into our children even while they are still in the crib! This directly counters any justification we may have felt in putting off our children's education until they're ready to engage in adult conversation.

•XIII•

In the first chapter of his *sefer Beis Yisroel* [sif 3], the great Gaon, the Chofetz Chaim, gives the following advice to parents: The true way to instill in children belief in Hashem and His Torah and insure that they will become G-d-fearing individuals dedicated to fulfilling Hashem's mitzvos—is to educate them about Gan Eden (a paradise where pleasures are unimaginable and eternal) and to inform them that this paradise—designated exclusively for the G-d fearing—awaits them in the future. (As it says in the fourth chapter of *Pirkei Avos*—one hour of bliss in Gan Eden is better than all the imaginable pleasures of this world.) We should also let our children know that there is a Gehinnom (hell), for sinners who stray from Hashem's will, where fires are sixty times hotter than any fire known to mankind. This awareness, the Chofetz Chaim advises, will serve as both an incentive and a deterrent to children, so that on their journey through life they will carefully consider their options and decisions.

However, one may wonder if the promise of a reward is

the preferred method of educating children in service to Hashem. We should therefore understand that the Chofetz Chaim is essentially advising that we employ the lesson of Rav, *"Shem'toch shelo lishma, ba lishma*—Someone who engages in Torah and mitzvos for ulterior motives, will eventually gravitate to do the mitzvos purely for the sake of Heaven" [*Masechtas Pesachim* 50b]. Thus, for young minds not yet mature enough to serve Hashem altruistically or out of love, we train them with the lure of Heavenly reward and the threat, *chas v'shalom*, of eternal damnation.

In a letter found in the *sefer Kraiyna D'igrasa* [105], the great Steipler Gaon, zt"l, issues the same instructions to parents. He writes that one should implant in children fear of Hashem, fear of Heavenly punishment, and awareness of the reward in the eternal world for the performance of mitzvos. It is therefore incumbent upon us to make this idea part of our everyday life and to refer habitually to *Olam Habah*. We should praise our children's good deeds using a comment like, "You sure acquired for yourself a nice chunk of *Olam Habah* for that mitzvah!"

━━•XIV•━━

HaGaon Rav Moshe Feinstein, zt"l, also encouraged parents to pray that they will be successful in guiding and educating their children. Similarly, the Steipler Gaon writes that we have to continually pray that our children will prosper in *yiras Shamayim* —fear of Hashem. The *Mishnah Berurah* [siman 47:10] advises that we pray for our children each morning in the *bracha ahavas olam* (presumably when we ask for Divine assistance *l'lamed* (to teach), and again in the *birchas* haTorah, when we say, *"V'nihyeh anachnu v'tzetzaeinu lomdei...*—May we, and our children learn ...." We should also focus on our children's chinuch in *U'vo L'tzion*, when we say, *"L'ma'an lo niga larik, v'lo neiled l'avehala*—May we not weary ourselves for naught, nor beget children in vain."

The Chazon Ish composed a tefillah for mothers to say for their children in *Shema Koleinu* in the thrice daily *Shemoneh Esrei*. (This tefillah can be found in the *Igros Chazon Ish* [cheilek 1:74].) Another suitable moment for women to pray for their children is just after they light the Shabbos candles. Finally, the Shelah HaKodosh writes that Erev Rosh Chodesh Sivan is a particularly auspicious time for parents to pray for the their children's success [*Inyanei Tefillah*].

━━ • XV • ━━

The *Kitzur Shulchan Aruch*, in its brief discussion of the mitzvah of chinuch [siman 165:1], states that one should place special emphasis on truthfulness, and strictly supervise children so that they never lie. It is probable that he emphasizes this particular attribute because the Gemara, teaches us that, *"Chosomo shel HaKodosh Baruch Hu emes*—The seal of Hashem is truth" [*Masechtas Shabbos* 55a]. This means that just as we know the author of a letter by their signature, so, too, in order to say that something emanates from Hashem, it cannot have any vestiges of falsehood. Therefore, if we would like to raise our children in Hashem's ways, we must stamp out lies and falsehood during character development. Here, too, it is mandatory that we, ourselves, are completely honest. Otherwise, all the lectures we give our children will be scorned and ridiculed by them as hypocritical, parental drivel. Examples of some easy hazards when our standards of honesty are not as high as we expect from our children: the phone rings and we tell our child to say that we are not home, or a *meshulach* (charity collector) rings the doorbell and we yell to the child to say that their father or mother is already sleeping. Such parental failures do not help impress upon children the importance of always being truthful!

A particular egregious example of our mixed messages concerning honesty is told about parents sending their child to a sleep-away camp for the first time. They impressed upon their child how they had spent so much money to enable their child to be in an ideal place to breathe the Torah ruach, and learn *middos tovos* (good character traits). Then, they warned the child to live up to his good name, to always be scrupulously honest and never make a chilul Hashem. Finally, they requested that as soon as he arrived at camp, he should telephone them and let them know that he had arrived safely. But, since it would be a shame to "waste" money on a long-distance call, he should make a collect call, and tell the operator that his name is Shoindue (Yiddish for, "I'm here!"). The parents, of course, do not accept the phone call. This kind of behavior is lethal to the future integrity of children.

An excellent illustration of what a substantial role honesty plays in the makeup of a ben Torah can be found in *Rus Rabbah* [5:11]. There, the *Medrash* cites the posuk in *Rus* where Rus HaMoaviya (Ruth, the Moabite) is quoted at length [2:21]. The *Medrash* is troubled by the fact that after her conversion, Rus is still referred to as Rus HaMoaviya. Once someone turns over a new leaf, we are forbidden to mention their past (as the Rambam rules in *Hilchos Teshuva* [7:8]). The *Medrash* answers that since Rus slightly altered the order of Boaz's sentence when she related the words of Boaz to Naomi, the word HaMoaviya is pointing out that the Moabite quality in her was still present, for a Jew-from-birth would have never even changed around the order of someone's words when retelling something in their name. Woe to us! How far have we strayed from the ancient Jews! How often do we pepper a story when retelling it, adding our own finishing touches and trimmings!? From this *Medrash*, it is clear that the Jewish identity is inexorably tied with our loyalty to the truth.

—•XVI•—

The Gemara teaches that, *"Bikvosa d'mshicha chutz-pah yasga*—Around the time of Mashiach, there will be a pro-liferation of impudence" [*Masechtas Sotah* 49b]. This is defi-nitely manifest in our generation which is witnessing an un-precedented amount of disrespect toward leaders, elders, par-ents, and spouses. Nowadays, people have the audacity to look their benevolent creditors in the eye and say, "I'm not paying—sue me." Congregants berate their Rabbis with the accusation, "As long I'm paying your salary, how dare you talk to me like that!" Yeshiva children talk to their English teachers with a lack of respect that borders on the incredible, and many marital problems escalate to open warfare because couples lack any fundamental concept of marital respect!

Part of this problem stems from the fact that parents are *not* proper role models. If parents allow their children to hear them berate each other and hurl harsh words and accusations back and forth, their children will grow up with this prescrip-tion for solving problems. Furthermore, discussing the flaws and weaknesses of a Rav or yeshiva principal in front of the children (even if it is true) does not help foster a sense of respect and honor to authority. Frequently, parents are dismayed when this cavalier attitude backfires in later years. All too often, chil-dren who grow up lacking the foundation of respecting every-one except the Gedolei Hador (or sometimes only an already deceased Godol Hador!) also turn on their parents and display total disdain toward the mitzvah of *kibud av v'eim* (honor of father and mother).

—•XVII•—

Another way to instill in children a sense of respect to authority is to train them from a young age to fulfill the mitzvah of, *"Mipnei seiva takum v'hadarta pnei zakein*—To stand up for the elderly and to revere the one who has acquired much Torah knowledge" [*Vayikra* 19:32]. What is the purpose of this Biblical command? We can hardly think that it is for the benefit of the recipient, namely the elder or Torah Sage, because honor is not a coveted acquisition by the wise. Quite the contrary, the Mishna in *Pirkei Avos* [4:21] cautions us to beware of honor since it is one of the evils that propels a person from this world! Therefore, the purpose of this precept must be to implant the sense of *giving* honor, to groom people in the habit of respecting the experience of the elderly, and respecting those of superior knowledge, and to honor the Torah sage. An ability to give honor is an extremely important trait for our young to acquire.

— • XVIII • —

While on the subject of respect, it is imperative to educate children to always be reverent while in shul. We have discussed this at greater length in a different chapter ("The Sin That's Too Heavy To Bear") but it is sufficient for now to establish that there is a definite link between fathers who talk about sports, styles, the stock market, and the latest gossip, with the children who run around the halls and aisles in shul, and disturb the tefillah. We must keep in mind that if adults observe a cavalier attitude to davening and *kedushas* Beis HaMedrash, our children will manifest the same inclination in their more childish manner!

— • XIX • —

Another significant subject to teach our children concerns something we find in *Devarim*, "*V'lo yeiraeh b'cha ervas davar v'shav me'acharecha*—That I (Hashem) may not see in you (Bnei Yisroel) a matter of nakedness and turn away from you" [23:16]. The Chofetz Chaim points out that Hashem never says He will forsake us with the exception of the sins of licentiousness and immorality.

It is so important, therefore, if our aspiration is to make our home a true *Mikdash Me'at* worthy of the presence of the *Shechina*, that we strive to keep the invasion of American *ervas davar* (lewdness) from entering the portals of our *bayis ne'e-man*. It goes without saying that this includes the blatant immorality present in the modern day "R" rated home videos, cable TV movies, the (so-called) soft pornography present in many television programs and advertisements, and the lewdness of some magazines. This is perhaps one of the greatest challenges for our generation because the 'tube' offers one of the quickest ways for a tense and frustrated couple to relax after an exhausting and trying day. The electronic screen also offers one of the simplest and quickest solutions to getting the children out of our hair. We must realize that our *tznius* (Jewish modesty) is one of the traits that carries the promise that we will have extraordinary descendants. The Gemara teaches us that in the merit of Rochel Imeinu's (the Matriarch Rachel) modesty, she earned the privilege of being the ancestress of Shaul HaMelech (King Saul), who, in merit of his own modest behavior, was blessed with Esther HaMalka (Queen Esther) as his progeny [*Masechtas Megillah* 13b]! We should therefore strive to instill in our children strong inhibitions concerning modesty.

In the immoral surroundings in which we live, a theme of our teaching should be that one of the merits for which our ancestors were redeemed from Egypt, and weren't condemned to perpetual slavery, was that we didn't forsake our distinctively modest Jewish garb. We, too, should be steadfast in our dedication to the tenets of modesty and not succumb to the immoral ways of our corrupt society.

⚬ • XX • ⚬

The Gemara teaches us that any mitzvah which we initially accepted with joy—like the precept of circumcision—we still perform with delight. However, those mitzvos which we originally accepted with misgivings, we still have trouble with [*Masechtas Shabbos* 130a]. This Gemara is not just a historical oracle. It is an important educational technique. It reveals how important it is for us to enthusiastically introduce mitzvos to our children.

For example, our young children hear us commiserating about how we have to shlep out to the succah in the cold, and that by the time we sit down the food is already cold. Then they hear us further complain that the evergreen needles from the *schach* (Succah covering) are always falling into our food, should we be surprised when our children grow up with an inborn disdain for this lofty mitzvah. However, if we correctly portray the rarefied mitzvah of sitting in the succah as one of only two mitzvos into which a person immerses his or her entire body, fully clothed, and that it is an exciting opportunity to serve Hashem in a wonderful way, the child will grow up with a much more rewarding legacy. [The other mitzvah which a person immerses one's whole body into is *yeshivas* Eretz Yisroel (dwelling in the Land of Yisroel) and not mikvah—for one doesn't enter the mikvah with shoes on one's feet.]

Similarly if a woman vocally expresses a negative attitude about cleaning the house for Pesach, her children will associate Pesach with negativity. And a father's attitude when he has to sit through a chazan's lengthy rendition of tefillas *Mussaf* will convey a great deal to his children about davening.

Horav Avigdor Miller, *shlit"a*, explains that when it rains, if we voice our dismay and groan that it's such a gloomy and depressing day, and the rain has spoiled all our plans, then the observing child will grow up programmed to be moody and despondent on a rainy day for the rest of his or her life. As Dovid HaMelech (King David) advises in *Tehillim*, we should share with our children the attitude of, *"Ivdu es Hashem b'simcha*—Serve Hashem with joy" [100:2].

This approach should even be more pronounced when it comes to the mitzvah of Torah study. Our sages teach us, *"Ein simcha k'simchas haTorah*—There is no joy like the happiness of Torah learning." Horav Moshe Feinstein, zt"l, used to put his sons' clothing on the radiator overnight, so that when he awoke them to go to yeshiva in the early morning cold, he would dress their shivering bodies in the inviting steaming warmth of their preheated clothing. He did this in order that they would have a desire to arise to study Torah! What a marvelous positive reinforcement!

•XXI•

In infusing our children with enthusiasm and joy, we should realize that this is not only an educational tool for proper mitzvah observance. It will also be a critical asset for them when they marry. In *Hilchos Ishos* [15:19], the Rambam teaches us that one of the primary responsibilities of a spouse is, *"Shelo yihye atzev*—That one should not be sad, gloomy and despondent." If one mate is continually negative, this will pull down the other and darken his or her life as well! Cultivating a cheerful world view in your children will have dramatic consequences throughout their entire lives.

•XXII•

Hand in hand with the development of a cheerful and sunny disposition is the importance of steering clear from the destructive habit of complaining. Complaining erodes the pleasures of many marriages and can make a person a social pariah. No one enjoys the company of a habitual whiner. The Medrash teaches us the devastating repercussions of complaining. We are warned, in *Bereishis Rabbah* [chapter 62], that when Yaakov told Pharaoh [*Bereishis* 47:9], "*M'aat v'reim ymei shnei chayai*—My years were few and bitter," Yaakov lost thirty-three years from his life span. Similarly, Adom was criticized for complaining about Chava when he said, "The woman which you gave me, she gave me the fruit from the tree..." [*Bereishis* 3:12]. Likewise, the generation of the *midbar* (desert) was blamed for complaining about the miraculous manna saying, "*V'nafshinu katza b'lechem*—Our souls are disgusted with this bread" [*Bamidbar* 21].

In *Eicha* [3:39] we find a beautiful posuk about complaining, "*Ma yisonen adom chai*," which Rav Shimon renders (in *Agadas Bereishis*), "Why does a person complain, if he is fortunate enough to be alive?!" The lesson in *Pirkei Avos*, "Who is rich? He who knows how to be satisfied with his lot" [4:1] is the same: Teaching us to focus on what we *have* rather than on what we lack. In our chinuch, it is incumbent upon us to set a similar example: Complaining is not the way to handle adversity. This is especially true on Shabbos when we are expressly admonished, "*Shabbos hi m'lizok*—Shabbos is a time to avoid yelling out" [*Shabbos* 12a].

(Elsewhere we will discuss, *bezras* Hashem, that another reason people complain is to gain attention. The spouse or parent of a complainer should be sensitive to this and look beneath the complaining—often they will see a subconscious reaching-out to you for more time and more attention.)

➤ •XXIII• ➤

Especially important for our children's healthy mental equilibrium and disposition is the way we conduct ourselves at two critical points of the day: before they get on the school bus, and when they arrive back home. A child who departs to school after witnessing his parents in a screaming match will be distracted for a good part of his morning studies mulling over the unpleasant scene and feeling somewhat agitated. This happens even though the parents are focusing on their children—juggling one child's last-minute test preparations, another child's peanut butter and jelly sandwich, and trying to feed the baby. Similarly, a child who knows that he will be accosted as soon as he steps into the house with negativity in a flurry of commands, like, "Where's your homework?!" or "Clean your room, wash yourself, and be quick on your feet!" will not have that extra incentive—as the school day wanes with his sapping strength—of looking forward to going home and getting some warmth and personal attention.

In the wonderful *sefer, Chinuch Labonim*, it is suggested that putting on some pleasant music during the early morning rush can have a calming influence on everyone's frazzled nerves. This may help immensely. Once we become aware of how we can condition children with positive or negative feedback we can change our behavior whenever we see them. When our children return home after a long grueling school day, giving them five minutes of undivided attention and warmth will make a world of difference in fostering a special relationship with them!

∼• XXIV •∼

One of the most common complaints that crops up in many a marital dispute is the claim that, "He (or she) is always criticizing me," or "She (or he) is always finding fault with whatever I do." We must recognize that this is, to a great extent, a natural consequence of our chinuch process. In yeshiva, the boys and girls are constantly hearing critical "shmoozen" designed to upgrade their spiritual level. At home, too, we are quick to point out the deficiencies of our young charges. While all this is an absolute necessity in the molding of our youth into proper Bnei Torah, it is inevitable that this approach will lead them to be critical minded of others as well. Therefore, we must continually keep in mind what the Baalei Mussar habitually say: A human being was given two eyes; one to judge himself or herself critically and the other to judge others favorably. Indeed, the Torah mandates, in *Vayikra*, "*B'tzedek tishpot amisecha*— Judge your friend charitably" [19:15]. The Gemara understands this to mean that we should "*Dan es kol adom l'kaf zechus*— Judge every person meritoriously," richly giving others the benefit of the doubt [*Masechtas Shavuos* 30a]. This notion of judging others favorably is taught to us twice in *Pirkei Avos* [1:5] and is included as one of the forty-eight ways to acquire Torah listed at the end of *Pirkei Avos* [6:7], where it is pointed out that fair-mindedness is an absolutely necessary aspect in the successful development of a true Ben or Bas Torah. Its acquisition is also a positive step towards promoting *achdus* (unity). In our day and age when there are so many shades of "Orthodox Jewry," the talent of not being immediately critical is crucial in fostering shalom among all of Klal Yisroel!

•XXV•

Successful married couples are also acutely aware of how important it is to be caring, affectionate, and sympathetic in a marriage. And the best way to nurture this in our children is to continually set an example of these traits for them to observe and absorb, day after day. We give them an inspiring lesson when we relate to them, "I'm doing this because I know it makes your father (or mother) happy," or when they see us readily sacrificing time and effort in order to make our spouse happy.

The Art Of
Giving Kavod

Every year there are two Jewish periods of mourning. The first is during the summer when we mourn the loss of the Beis HaMikdash (Holy Temple) for a three-week period. These three weeks culminate in the fast day of Tishah b'Av. During the time of the Beis HaMikdash, blessings of financial success emanated from the *Shulchan* (the Table in the Temple), while the *Mizbeiyach* (altar) helped atone for sins and ward off sickness. Thus, nowadays, with rocketing unemployment and so many falling sick (*lo aleinu*), we heavily miss our Bais HaMikdash.

Our second period of national mourning takes place during the thirty-three days of *sefira*, a period longer than Succos and Pesach combined, and equal to two-thirds of all the Shabbosim of the year. During all the days of *sefira* we abstain from music and haircuts in memory of the 24,000 disciples of Rabbi Akiva who died a painful death from diphtheria [*Yevamos* 62b]. This calamity rocked the collective Jewish soul and left an indelible impression on our national psyche.

The Gemara explains [*Yevamos* 62b] that these disciples died because they did not show proper *respect* for each other. The Gemara does not say they disgraced each other. Rather, they were severely punished for simply not respecting one another!

Talmudic analytic methodology features a device known as a *kal vechomer*. This argumentative formula works as follows: If I am tired now, and it's only the beginning of the week, imagine how tired I will feel by the end of the week! Thus the following logic can be utilized in our discussion of Rabbi Akiva's disciples: If there is such a severe punishment for not honoring one's colleague, imagine how dreadful the punishment must be for not honoring a parent!?

Honoring Parents

It is therefore important that parents spend time training their children in the mitzvah of *kibud av v'eim*. You may consider this self-serving given that this mitzvah only benefits you, the parents. The Torah teaches us, however, that, in fact, by emphasizing this mitzvah, parents are bestowing on their children the gift of life since the reward for honoring a parent is a lengthening of one's days [*Shemos* 20:12].

Here are some signs that your children may not have absorbed all the Torah they should have: If you notice, for example, that when your son returns from shul he fails to hold open the door for his father or that he breezes into the house in front of his father, it's your job in this case to investigate why he hasn't learned the importance of this mitzvah. Similarly, when your daughter has a screaming match with her mother on Friday afternoon, it's time to find out why she has not internalized all the discussions about respect and *derech eretz* that she has listened to over the years.

One of the most important lessons we learn from what happened with Rabbi Akiva's students is that it is possible to have a superb teacher and hear eloquent and important lectures and still fail to absorb the lessons! Indeed, there was a great Talmudic scholar named Geniva, to whom the Rabbis specifically instructed students not to show respect [*Gittin* 31b]! The Rabbis explained that since Geniva was quarrelsome, this proved he wasn't absorbing his Torah—for the entire Torah was given to promote peace in the world and Geniva invariably caused conflict. (See the final Rambam in the Laws of Chanukah. Rambam cites the verse, *"D'racheha darchei noam, v'chol n'sivoseha shalom*—Its [the Torah's] ways are pleasant and all of its paths are paths of peace.") We must stress to our loved ones that the directives of honor and kindliness which we study daily are intended to be actively practiced!

Of course, one of the best ways to educate children in the art of honoring parents is for them to witness how *their* parents act toward their parents. In the midst of hectic schedules, parents can demonstrate how they stand up for their parents when they enter a room or how they telephone their parents, or shop for them. Teaching by example is the most time-saving method to pass on traditions to your families!

Honoring Spouses

Another *kal vechomer* is as follows: If dishonoring colleagues brings the punishment of diphtheria, imagine the punishment for not honoring one's spouse?! Judaism is extraordinarily insistent on honoring one's mate. Every man promises in the *kesuvah*, *"Ana efalach v'ohkir, etc., k'goov'rin y'hodain, etc., b'kooshta*—I will work..., honor..., etc., my wife like Jewish people who work, honor, etc. their wives with truth!" Thus, in the marriage agreement, a husband pledges to show his wife special honor (i.e., more honor than he grants the average person). He gives his word that this honor will be granted honestly, and not just when other people are watching. Furthermore, a husband should learn to honor his wife by becoming aware of his wife's strong points, and not just by dutifully fulfilling his marital agreement.

This notion of honoring one's spouse has been the practice of Jews throughout the ages. (Thus the mention in the *kesuvah*: "like Jewish People," etc.) It is of primary importance for a husband to demonstrate honor to his wife—it's not as many assume only of secondary importance. A departure from this behavior threatens the fabric of a Jewish home—the centerpiece of Judaism.

Honoring one's spouse confers a multitude of benefits. The Gemara teaches us, "*Ohkiru l'nsheiychoo ki heichie d'tisassru*—Honor your wives so that you will become rich" [*Bava Metzia* 59a]. (Is it any wonder there are so many impoverished people nowadays!)

The flip side is also true. In the Laws of Marriage [chapter 15, halachah 20] the Rambam teaches us that a woman should honor her husband and view him as a nobleman or king. Of course, the best way for a woman to become a queen is to treat her husband as a king! (This follows the popular adage—the most efficient way to get anything is to first give it!)

Thus we discover that the Jewish "palace" consists of husbands and wives absolutely committed to showing mutual respect for one another. It follows that to ensure that children have stable and successful marriages, parents must model a good marriage—personally demonstrating to children how a husband and wife should respect each other. This means never fighting or raising your voice toward your spouse within their view! Rabbi Dr. Abraham Twerski once said something so wise about this: If, for *hashkafic* reasons, you choose not to openly show physical affection in front of your children, be consistent and don't let them witness conflict and disagreement either. Otherwise, you're sending them confusing signals.

On a practical level, be sure to avoid talking badly about your spouse to friends, parents, in-laws, etc. This is not only unseemly behavior towards someone whom you have publicly promised to honor but it puts everyone in an awkward position. Make it a habit to act loyally and always defend the honor of your spouse. Actively purge from your behavior the caustic or sarcastic manner you may be tempted to use while you are under stress or are in a bad mood!

In addition, maintain the same high standards with your spouse as you adhere to when you're in the company of a distinguished person. Offer your best in dress, food, temperament, etc. to your spouse just like you would with anyone you genuinely respect. This may not be easy but it will make your life richer and happier! You'll have to become aware of becoming susceptible to the dynamic in which familiarity breeds contempt. In addition, you are usually with your spouse during times when you may not be at your best—such as early in the morning before you are fully awake, late in the night when you may feel like a washed-out dish towel, and Friday night when your eyes are closing! To preserve the sanctity and happiness of a Jewish home you'll have to acknowledge that it takes determination and ingenuity!

Honoring Torah Authorities

There's one final *kal vechomer*. If, as mentioned previously in reference to Rabbi Akiva's students, the punishment is so extreme for not honoring one's colleague, imagine the punishment for not showing honor to a Rosh Yeshiva, Rabbi, Mechaneches, or other Torah authority! It is of the utmost importance to raise children to respect Torah leadership. On Shabbos after davening, a father who takes his child to say "Good Shabbos" to the Rabbi is giving his child a treasured gift! For these are the children who will continue to go to the Rabbi with halachic queries when they are adults.

Woe to the parent who belittles the Rabbi's speeches, or dashes out when the Rabbi reaches the pulpit, or who guffaws that the most pleasant thing he hears in shul is, *"chadaish yamainoo k'kedem—yisgadal v'yiskadash,"* (signifying that the chazan will proceed directly to *Mussaf* without pausing for the Rabbi to speak). Little does this man realize that this kind of behavior can be the direct cause for his son opting to daven in a shul without a Rabbi when he's older—or deciding that he wants no connection with Rabbis altogether!

What a tragedy! Where will a child like this go later if his marriage (*chas v'shalom*) begins to flounder? Where will his business associates go if they have a monetary disagreement with him? He will be left swimming in the oceans of *olam hazeh* without any navigational equipment! Furthermore, a Rabbi sets the tone for each specific Jewish calendar event, gearing us up for the solemnity of the Rosh Hashana season, clarifying for us the lessons of Succos and Pesach, defining for us the joviality of Purim, etc.

Who could surpass the effect of a Rabbi teaching children the importance of wearing seat-belts, or the dangers of cigarette smoking? Do you honestly want to give up the benefits of a Rabbi's guidance? If the answer is no, you'll have to concentrate on teaching your children to actively fulfill the great mitzvah of *"mip'nei seiva takum v'hadarta p'nei zakein—*to stand up for the elderly and to revere the Torah Sage" [*Vayikra* 19:32]. And in the merit of showing respect to all of the above mentioned, may we merit the rewards of long life, a healthy and happy home, and much Torah *nachas!*

Stress Management

I t is astonishing to note the startling similarity between the Jewish plight during the time of the Pharoahs in Egypt and the circumstances we find ourselves in today.

You may be thinking, "How can you even begin to compare the Jewish experience in Egypt with our current situation in the United States!? During the Jews' stay in Egypt we were slaves and suffered scorn and derision, doom and despair. Today in the United States, the Jews live in a free country, a land with a variety of technological marvels, all of which make our daily lives so much easier. We've even earned a relative amount of equality with our neighbors!"

So let us consider my proposed analogy:

When Moshe arrived from Midyan with the message that Hashem had appointed him to deliver the Jews, he was believed. As the Torah testifies, "*Vayamein haam vayishmue—* The nation believed and listened" [*Shemos* 4:31]. This was partly due to the fact that Moshe showed Bnei Yisroel three signs to prove that he had been chosen by Hashem—the stick converting to a snake, his hand becoming leprous, etc., and the water changing to blood. Moshe Rabbeinu also gave the secret password that Yosef HaTzadik had entrusted to the noble Serach Bas Asher (whom Yosef knew, through prophecy, would still be alive when Moshe would arrive).

Before Yosef died, he told Bnei Yisroel that one day a Jewish savior would come. Yosef gave Serach a key to determine this savior's authenticity, and the savior would have to reveal the exact password which Yosef had given to Serach. When Moshe arrived, Bnei Yisroel promptly brought him to Serach. By revealing the code phrase, *"pakod yifkod—you shall surely be remembered"* [*Shemos* 13:19], he was quickly accepted. From that time forward, he was absolutely accepted by the Jews. (It is appropriate that Serach—who lived long enough to see Dovid's kingdom as a reward for revealing to Yaakov that Yosef was still alive—was the vehicle used to jump-start the delivery of Bnei Yisroel from Mitzrayim!)

Why then, does the Torah testify, only a short while later, that Bnei Yisroel as a whole, and not just a vociferous minority, did an about face and, according to the posuk, *"V'lo shamu el Moshe—*Bnei Yisroel did not listen to Moshe." [*Shemos* 6:9]? The posuk states Bnei Yisroel did this, *"M'kotzer ruach u'mei'avodah kasheh—*Because of shortness of breath and the harsh work!" [*Shemos* 6:9]. Simply stated, they did not listen to Moshe because they were exhausted. The intense pressure of their lives as Egyptian servants, caused them to literally have an inability to catch their breath. As mentioned in the Haggadah on Pesach, *"V'es lachatzeinu zu had-chak." Lachatzeinu* is defined as the pressure under which Bnei Yisroel lived during the days in Egypt!

For a little notion of the intensity of this pressure, it's helpful to acquaint ourselves with a few facts. The Medrash states that each Jew had to produce six hundred bricks every day! [*Otzar HaMedrashim* 9]. (The holy Steipler Gaon, zt"l, explains the number of bricks is derived from the fact that the Torah uses the word *perech* [crushing labor] twice—which in gematria equals six hundred.) If, at the end of a day, a slave was short even one brick, one of his children would be taken in its place and cemented into the walls of Pittom and Ramses! (Perhaps this Jew even had to choose which child!) Imagine the desperation in which each man worked! He couldn't waste even a breath as his children's lives hung in the balance. He worked under this kind of pressure for endless days.

But this was only the beginning! Pharaoh saw, to his amazement, that the Jews still had the energy and time for religious aspirations! Moshe even asked Pharaoh to allow the Jews to go to a three-day meeting with Hashem in the desert! Pharaoh responded by intensifying the pressure, taking away the raw materials for the bricks, and insisting that, although the production quota was the same, they would now have to procure their own straw.

But Pharaoh could have made life even more difficult, he could have raised the quota, from 600 to, say, 1,000 bricks. In the yeshiva at Volozhin, they commented that Pharaoh did this to forestall the redemption. Pharaoh figured that if he pressured hundreds of thousands of Jews to find their own straw—with their children's lives hanging in the balance—they would fight with each other like cats and dogs for every blade of straw. With such internal strife, they would never merit the redemption!

There's another angle to Pharaoh's scheming decree. Pharaoh understood that as long as one can see an end to his or her travails, it's possible to cope. 600, 700, even 1,000 bricks! It just meant they had to work harder. But at least they knew that it was in their control. However, with this second decree, a Jewish man woke up in the morning not knowing where the next piece of straw would come from. This was the ultimate pressure! From one moment to the next they did not know what their fate would be!

This is the reason, *"V'lo shamu el Moshe*—They didn't listen to Moshe."* To the exclusion of anything else, their every moment was occupied with the pressure of survival. They could not rationally cope with Moshe Rabbeinu's prophesy. The Torah states openly that this was Pharaoh's nefarious intention. *"Tichbad ha'avoda al ha'anashim v'al yishu b'divrei sheker*— Make the work heavier on the people, let them not dwell on foolishness"* [*Shemos* 5:9].

Is this analogous to our day and age? We live in a generation sometimes dubbed the prozac (anti-depressant) generation. We have seen a climb from mild over-the-counter drugs— such as mylanta, maalox, and digel—to the prescription drugs of zantac, tagament, axid, pepsid, and prilosec. All are for the treatment of ulcers, etc., due in part to mounting pressures. Dismayingly, more and more people resort to the anti-anxiety drugs: valium, xanax and the like in order to cope with the crushing stress of present-day urban America. Quite a few people even turn to prozac and its ilk for help in coping with growing despair.

While we thank Hashem for the gift of these drugs, and for the doctors who know when and how to prescribe them wisely, we must reflect on our intense and pressure-filled society that makes them needed by some people in the first place. The now not uncommon use of psychologists, psychiatrists, and marriage counselors also points to this alarming trend.

Although, thank G-d, many of us don't need anti-depressants, ulcer medicine, or visits to a mental health specialist, we surely would admit, that all too often, we find ourselves without a moment to catch our breaths. We would readily apply to ourselves the descriptions of *kotzer ruach* and *avodah kasheh* (keeping in mind such things as car pools, homework, bills, doctors, dentists, orthodontists, carburetors, transmissions, shoe stores, food shopping, tuition, taxes, termites, etc.). [If you're reading this on Shabbos, please don't get depressed!]

In addition, the similarities to Pharaoh's time do not seem so absurd when we are aware of so many Jews who can't earn enough to make ends meet. (Thus they feel tuition pressure from their children's yeshivas.) Or we've heard of the many *acheinu beis Yisroel* out of work and in the throes of desperation, not knowing from day to day what's going to happen.

All this pressure adds up to strained relations—so it's understandable why there is also so much marital tension nowadays, and why we find so much strife in the Jewish community. The result of all this pressure is *v'lo shamu*! We don't listen to one another. We have neither the patience nor the level-headedness to act rationally with our spouses, with our peers, or with our children!

However, all is not bleak! Once this problem is identified, our beloved Torah contains all the answers concerning how we can better cope with our stress and with the daily vicissitudes of life. By looking to the Torah, we will enhance our quality of life and strengthen our relationship with Hashem, our loved ones and Klal Yisroel.

For starters, the Ohr Hachaim HaKodosh[1] gave the following short, but immensely important, commentary on the words, *"M'kotzer ruach* (Klal Yisroel's shortness of breath). *"Ulai ki l'tzad shelo hayu Bnei Torah lo shamu ulzeh yikarei kotzer ruach, ki haTorah marcheves da'ato shel adom—* Perhaps it was because Bnei Yisroel did not as yet have the Torah, and thus were not yet Bnei Torah. For this reason, they didn't listen to Moshe, since the Torah widens the minds of men!"

Thus, the Ohr Hachaim HaKodosh explains *kotzer ruach* as signifying lack of Torah knowledge and experience.

The result, he says, is a narrowness (*mikotzer*) of one's mind which results in an inability to cope sufficiently. The inference is obvious: If Klal Yisroel had had the Torah, they would have been able to cope much better with the high stress of their Egyptian daily life.

This is a powerful lesson for us all. During moments of financial pressure, the first thing often discarded is Torah study time. After all, it is reasoned, who has time for such luxuries when there are bills to be paid! However, the fallacy of such reasoning is that it doesn't take into consideration that the Torah we learn while we are under a lot of stress gives us *broita pleitzis* (wider shoulders) to survive and remain level-headed when pressure mounts!

Indeed, we should also understand the great benefits of Shabbos Kodesh in this area. It was Moshe Rabbeinu who suggested to Pharaoh that he give the Jews a Shabbos day. This is why it's called *matnas chelko* [*Bamidbar* 12:7]. The Torah states, "*Sheishes yomim taavod v'asisa kol m'lachtecha*—Six days you will toil and do *all* of your work" [*Shemos* 20:9]. Rashi points out that this is a directive to feel that all your work has been completed by the time Shabbos begins, and you haven't a worry in the world (despite the fact that, in reality, you have messages, faxes, clients, and bills which need attention!).

The mitzvah of Shabbos commemorates Hashem's creation of a perfect complete world that needed no more work! Shabbos was also intended to create an oasis for us where we are forced to transcend all our mundane pressures and be rejuvenated by a Shabbos Kodesh. The precious gift of Shabbos also gives us the strength to deal with daily stress!

Another insight into Bnei Yisroel's refusal to listen to Moshe comes from the comments of *Pesikta Zutrasa* on this verse. The Medrash explains that Bnei Yisroel did this because, "*Ki hakaas m'salek es hadaas*—Anger strips one of reason" (for the duration of the anger). This lesson is so important that people should write it on the paperweights on their desks and post it to their refrigerator doors! The Medrash reminds us that when people are angry, their brains go out of gear.

How frequently this lesson can impact our lives! When a parent is angry and strikes a child in a rage, the Medrash considers this a completely senseless act, since, one is *never* in complete control of one's senses while angry! Let's emulate the Adom Gadol, who, before hitting his child, would take the time to put on his hat and kapote (as before any important mitzvah), thereby giving himself time to cool down before disciplining his child!

Similarly, when an adolescent flies into a rage and says things to his parents which he shouldn't say, it's preferable *not* to react hastily. It's best not to immediately deduce that the child's yeshiva tutelage was for naught, and that he hasn't grasped the rudiments of elementary *kibud av v'eim* and respect for one's elders. Rather, the ideal reaction is to take a deep breath and acknowledge that someone who is angry is simply not rational! (Of course, our primary job is to train ourselves to avoid expressing the anger in the first place, and inculcate that attitude in our children.)

Under stress, marital problems can also escalate—a spouse can scream at the other spouse, "I hate you!" or heaven forbid, "I want a divorce." Do not let these words, uttered in a moment of rage, erode the magic of your marriage. These words, said in anger, are meant to be forgotten and not intended to be engraved in one's memory or mentioned during future disputes! As the Medrash says, *"Hakaas m'salek es hadaas,"* the person was temporarily out of his/her mind when the statements were made!

This Medrash teaches us to avoid trying to reason with someone who is in the throes of a tantrum. Just as one wouldn't try to debate with someone asleep, so, too, it's fruitless to reason with someone while he or she is in a rage! During the height of anger one is absolutely incapable of reasoning rationally. A wise tactic is to stall and calmly say, "I see we're both somewhat upset. Let's wait to discuss this until we cool down."

Another lesson from the drama of Mitzrayim: pressure and stress are meant to stimulate us to pray with greater intensity. This can be deduced from the verse, *"Vataal shavasam el Ha'Elokim min ha'avoda—Their prayers went up to Hashem from the midst of their harsh labor"* [*Shemos* 2:23]. However, if Bnei Yisroel only prayed while they were in such dire straits, how valuable is such forced devotion to Hashem?! The posuk is teaching us that they utilized the lesson of their high stress and pressure correctly: As a catalyst to turn to Hashem.

This was why the *Imahos* (Matriarchs) were initially barren: It stimulated them to prayer. For years, Leah's personal response was prayer when she feared she would end up marrying the hated Eisav! [*Bereishis, Rashi* 29:17]. We, too, should emulate this response during difficult times: Intensify our prayers, make our *bentching* more heartfelt, and when we say our amens in Kaddish (for life and peace) make them more resounding!

Finally, the Torah highlights a strange miracle that occurred during the Exodus, *"Ulchol bnei Yisroel, lo yecheratz kelev l'shono—Toward all the Jews, no dog barked!"* [*Shemos* 11:7]. Let's visualize the circumstances: All of a sudden and from all over Egypt, three million Jews left Egypt in less than eighteen minutes (the time it takes for dough to ferment)! We know that when someone passes a porch with a dog, it will most likely bark. Dogs react to strangers encroaching upon their territory. To make matters worse, commentators such as the Tur, Riva and Chizkuni explain that the Jews were all carrying sticks (*makelchem b'yedchem*)! Dogs often react more excitedly to people carrying sticks. To further describe the pressure the dogs must have felt, the Gemara [*Bava Kama* 60b] teaches us that when the Angel of Death arrives in a city, all the dogs start screaming, barking or howling! On this night of Pesach, the *mashchis* (destroying Angel) was in Egypt at full strength. Imagine the temptation for the Egyptian dogs when *millions* of people passed in front of them. Yet, the dogs uttered not a whimper while the Jews exited.

The Medrash [*Mechilta Mishpatim* 20] teaches us that dogs were rewarded for this: Dogs will forever be the first to receive any meat found unfit for consumption, i.e., if, during processing, any meat is found to be *treifah*. As the posuk says, *"U'basar basade treifah lo socheilu lakelev tashlichun osso* —meat that is rendered treifah, throw it to the dogs" [*Shemos* 22:30].

What is the lesson in this? We can apply this to ourselves—if one resists the temptation to "bark" while under mounting pressure and incredible strain (think of Friday afternoons, etc.), Hashem will provide one with His sustenance (in the same way that Hashem rewarded the dogs). Of course, this may take superhuman effort since, all too often, the opposite occurs and, when things begin to slide, the volume of the voices in our homes rises considerably.

May Hashem give us all the strength and wisdom to cope with the *nisyonos* (tests) of everyday life, (foreclosures and shut-off notices, instead of pogroms, etc.) and may we merit only good health, happiness and many Torah blessings!

---

1. (It is written that the venerable Admor and Torah great, the Divrei Chaim, had a Rebbe dismissed because he refused to add the title 'HaKodosh' at the end of the Ohr HaChaim's name.)

What To Look For On A Date

Before we discuss what to look for in a date, it's helpful to bear in mind the adage: Date thyself first. What does this mean? Make sure that you have—or that you are refining into your character—many of the characteristics which you admire and seek in a spouse.

You may think—Why waste all this effort dating, investigating, pondering, and consulting if it's all *bashert* anyway. We all know Hashem decides who is for whom forty days before the creation of an embryo. It's all preordained! Well, this line of reasoning is as ridiculous as someone who crosses Ocean Parkway on a red light thinking, if it's not my time to leave the world, all those cars and trucks will get flat tires before they hit me! Don't try it! You'll become a pancake fast!

Obviously, Hashem wants us to make proper *hishtadlus* (attempts). In the case of dating, this means making sure that your choice affords you the best chance of achieving happiness and gaining spiritual success.

Choosing the person you will marry is the single most important decision you will make in your entire life. Barring the tragedies of divorce or death, it will determine your life and your ability to find happiness for the rest of your worldly existence. It will determine what your children and grandchildren will be like and impact greatly upon how they will succeed or fail in life.

Marriage is a long-term merger and will endure for all of this world and through eternity. Indeed, marriage does not end at the grave! The town of Chevron is also known as Kiryas Arbah—the City of Four Couples (Adom and Chava, Avraham and Sarah, Yitzchok and Rivka, and Yaakov and Leah are buried there). They are called *zugos* (pairs) because—even after death—they remain couples! This demonstrates how the person you choose for a life-long partner has far-reaching ramifications and therefore deserves your careful consideration.

Think of other major decisions you may have to make. When buying a car, for example, you turn to someone with more experience than you. After all, it's an expensive purchase and you hope to drive it for a long time. You may also carefully consider a long list of options—American vs. Japanese, used vs. new, debating which items would meet your particular needs.

Any big decision is made more easily by reaching out to people around you and gathering all the information you can. Similarly, when looking to find a mate for life, it's a good idea to take counsel from those around you. Consult with the people who love and care about you and go to the people who have been your spiritual guides or who have watched you grow up. They can help provide guidance about the qualities you will need from your future mate.

Nowadays, we are witnessing an escalating number of divorces among young couples. We watch the heartbreak of young children shuttled back and forth between warring ex-spouses, each feeding the children with hatred against the other.

We witness the sad lives of couples filled with hatred instead of love, and bitterness instead of happiness. This sight should have a galvanizing effect. It should strengthen our resolve to cultivate traits in ourselves which will make us a strong marriage partner and mobilize us to scrutinize, even more carefully, any candidate poised to be our future life's partner.

So, let us now look at some important areas of life one should investigate when considering a prospective suitor.

Health

Mental health and stability should be your primary concern. Life throws many challenges our way, from the strains of childbirth to the burdens of earning a living, and if one is emotionally unbalanced this multiplies the usual stresses on any marriage. Therefore if you hear reports of chronic depression or frequent mood swings, tread carefully. Rumors of a possible mental breakdown should be thoroughly checked into. (As to the responsibility of friends, etc., to disclose this information, the guidelines are beyond the scope of this *sefer*. This delicate and complex halachic issue should be discussed with a competent Rabbi or Rosh Yeshiva.)

As to the issue of physical health, Rabbi Avigdor Miller gives a practical piece of advice. If you're not sure of your date's health and stamina, suggest a vigorous walk for the next time you get together and see how they appear after that "ordeal." More than anything else you want to make sure that your candidate is healthy both in body and mind.

Included in the category of health is smoking cigarettes: Why should a young girl settle for someone who could leave her a young widow?! Why should she put herself into a situation where she and her children can be poisoned by second-hand smoke? Is there any reason she should constantly be aggravated by having all her sheitlach reek of tobacco? Similarly, parents should be aware that by being lenient with their sons concerning smoking, they are not only allowing their son's life to be endangered, but his field of shidduchim will be greatly reduced! I have taught many seminary classes and scores of girls have assured me, in unison, that they would never consider dating a boy who smokes cigarettes!

Leiv Tov

When the great Torah scholar and teacher, Rabbi Yochonon ben Zakkai, sent his four great students to search for the best attribute in the world, Rabbi Elozer ben Arach returned espousing the quality of *leiv tov* (a good heart) [*Avos* 2:9]. Rabbi Yochonon agreed that this attribute was superior to all others. One of the reasons he may have asked his talmidim to research this subject was to teach them and us what to look for in a mate. His conclusion, based upon his choice of several noble traits, reveals to us how important it is to look for someone kindhearted. Indeed, in parshas *Chayei Sora* (containing the Torah's model for what to look for in a spouse), when Eliezer pursued a worthy mate for Yitzchok, he sought someone with a passion for chesed.

This quality manifests itself in a marriage in countless ways. If your spouse is kind, he or she will help you when you are weary, console you when you are defeated, calm you when you are feeling agitated. He or she will commiserate with your setbacks, and soothe your bruised ego. Kindness translates into help in the kitchen and patience when bathing the kids. It means going the extra mile for each other. How priceless is the commodity of caring in a marriage! Rav Shimshon Raphael Hirsch portrays this succinctly when he teaches us that the root of the word *ahava* (to love) is *hav* which means to give, for giving is the greatest expression of love!

Leiv tov also includes consideration. Consideration will manifest itself during the dating process when someone takes pains to date you in places where you won't be embarrassed by friends and acquaintances spotting you. You can tell if someone is considerate if they bring you home early enough so that you are able to function well the next day at work (if that's what you want). A considerate spouse will attempt to anticipate your needs and desires and continually strive to make the marriage bond more fulfilling.

Finally it's pertinent here to mention self-centeredness. Strive to find a partner who is not solely obsessed with the big three—namely, me, myself, and I! Some people can only focus on the rest of the world with their peripheral vision. It is not a pleasant experience to proceed through life with a partner who will fit you in whenever he finds a spare moment!

Religiosity

Shlomo HaMelech teaches us, *"Isha yiras Hashem, hi tishalal—*The G-d fearing woman, she is to be praised" [*Mishlei* 31]. If you want a Torah home, find a mate who has Hashem in their thoughts (see the chapter "A Prescription for Ruchnius"). The *mezuzah* at the portal of your home promises Divine protection when the inhabitants live by its message, namely that Hashem is in each and every room. This is why the name of Hashem that is placed on the very front of the *mezuzah*—the Divine *Shada-y*—is an abbreviation for *shomer dalsos Yisroel* (He guards the doors of Yisroel). If thoughts of Hashem permeate the home, then G-d's protection will be present there as well.

With this in mind, here's a solid rule to follow: Always "marry up" in religiosity! Don't marry so that you can make your new spouse more frum. It's admirable to bring people closer to Judaism and be *mekarav rechokim*. But it's not wise to do so with your entire future or with the future of your descendants! Don't lock yourself into a situation where you are hampered by a disinterested or protesting spouse when, as you mature, you aspire to grow and develop spiritually.

The Torah teaches us at length, what a boy should look for in a girl. As mentioned previously, the narrative of Eliezer and Rivka is a tutorial on this subject. What about a parallel lesson for a girl to look for in a man (besides a *leiv tov!*)? I believe the lesson can be found in Rivka's first encounter with Yitzchok. The Torah relates [*Bereishis* 24:63], "*Vayetzei Yitzchok lasuach ba'sadeh*—Yitzchok went out to talk in the field." Chazal teach us that it was at this moment that Yitzchok instituted *Minchah*. And Rivka encountered him at this particular moment. The Torah records Rivka's reaction to her first encounter with Yitzchok. The verse states, "she fell off her donkey!" Then she asked Eliezer, "*Who* is this man?" The Torah reveals to us the impact that Yitzchok's devout prayer made on Rivka. Perhaps this is to teach us that an excellent way to determine a young man's piety and sincerity is to scrutinize the way he davens. If he is devout in his praying and *bentching* (providing it is not just a studied act), this is a clear sign of *yiras Shamayim* (fear of Heaven) and signifies depth of religious belief.

Dedication to Torah Study

Of course, a woman should look for a man dedicated to Torah. This will bring blessings of life and happiness to the home (see the chapter "Torah"). A man should look for a woman who has a deep appreciation of the importance of Torah, someone who will be proud of his Torah accomplishments, and who intends to raise a generation of talmidei chachomim.

I was delighted to find that Rav Yehuda HaChasid, in his

book *Sefer Chasidim* [156], advises one to pray—not only for himself, but for his children and grandchildren—to have a mate with the three specific qualities I mentioned in the previous three sections of this chapter: *yiras Shamayim*, religiosity, and kind-heartedness! Rav Yehuda HaChasid refers to this trio as the *chut hameshulish*—the triple cord which is not easily broken. He caps off this thought with a beautiful gematria demonstrating the connection between these wonderful characteristics. He points out that, remarkably, the words Torah, *yiras*, and *gemilos chasodim* each have the identical numerical value of 611!

Supporting a Family

How will a husband support his family? Will he have the ability to pay a mortgage, purchase medical insurance, provide tuition, etc.? Dovid HaMelech directly links having sufficient "provisions" with the presence of peace in the following posuk [*Tehillim* 147:14], "*Hanosein g'vulech shalom, cheilev chittim yasbi'eich*—He who puts in your borders peace and satisfies you with the fat of wheat." If there is not enough money, a husband is likely to be nervous and tense with the burden of mounting bills. He may become easily agitated. He won't have a head for lighter activities and may become too preoccupied to pay attention to his wife's needs and desires.

Even worse is the scenario which can come with unemployment. When a husband is home and around the house, he will have plenty of time to find faults with his wife's domestic skills. Little things can begin to irritate him. He may feel a great sense of failure. Many men measure their self-worth in their ability to support their family or do something useful with their lives. When a man fails to do this, he can feel emasculated and useless. A man who feels this way will not be pleasant partner! He may even grow jealous of his wife's successes and begrudge her happiness. Thus, it is crucial to assess a man's earning potential and occupational stability before you marry him.

However, the ability to make money is not enough. It's important to find someone who will take pleasure in his chosen profession. The Mishna teaches us, *"Eh'hov es hamlacha—* Love your work"* [*Pirkei Avos* 1:10]. Since the majority of a man's waking hours are spent busy at work, if he finds his work fulfilling and satisfying, this sense of fulfillment will spread into his home and to his relationship with his wife and children.

Furthermore, a husband who is gainfully employed will have a healthier dose of self-respect. And someone with self-respect will be more likely to respect and honor his wife. For this reason, in the *kesuvah*, the husband first obligates himself, *"Ana afalech—*I will work." Only after this does he pledge, *"Ana okir—*I will honor her." This is natural, since a person who feels good about himself or herself is better able to show respect to someone else!

If a girl is dating a young man who has been learning all his life, and who plans to remain in kollel after he marries, it's a good idea for the girl to discuss his long-term plans with him. If he expects a young woman to support him, the young woman must be brutally honest with herself. She must carefully determine if she is able to juggle the responsibilities of being a wife, mother, and full-time breadwinner. (There are many fine women who can succeed in managing this full load at once, but it is *not* for everyone.) When anyone assesses their own abilities and desires, it is crucial to be absolutely truthful to themselves and to the person they are considering marrying.

While marrying a boy who sits and learns might be the "in" thing with all of a girl's friends, not everyone is cut out for this challenging lifestyle, and when a girl goes through with this and finds herself overwhelmed, she can bring misery to her entire family. Careful consideration is warranted to determine whether you have the strength and stamina to maintain this life over the long run.

When dating a learning boy, find out if he is productive and happy with his learning and make sure he's not doing it for lack of any other option or because his parents want him to do this. Once again, a fulfilled and accomplished husband makes a better partner.

In checking out a bochur's learning acumen, a good starting point is the young man's mashgiach or menahel. Whenever possible, phrase your question without a negative side. This will make it easier for the menahel to answer you, without feeling he's hurting the young man. Thus, you might say, "My daughter is very interested in supporting a young man for several years in learning. Do you think so and so is cut out for long-term study or do you think he'll be happier doing something else?" Both sides of the question are respectable and makes it easier to get a full answer to your query.

As a young man, what are you looking for in your future wife? Are you searching for a girl who will stay at home with the children, one who wants to wait for them by the bus stop each and every day? Do you seek a wife who will personally teach the children their first words? Do you hope to find a wife whose entire life will revolve around her husband, children, and home?

If so, in today's difficult financial climate you must be prepared to shoulder the entire fiscal burdens of life. Then, you must carefully determine if this kind of lifestyle will be fulfilling enough for the young lady. While this was the overwhelming norm for a young Jewish girl fifty years ago, it is now not as frequently true. If a young lady will be miserable sitting at home surrounded by diapers and eggshells, the home will not be a place of harmony and tranquillity. It is your job to assess if the pursuit of *"tzofia halichos beisa*—to oversee the ways of her home" is something that your spouse-to-be will find sufficiently satisfying and fulfilling.

When dealing with a career-minded young man or woman, it is important to investigate their potential to be a workaholic. (Young men should be aware that the destructive possibility of this situation is even worse when it is the woman who is the workaholic!) While initially you may be impressed by someone being beeped twice and having to make three cell phone calls to clients while on a date, this may actually be an alarming signal! If he can't even give you his undivided attention while he's dating, do you imagine he'll find the time to help bathe the kids in five years? If he's already busy during your first hours together, do you think he'll come with you to the children's siddur parties?

Finally, imagine your future with this kind of man—will you feel compensated by his potentially big paycheck for the many nights you fall asleep in an empty bedroom while he is busy furthering his career?

Disposition

There is one kind of disposition that is almost universally perceived as the most attractive—a cheerful and sunny disposition. This is so important. In *Masechtas Kesuvos* [111b], Rabbi Yochonon teaches from the verse *"oolven shinayim meichalav-al tikrei oolven shinayim ela oolvon shinayim maichalav*—Read rather that showing the white of the teeth (namely, a smile) is more important than milk."* We know how essential milk is to a family's health, yet smiling is considered even more important! If there is tension or gloom, friction or apathy, the aura and environment of the house will suffer. A home with humor and good cheer, laughter and giggling is a joyful atmosphere in which to live and a terrific environment to in which to raise children.

Often a young woman will confuse the fine trait of responsibility with her date's serious demeanor. She may later discover—to her chagrin—that her new husband is taciturn and morose, or even worse, bitter and surly! Remember, nothing diffuses a fight as quickly as the ability to laugh at oneself!

Let's remember that we are charged, *"ivdue es Hashem b'simcha*—to serve Hashem in a state of joy" [*Tehillim* 100:2]. The final *bracha* of the Sheva Brachos begins with, "...*Gila, rina, ditzah, v'chedva*—Gaiety, song, exultation, and happiness," and only then, *"Ahava v'achva*—Love and togetherness." This re-emphasizes the theme that love can be achieved only after happiness and joy exist!

For this reason, when dating, make it a habit to smile often. And study your date carefully—the ability to be happy shows in a quickness to smile and an easy laugh. Finally, remember a girl looks infinitely more pretty when she's smiling. So smile often! You'll make a much better impression.

Warmth

Evaluating how warm a prospective mate is will correlate with how affectionate and caring they will be in the marriage. Such a determination can make the difference between a life of bliss and a perpetual existence of disappointment! How often in marriage counseling does a therapist hear, "she's like a block of ice" or "he has as much feeling as a stone." Igniting the fires in such marriages is a formidable task! So start off the right way with a warm and emotionally-responsive mate!

Temperament

The Gemara explains that there are three barometers

which reveal a great deal about someone's character: *"Kiso, koso,* and *ka'aso*—His purse, his wine goblet, and his anger" [*Masechtas Eruvin* 65b]. We'll discuss here the third barometer—the threshold of temper and inclinations toward self control. This characteristic in a potential spouse is particularly significant. The Gemara teaches, *"Ein m'ratzin es ha'adam b'shas ka'aso*—Do not attempt to appease a person when angry" [*Masechtas Brachos* 7a]. This is because when someone is angry, he or she temporarily is unable to think rationally. Thus it is futile to try to reason with him or her. Obviously, living with a person whose anger is easily triggered is not pleasant. Furthermore, the effects of anger and the tension have a devestating impact on the home's atmosphere and the upbringing of the children. As we are taught in *Koheles* [9:7], anger rests in the bosom of the fool. We would be wise to avoid such foolishness. Moreover, Rav Yehuda HaChasid in the *Sefer Chasidim* (#951) advises us that if a woman is quick to anger, a man should not marry her even if she has the attribute of modesty! Similarly, he cautions (#391) not to match a girl with a young man who has an angry nature.

Spending Habits

The Gemara [*Masechtas Eruvin* 65b] gives advice on discerning a person's true colors from his purse. This means we should investigate if our suitor is stingy or giving. Will he or she be a tyrant about spending? Will you be held accountable for every last penny? This could become awfully difficult for you each time you need to buy something necessary for the home.

This can even be a problem in a wealthy family. One spouse might be driven to invest every available dollar in the stock market or into mutual funds (or even under the mattress) and not be prone to giving and sharing.

Finally, one's charity habits also reveal a lot about someone's personality. How someone spends or gives charity will reveal a lot about their level of empathy, their generosity, and their level of responsibility towards others.

Criticizing and Complaining

Couples in the throes of marital difficulties often lament that their spouse is always complaining or finding fault, etc. If you are with a date who regularly badmouths his or her parents, rebbeim, or friends, this is cause for concern. Similarly, someone who chronically complains and whines, may not have good problem-solving skills or a positive attitude. In *Pirkei Avos* [4:1], Ben Zoma teaches that a wealthy person is someone who is happy with his or her lot. Thus, the reverse is also true—a poor person is someone who is always negative, either complaining or discontented. The joy of life is diminished living with someone who is unable to be happy and whom you can never please. Someone like this will always notice and point out what's missing and will rarely see the happier side of life.

Courtesy

Watch carefully to ascertain whether or not your date is courteous. From the Tanach [*Tehillim* 43:13], we learn the importance of courtesy and politeness, *"Mi ha'eesh ha'chafetz chaim, ohaiv yomim, liroes tov, n'tzor l'shoncha meira—Who is the one who desires life, wants quality days, this person will guard his tongue from speaking evil!"* Thus, it is eminently clear that a good life is linked to a quality mouth. So, too, it states, *"Hamaves v'hachaim b'yad haloshon—Death and life is in the hands of the tongue"* [*Mishlei* 18:21]. Particular scrutiny should be used since, while a couple is dating, graciousness and chivalry can be a studied act and it is relatively easy to hide a rude and unruly side. But if one can't be courteous in the most ideal circumstance—i.e., a date—you can be sure that they will be unable to act considerately or courteously under the stresses of marriage.

Intellect

While you are not marrying a *chavrusa* (study companion), and having a desirable family and home life is not necessarily contingent upon matching IQ's, there are many pitfalls when one partner's intelligence or education lags far behind the other. Stimulating conversation, for example, could be difficult to maintain through the years. Helping a spouse, or consoling him/her in times of need, may be formidable for a weaker partner. Socializing with each other's friends can also become a challenge since the two sets of friends will usually be worlds apart in interests and in conversational style. So make sure to add to your check list of important characteristics in a mate—intellectual compatibility.

Flexibility

Flexibility is an often overlooked characteristic. But the ability to bend if necessary is important. It is incredibly difficult to live with someone who must always have his or her own way and is blind to anyone else's side of things. Someone rigid and stubborn will not make a good life partner.

Introvert, Extrovert, or Somewhere in the Middle?

Check out the social disposition of your dates. Are they happier remaining indoors evenings with a hot cocoa and a book, or do they thrive on being with people at every opportunity? Do they want to fill their home with parties and guests or do they prefer a more private, quiet existence? Do they look forward to squeezing out the social juice from every wedding and bar mitzvah, or do they make plans for the earliest time they can acceptably leave and go home? Remember, to a great extent once married you'll be locked in to your spouse's preferences, so investigate carefully before you leap!

Listening Skills

Good communication is important to any marriage and a vital element of this is the art of being a good listener. Whenever you are on a date, evaluate carefully if your date is really listening to you, or if they are just waiting for you to stop talking so they can speak again. Pay particular attention not to monopolize the conversation during a date. While you may have a delightful time talking up a storm, don't forget the purpose of the date—which is to get to know the other person—impossible to achieve if you are always talking!

Physical Appearance

Make sure you are contented with the "looks" of your potential mate. Everyone says that beauty is skin deep (cf. *Masechtas Kiddushin, "Hanosei isha l'shum noi, etc.").* This simply signifies that you should not be swayed solely by someone's external appearance. However, don't marry someone whose physical appearance does not attract you! You will only find yourself looking jealously at others for the next twenty years. This is why the Gemara mandates not to betroth a woman through an agent, lest you find yourself subsequently displeased with her appearance. It can lead to a divorce!

The fact that the Torah makes note of the physical beauty of Sara and Rochel (among others), and praises them in this regard, indicates that a pleasing appearance is a positive attribute, and one to be pursued when possible. This is confirmed by a Gemara in *Masechtas Yevamos* [63b], where it is observed that every single day for a man with a beautiful wife, is as pleasurable for him as are two days for someone else!

Similarly Rebbe Yehuda HaChasid in the *Sefer Chasidim* [#490] teaches that a matchmaker should not pressure a young woman to marry someone whom she doesn't find handsome! This is a transgression, he explains of, *"Lifnei eivair lo seetein michshol—Don't* put a stumbling block before the blind" [*Vayikra* 29:14], for it only will make her unhappy and tempt her to gaze at and covet other men.

You might counter that Shlomo HaMelech states [*Mishlei* 31], *"Sheker hachein, v'hevel hayofee—Charm* is false and beauty is only vanity!" In response, the Vilna Gaon, zt"l, explains that this charm and beauty are like zeros. Without fear of Hashem before them, they are indeed worthless. But if a woman is invested with fear of G-d, every zero makes the total package bigger!

In general, pay particular attention to those who are close to you and who love you. If they say that your date is bad news or not for you, seriously consider their points. Remember that you may be plagued by overactive hormones, or bowled over by being the center of male or female attraction, but your older relatives or friends often have a more logical perspective, invested with years of experience in the pitfalls of a married couple's life. At the same time, firmly assert yourself and take a good look inward if your family emphatically wants you to marry someone. Never follow their wishes if your heart is not in agreement. Remember, you will have to live with this person the rest of your life. No one else will!

Recreational Activity

It's astonishing how many people forget to discuss what they enjoy doing for recreation with a prospective partner. While this might seem trivial, free time is the glue that helps many marriages remain strong, fresh, and full of vitality. During leisure time, a couple can strengthen their marital union. If you both enjoy unwinding in the same way—whether it is by jogging or by playing scrabble, the ability to do it together will make your life much closer and happier.

Investigating the Family

Checking out the family background (*yichus*) of the person you are dating is vital for many reasons. First, one of our primary life goals is to bring a new generation of children into the world, and raise them to be G-d-fearing and kind human beings. The genetics of your spouse plays a crucial role in determining the makeup of your children. Don't underestimate this!

Of more immediate concern, is the inevitability that children will learn from their parents' behavior. Thus, if both parents are gentle and courteous, their children will most likely follow in their footsteps. I once heard the following wise advice from Rabbi Dr. Abraham Twerski. He related, "I'd rather my daughter find a mate whose father helps in the kitchen, than one who is a rich!" A child from a stormy marriage or a divorced family may have learned poor communication skills and bad habits such as screaming and fighting from their parents. (However, there are children from divorced families who after witnessing an unhappy marriage make a concerted and successful effort not to fall into similar problems as their parents, and who become wonderfully devoted husbands or wives!)

One should also consider, in terms of religious lifestyle,

what he or she was accustomed to at home. Did their family enjoy a beautiful and meaningful Pesach seder? What were their Purims like? Did they decorate a gorgeous succah? Did their family prepare for Shabbos with gusto, and then celebrate it with zemiros and divrei Torah? Did the sweet melody of Torah learning exist in their home? These practices often become second nature, and while these habits can definitely be learned and incorporated in one's life and practiced to perfection, it is a clear advantage if your spouse practiced such behavior and absorbed it from his/her youth.

Another reason to check out someone's family background is so that you can get to know the parents a little bit. It's important to examine their attitude towards their child. Marriages can disintegrate because of the interference and meddling of in-laws! You should also investigate if there is a destructive potential in the family. This is particularly true if you hear that a married child of this family is already experiencing such turbulence.

Rav Yehuda HaChasid in the *Sefer Chasidim* [247] advises that when investigating a girl, one should find out about her mother, as many girls take after their mothers. This is based on a Gemara in *Masechtas Kesuvos* [63a] which states, *"K'ovdei ima kach ovdei b'rata*—Like the ways of the mother, so are the ways of her daughter."* He then adds that it helps to look into the mother's sisters as well. When it comes to investigating a boy, Rav Yehuda HaChasid cites [375] the famous Gemara in *Bava Basra* [110a] which comments that most boys take after their mother's brothers. He also adds a novelty: Most boys emulate their grandfathers. This is an especially helpful pointer when the mother of the boy you are dating has no brothers.

Some Important Questions

We've gone through a host of characteristics for you to

look for in a prospective spouse. Once you've ascertained that you've found a match in terms of desired attributes, you'll have to begin to consider lifestyle choices. It's best before the marriage proposal to discuss all critical issues since once you're married, you will have to compromise, be miserable or fight about these issues.

Here is a list of some crucial topics that you should discuss with a prospective spouse:

1. Where will you live? Do either of you dream of living in Eretz Yisroel? Are either of you determined not to move far from your parents? Do you have a desire to spread Torah in the hinterlands far away from the Torah centers of your youth? Are you insistent on raising your children where there are dozens of choices in yeshivas? Do you want to live in the city or in a suburb?

2. Will you have a television in your house? This single decision can drastically alter both of your and the lives of your future children!

3. Do you aspire to raise a large family? Although this is clearly a purely halachic matter, it's good to discuss it before getting married.

4. Discuss your expectations in the *tznius* (modesty) department. How do you expect your wife to dress? What will be your position about your spouse having opposite sex, platonic friends? Discuss these things beforehand rather than wait to be surprised later!

5. Make sure your prospective mate is committed to making their spouse their first priority in life. This is what marriage is about—as is written in *Bereishis* [2:24] "*V'davak b'ish-to*—To cleave to his wife" which means to be loyal to her above anyone else! So, too, in the *kesuvah*, a chasan pledges, "*ana okir*—I will honor her."

We know that a Jew is required to honor every Jew as it

states in *Pirkei Avos* [2:10], *"Y'hei kavod chavercha chuviv alecha k'shelach*—Let the honor of your friend be as precious to you as your own [honor]." So when the husband commits himself to honor his wife it must mean something more, namely his wife more than anyone else! This is consistent with, *"Um'chabda yoseir migufo*—Honor her (your wife) more than yourself!" [*Masechtas Yevamos* 63b].

In fact, Rav Pam, *shlit"a*, explains that one of the reasons for the minhag of the bride walking around the groom under the chupah is to symbolize that, from now on, her husband will be the center of her universe. Therefore, ask yourself if you love your prospective mate enough to pledge your unswerving support and total dedication and devotion to him or her for the remainder of your life! In a good marriage, husband and wife save the best of themselves for each other!

Handling Rejection

Sometimes you date someone with whom you become enamored. If the feeling is not reciprocated and he or she says no, you may feel tempted to brood over it. It's healthiest to move on as quickly as possible. The *Sefer Chasidim* [#514] learns this from Eliezer, Avraham's servant, who told Lavan and Besuel, "If you don't agree, tell me and I will go to the right or to the left" [*Bereishis* 24:49]. From this we learn that if one is rejected, the matter should be pursued no further. The best thing to do is to immediately turn one's attention to other prospects! (How sad it is that many people waste precious years of their life fruitlessly enamored with someone who does not feel the same.)

Once I heard Rabbi Gershon Weiss (in the name of Rabbi Dovid Kronglass, of blessed memory) say that even more important than seeing if you like a certain girl is to determine if she likes you!

Sometimes, after dating for a long time and feeling close to someone, the relationship suddenly breaks up and your suitor picks up and becomes engaged to someone else! Although this is emotionally difficult, the *Sefer Chasidim* [#521] advises, "*Gam zu l'tovah*—This too is for the best." Since your prospect married someone else, it is clear that that person (and *not* you) was their intended. If you had tried to interfere you would have had to die (or get divorced) to allow the other match to take place!

Being Yourself

Sometimes young men and women encounter a frustrating phenomena: The people they like say no, while those that they have no interest in would like another date! This leaves a young person perplexed and worried. The cause of this dynamic may stem from the way a person projects himself or herself on a date. Many people act in a way that they think is appropriate for a date, and they neglect to show their authentic self. They do not project a true picture of who they actually are. Thus, prospects who are saying yes (or no) are, in reality, reacting to an "image" which they are receiving, and not to the person who's really there! So be yourself on a date! Show your authentic self—reveal your warmth, humor, etc. And if someone rejects you, realize that it just wasn't meant to be.

When the Date is a Washout

Once in a while you may go out with an obvious mismatch. It is immediately evident that the person you are with is not for you. Even so, it's very important to give the date a good time! First of all, you're rejecting this person as a prospective mate *not* as a human being. In addition, you don't want this person badmouthing you to everyone and saying how poorly you behaved. This is also a prime example of *"V'ahavta l'reiacha k'mocha*—Love your fellow like yourself" [*Vayikra* 19:18]. It may help to imagine yourself in their shoes—you wouldn't want someone to treat you shabbily just because you weren't a good match for them. One of the best rules of behavior is to treat others as you would like to be treated. So be grateful that the person even considered going out with you. Try to make the evening as pleasant as possible. In the process, practice your conversation and etiquette skills so you'll even be sharper for the next prospect.

Praying for a Mate

At the beginning of this chapter, we discussed the importance of carefully choosing a life's mate. The Gemara advises that one should pray for a worthy partner beginning at a young age [*Masechtas Brachos* 8a]. The Gemara cites the verse, *"Al zos yispallel kol chosid aylecha l'eis m'tzo*—For this, all pious individuals should pray toward the time of finding" [*Tehillim* 32:6]. Included in the meaning of this verse, the Gemara explains, is the advice that one should pray toward the time of finding a wife. Similarly, *Sefer Chasidim* recommends that parents should fervently pray for their children to find worthy spouses. We can invest a lot of effort into raising our children, but much of it can fall by the wayside if they fall prey to an unworthy mate.

I hope these words will help you formulate your priorities as you venture into the world of dating. I also hope this serves as an initial syllabus for parents as they advise their children. May it be the will of Hashem that everyone will find their partner quickly and easily, and may all of us enjoy happiness with our partners, our progeny, and from their spouses!

The Essence And Beauty Of Shabbos

Importance of Shabbos

The importance of Shabbos, and the profound love and awe Jews committed to Shabbos feel, has been described many times. But few descriptions match the tragic but inspiring incidents common during the Holocaust—reports of Jews who were so bound to the mitzvah of Shabbos that they would rather lose their lives than violate this mitzvah.

To further their hideous goals, the Nazis, *yemach shemam v'zichram* [may their names and memory be blotted out], desperately needed tin craftsmen. Finding skilled tin workers during the war was not easy and, as a result, they were severely shorthanded. Their needs were so acute, that they even plucked a Chassidic Jew out of Auschwitz and put him to work laboring for their war effort. This Jewish man was removed from the concentration camp and given unheard of privileges. As a result he saved many Jews from the gas chamber.

Despite all this, he was plagued by a burning issue. One day he smuggled himself back into Auschwitz and into the barrack of the late Klausenberger Rebbe, zt"l. When he succeeded in meeting the Rebbe, he posed the following chilling query. As slave laborers, all Jews were forced to desecrate the Shabbos. According to halachah, to biblically desecrate Shabbos, one must do a complete act. The Jews in the concentration camps were generally forced to work in the rock quarries where they rarely did a complete act. This chosid, however, was commanded to perform precision tin work. As a result he completed many acts on Shabbos. Therefore, he asked his Rebbe if halachically he would be permitted to purposely burn his hands to end his ability to do his work. In doing this, he exclaimed, he would be sent back to the camps where he wouldn't have to desecrate the Shabbos as much.

The Rebbe firmly answered that people were killed all the time in the camps. For this reason, he categorically rejected the chosid's plan to mutilate his hands and thus be returned to the concentration camp where his life would be in danger. The chosid, however, persisted. How could his existence be considered "life" if he had to continuously desecrate Shabbos? The Rebbe impressed upon him the fact that his unique status gave him the possibility to save other Jews and he had *no* right whatsoever to give that up. At that, the chosid was convinced and continued outside the camp with his forced labor.

This true story demonstrates how profound the love and awe for Shabbos is in a Jewish soul [heard from Rav Gershon Weiss, *shlit"a*]. However, determining the essence of Shabbos is more difficult.

Hashem is Our Boss

I was once approached by a gentile neighbor. Her college professor, she said, had made the preposterous statement that the Bible should be considered fiction. To bolster his claim, he cited the laws of Shabbos. He exclaimed, "They call it their day of rest, yet, if they need to visit someone on the twentieth floor of a skyscraper, they climb twenty flights of stairs. If the synagogue is two miles away, they have to walk. If it's a sweltering hundred degrees outside and the air-conditioner had not been turned on before Shabbos, they must suffer the blistering heat for the entire day. Some day of rest!" She mentioned to her professor that her neighbor was an Orthodox Rabbi and that she could ask him what all this meant.

I told her that there is a paragraph in the Shabbos liturgy, almost universally sung in synagogues each Shabbos morning. It starts off, "*Keil adon al kol hamaasim*—The Almight-y is the Boss over all His creations." This is a major theme of Shabbos. In the working world, the more you are paid, the more your boss or employer can ask you to do. Thus, if you are paid eight dollars an hour, there is only so much you can be expected to do, but once you are paid fifty dollars an hour, you are required to be responsive to greater demands. If you are paid even more—let's say one thousand dollars an hour, your boss can expect an even greater degree of compliance and work.

Hashem is our absolute Boss, and so whatever He may ask of us we must do. Once a week we remind ourselves of our joyful subjugation to Hashem by desisting from every possible creative labor. This affirms our acknowledgment that we are under the complete command of our Divine Commander. Thus, the focal message of Shabbos is that we are bound to Hashem. It is for this very reason that Jewish males do not put on tefillin on Shabbos, for tefillin, which remind men of their bond to Hashem, are unnecessary on Shabbos.

A Spiritual Day

The essence of Shabbos is discussed in the Gemara which relates that Hashem told Moshe, *"Matana tova yeish li b'beis genazi V'Shabbos sh'moh*—I have a wonderful present in my vault and Shabbos is its name" [*Masechtas Shabbos* 10b]. What was it Hashem stored in a celestial treasure chest? Certainly, not kishka or gefilte fish! And why would Hashem need to keep this valuable item securely hidden? The only possible reason is that He had to hide it from the angels. The angels, who were purely spiritual beings, would covet neither a seven-layer cake nor an afternoon nap! We must infer that the special nature of Shabbos dwells in its spiritual nature rather than in any of its material attractions. Similarly, the Gemara [*Brachos* 57b] relates that three things have a semblance to *Olam Habah* (the World to Come), and one of them is Shabbos. And we know that in *Olam Habah* all the pleasures will be of a spiritual nature.

Delighting Hashem

If Shabbos then is not just a day of physical collapse, nor an escape from the rigors of the week, nor merely a day off for pursuing pleasures of the body, what should be the authentic aims and goals of correct Shabbos observance?

The Gemara states, *"Kol hamaneg es HaShabbos nosnin lo mishalos liboh*—Whoever delights in the Shabbos is given his heart's desires" [*Masechtas Shabbos* 118b]. The Gemara cites proof for this from *Tehillim*, *"V'hisaneg al Hashem, v'yiten l'cha mishalos libcha*—When you delight Hashem, you'll be given your every wish" [37:4].

Hence, one focus of Shabbos is to give Hashem delight. In fact, the Shabbos liturgy is inaugurated with a resounding, *"L'chu n'rannah LaHashem*—Let us go sing to Hashem." In addition, the song of the day for Shabbos states, *"Mizmor shir l'yom HaShabbos, tov lehodos LaHashem*—A song for the Shabbos day, for it is good to give thanks to Hashem." We are repeatedly reminded that the centrality of our activities on Shabbos must be devoted toward Hashem.

Indeed, the Gemara relates that centuries ago the Roman Emperor, Caesar Turnus Rufus, asked Rabbi Akiva, *"Ma yom miyomayim*—What's so special about this day more than any other day?" Rabbi Akiva answered plainly, *"D'mari tzavi*— The Master desires it" [*Sanhedrin* 65b].

Thus Shabbos's uniqueness lies in the fact that it is Hashem's special day. This is the meaningful dimension to the Shabbos cholent and patcha. All the special Shabbos foods are to honor Hashem and give delight to the Creator Who has bestowed upon us this wonderous world which He formed in six days. This is why the Gemara carefully states, *"Kol hamaneg es haShabbos*—Whoever delights *the* Shabbos," and does not state *B'Shabbos* (*in* Shabbos) [*Shabbos* 118a]. Our job is not simply to *take* delight from Shabbos, but to *give* delight to the Shabbos.

In the same vein, the simple meaning of the posuk, *"V'yom hashveeie Shabbos LaHashem Elokecha*—The seventh day is Shabbos for Hashem your G-d," [*Shemos* 20:10] is to be understood quite literally. We must devote the Shabbos day to Hashem and not use this day for any of our own pursuits and desires! This can manifest itself in a multitude of ways. For example, if one has a fever on Shabbos and can't venture outside to shul, one should still put on one's Shabbos garments. In so doing, one is powerfully demonstrating that the fancy clothing is *not* being worn for others to see but primarily to bestow honor on the Shabbos. Similarly, one who makes sure to eat the third meal every Shabbos—even on a short winter Shabbos or even when one isn't particularly hungry—proves that the meal is eaten exclusively to honor Hashem and not due to hunger or convenience.

Incidentally, this kind of motivation supports one reason Ashkenazim use the term *shalosh seudos* (three meals) for the third meal, and not the more grammatically correct name used by the Sephardim—*seuda shlishit* (third meal). For when we consistently eat the third meal, we demonstrate that all three meals are eaten in honor of Hashem. Thus, it is called "three meals" for it sheds light on our motivation for eating all three meals.

Melavah Malka

Another important way to ascertain that our Shabbos observance is on the right track is to examine our attitude concerning the mitzvah of Melavah Malka (literally, to escort out the Shabbos Queen). After Shabbos, we resume our hectic lives and are quickly engrossed with whatever we may have put aside before Shabbos. Some people feel the need to immediately leave their house and do something, a by-product emotion from the void created by the departure of the *neshama yeseira* [the additional Shabbos soul] which leaves us after havdalah is said. However, to show a genuine respect and honor for the departing Shabbos, we should postpone these other interests and make it our business to sit down and eat in honor of the departing Shabbos, even though we may already have had enough eating during the last twenty-four hours.

A testimony to the supreme significance of Melavah Malka can be seen in the *Orchos Chaim Leharosh*. The Rosh mentioned 155 short snippets of advice which he considered absolutely essential in life. Though hardly any single item is mentioned twice, the Rosh mentions the mitzvah of Melavah Malka in number sixty-nine, and then again in number nineteen (of the Shabbos day).

What a wonderful habit to inculcate in one's family:

Gather around for a short Melavah Malka. You can be sure that you will be giving your descendants a lasting legacy. If they grow accustomed to the practice in their parental home, they will surely adopt it in their homes when they marry. You will be credited with starting a dynasty of honoring the Shabbos!

Waiting to Eat: Self-restraint on Erev Shabbos

Another barometer of correct Shabbos observance is the practice of abstaining from any heavy eating on Erev Shabbos. This practice ensures a hearty appetite on Shabbos night. The Gemara relates a scary incident concerning a certain family-line. On Erev Shabbos they always ate a fixed meal. Eventually, they became extinct. One might wonder, what was so terrible about this custom? If they entered Shabbos already satiated and in a suitable state of oneg, should that have detracted significantly from their Shabbos spirit? It turns out the answer is yes! They were punished for failing to allow themselves the active honor of eating to delight the Shabbos [*Masechtas Gittin* 38b].

Shabbos: The Goal of the Week

The Ksav Sofer sheds a penetrating insight into the essence of Shabbos. He wonders why Hashem deliberately chose to give Bnei Yisroel the mitzvah of Shabbos in the wilderness. He could have bequeathed it previously to Avraham Avinu, as He had the cardinal mitzvah of bris milah. The Ksav Sofer comments that Hashem did this to emphasize that Shabbos is not merely a rest day from the rigors of the frenzied work week. In fact, Shabbos was given in the desert where there was no work week at all and when everything was provided by heaven—from the miraculous manna to the waters from the well of Miriam. Hence, it is evident that there is more to the exalted mitzvah of Shabbos than just a twenty-five-hour vacation from work!

HaGaon, Rav Reuven Feinstein, *shlit"a*, explains that this is one of the critical differences between the Jewish Shabbos and the gentile Sunday "Sabbath." The gentile "Sabbath" is at the beginning of the week, since its function is to relax a person for the hard week ahead. Shabbos is at the end of the week, which makes the seventh day the focus and goal of the entire week. A Jew trudges through the materialistic week, aspiring and pining for the eventual goal, the spirituality of the Shabbos day.

Indeed, in each *shir shel yom* [song of the day] in our daily prayers, we say, *"Hayom yom echad L'Shabbos, or sheni L'Shabbos...*—Today is the first day towards Shabbos..., or, This is the second day towards the Shabbos...." Similarly, in the famous song *Echad Mi Yodeah* (Who Knows One) recited at the end of the Pesach seder, we sing, "Who knows seven? I know seven—*shivah y'mei Shabbata*," which literally means, "The seven days of the week." Thus instead of identifying the number seven with the Shabbos day, we say it stands for all seven days of the week, with all of them pushing us towards the goal of Shabbos. Indeed the great Gaon, Mori V'rabi, Rav Moshe Feinstein, zt"l, used to say that the Russian atheists sought to change the seven-day week to a different numeration, for they realized that the seven-day week symbolizes G-d's creation of the world.

A Difference between Shabbos and Yom Tov

Sefer Toras Haavos sheds another insight on the rarefied Shabbos experience. It introduces us to a basic difference between Shabbos and Yom Tov. On Yom Tov, he explains, Hashem comes to us. On Shabbos, however, we are given the great privilege of being allowed to go to Hashem. Indeed, this is another reason why Shabbos is akin to the future world—in *Olam Habah*, the righteous will be allowed to enter into Hashem's presence.

Shabbos, the Desire of the Days

In the Shabbos liturgy, we say, "*Chemdas Hayomim osoh karasa*—You [Shabbos] are called the desire of the days." The Medrash offers an intriguing explanation for this cryptic statement. Originally, the Medrash states, Hashem planned to create the world in six days, with each day comprised of 28 hours. However, the days gathered together and proclaimed that they desired a King. So each day donated four hours, thus making a week include seven days of 24 hours, and creating for themselves a King—the Shabbos day. (Somewhat related to this, the Rambam refers to Shabbos as the Shabbos King instead of the usual title, Shabbos Queen.) [*Hilchos Shabbos* chapter 30, halachah 2].

Remembering Shabbos Daily

With this in mind, we can better appreciate the mandate of the posuk, "*Zachor es Yom HaShabbos l'kadsho*— Remember the Shabbos day, to sanctify it" [*Shemos* 13:3]. The Beis Shammai [*Beitzah* 16a] interprets this as a directive to remember the Shabbos, each and every day. The Gemara comments that Shammai the Elder made it a point to honor the Shabbos daily by purposely using every day of the week to make some purchase for Shabbos. He did this in recognition of the fact that each day contributed from itself (as explained above) to the creation of the Shabbos. Thus, it is only proper that during each and every day, we intentionally attempt to honor Shabbos.

The Chofetz Chaim writes in the name of a Gadol Hador of his generation that this Gaon had a beautiful habit of mentioning something about Shabbos every day in his lecture. In this way, he fulfilled the positive command of *"Zachor es Yom HaShabbos L'kadsho."* The Chofetz Chaim adds that even when one refers to something that transpired the previous week, one should be mindful to describe the event by including how many days before Shabbos it occurred, and thus sneak in a remembrance of Shabbos [*Sheim Olam* chapter 4].

In yeshiva, I remember some bochurim who had the marvelous habit of marking food items (such as soda bottles) which they had bought for Shabbos with the words *l'kavod Shabbos Kodesh*. The theme of making Shabbos a part of our thoughts throughout the entire week is also expressed in the posuk, *"V'shomru Bnei Yisroel es HaShabbos"* [*Shemos* 31:16]. The word *v'shomru* can be translated to mean "to wait" as well as "to keep," as we find in reference to Yaakov Avinu where it says, *"v'aviv shomar es hadavar"* [*Bereishis* 37:11], that Yaakov waited for the fulfillment of Yosef's dreams. Similarly, Klal Yisroel continually waits and pines for the Shabbos day.

Yetzias Mitzrayim and Shabbos

There are several meaningful connections between *yetzias Mitzrayim* (the departure from Egypt) and Shabbos. In the second set of *luchos* (the tablets received by Moshe at Mount Sinai), the Torah links Shabbos with *yetzias Mitzrayim*, stating that we should observe the Shabbos in memory of the Exodus. *Yetzias Mitzrayim* is also prominently mentioned in kiddush, when we chant that Shabbos is *"zecher l'yetzias Mitzrayim."* On a simple level, the commentator Sforno explains that our refraining from work on Shabbos commemorates how Hashem freed us from the harsh servitude of Mitzrayim and allowed us to rest.

In *Masechtas Pesachim* [117b], *Tosefos* adds that in the gematria known as *at-bash*, the Hebrew word *perech*, which is used in the Torah to describe the harsh labor the Egyptians forced upon us, equals the word *v'gal* (numerically, both equal thirty-nine). From this, *Tosefos* proves that our enemies forced us to engage in all the thirty-nine labors prohibited on Shabbos. Hence, when we rest from these precise activities on Shabbos, we vividly commemorate how Hashem saved us from Egyptian domination.

Progressing to Holiness

The Bostoner Rebbe, Rabbi Levi Yizchak Horowitz, *shlit"a*, addresses the relationship of Shabbos to *yetzias Mitzrayim*. He explains that after a materialistic work-week spent in a sometimes hostile environment amongst non-Jews, Shabbos is an oasis of purity. So, too, we left Mitzrayim, the land of lewdness and *tumah* (impurity), and entered the pure environment of the *Ananei HaKavod* (protective Clouds of Glory), receiving the miraculous *mun* (manna) and *be'er shel Miriam* (well of Miriam). It is this progression from mundane banalities to holiness that stresses the link between *yetzias Mitzrayim* and Shabbos.

World Maintenance

Another lesson is taught to us through this linkage—Hashem not only created the world, He is constantly maintaining it as well. This aspect of Hashem's connection to the world is attested to by *yetzias Mitzrayim*, where Hashem manipulated the *teva* (natural forces) in numerous ways to demonstrate that He keeps a hands-on control over the world.

More Connection to *Yetzias Mitzrayim*

The Yalkut tells us that the Jews merited leaving Mitzrayim in the *zechus* (merit) of keeping the Shabbos. The Medrash relates that Moshe advised Pharaoh that Bnei Yisroel would produce more if he gave them a day of rest. Thereby, Moshe procured the Shabbos day for them. In the Pesach Haggadah, various commentators tell us that one of the intentions of the ambiguous statement contained in the Haggadah, "*V'hi she'amda*—And it was this that stood up for us," refers to the Shabbos day, since about Shabbos, it says "*Shabbos hi LaHashem b'chol moshvoseichem*—It is Shabbos to Hashem in all your neighborhoods" [*Vayikra* 23:3]. Indeed, in the Haggadah, in the song *Echad Mi Yodeah* (Who Knows One?), when we are told how the numbers one through thirteen relate to *yetzias Mitzrayim*, Shabbos is mentioned as the significance of number seven, because in the *zechus* of Shabbos, Bnei Yisroel was allowed to leave Mitzrayim. Hence, the obvious explanation of why Shabbos reminds us of *yetzias Mitzrayim*: It was one of the catalysts for our deliverance.

Shabbos Celebrates the Perfection of Creation

Since Shabbos observance primarily commemorates the creation of the world, we, too, celebrate the Shabbos with the feeling that all of our business is totally completed.

We are taught, "*Sheishes yomim ta'avod v'asisa kol m'lachtecha, v'yom ha'shviyi Shabbos La'Hashem Elokecha*

—Six days you will work and accomplish all of your labor, but the seventh, a Shabbos, is for Hashem your Lord" [*Shemos* 20:9]. Rashi explains that the word *kol* (all) is included to teach us that even when one has unfinished business, at the moment Shabbos arrives, it should be as if a big burden has fallen off and one should feel as if all of the work has been completed. Perhaps Rashi mentions this to commemorate that Hashem created a perfect world, as it says, *"Vayar Hashem es kol asher asah, v'hineh tov ma'od—*And Hashem saw all that He had done, and it was very fine" [*Bereishis* 1:31]. All that He had made—with no unfinished business.

No Complaining

Similarly, we find in halachah that on Shabbos there is a particular formula we use when wishing well to someone who is sick. On Shabbos, instead of simply using the statement commonly used on the weekdays, *"refuah shelaimah*—have a complete recovery," we declare, *"Shabbos, hi m'lizoak u'refuah k'rova lavo*—Shabbos, when we refrain from shouting in pain, a cure is coming shortly." At first glance, the reason one is prohibited to complain on Shabbos is simply because it clashes with the obligatory lofty mood of the day, namely a spirit of oneg, delight. However, since we now know from the previous section that Shabbos commemorates a perfect creation, we can understand how this relates to sickness in a different light, since complaining on Shabbos is contrary to the symbolism of the perfection of the day.

Symbolic Foods

My father, zt"l, told me that his father, Rav Meir, of blessed memory (who was murdered by the Nazis, may Hashem avenge his blood) used to say that Shabbos is an pneumonic acronym for *Shabbos, Basar, Tocheil*; *Shabbos, Beitzah, Tocheil*; and *Shabbos, Batzel, Tocheil* (on Shabbos we eat meat, we eat egg, and we eat onion). We can easily understand why eating meat on Shabbos would enhance the joy of the day. The Gemara says, *"Ein simcha ela b'basar*—There's no joy without meat!" [*Pesachim* 109a]. So the mitzvah of eating meat would be to generate happiness.

However, what is the significance of eating eggs? I think eggs are appropriate for Shabbos in order to emphasize the essence of Shabbos: To commemorate *Ma'asei Bereishis* —the Creation of the World. Hence, eggs which symbolize birth are perfect for Shabbos. This is also one of the main reasons an egg is eaten at the seder—since the seder night commemorates the birth of the Jewish people. Thus, it is wholly appropriate to eat an egg on Shabbos to remind ourselves of the symbolism of birth and creation.

Eggs are also symbolic of mourning. This is brought up by the *sefer Ta'amei Minhogim* [page 174] which explains, from the *Knesses Hagedola*, that eggs are eaten on Shabbos to remind us that Moshe Rabbeinu was *niftar* (passed away) on Shabbos.

The custom of eating onions was explained to me by Rabbi Prager of the Noveminsker Yeshiva. The Vilna Gaon explains that if you look at many of the particular foods traditionally eaten on Shabbos, you'll find many of them have the *mispar katan* of seven. Thus, *yayin* (wine) is seven (1+1+5), *basar* (meat) is seven (2+3+2), *dag* (fish) is seven (3+4), and *challah* (bread) is seven (8+3+5 = 16; 1+6 = 7). Even *ner* (candle) is seven (5+2). If you keep this in mind, Rabbi Prager continued, this will illuminate the Shabbos *minhag* to slice the onion in half (before we cut it smaller), since *batzel* (onion) equals fourteen (2+9+3). Hence, when you cut it in half, it too becomes seven. I have also heard that a common species of onion has seven internal "rings" or layers. Thus in the onion lies yet another symbolism of Shabbos.

Fish On Shabbos

The *Shulchan Aruch* dictates in *Orach Chaim* [250:1] that one should eat meat and drink wine on Shabbos. The *Mishnah Berurah* [242:2] adds that fish should be eaten as well. In the *Biur Halachah* [242:1], the Chofetz Chaim explains (citing the *Toras Chaim*) that fish is appropriate because Shabbos has a semblance of *Olam Habah* as we sing, "*Me'ein Olam Habah*—A resemblance to the World to Come." Since we will eat the *livyoson* (a legendary fish), *shor habor* (a legendary 'wild' ox), and we'll drink special wine aged from the beginning of time, these are exactly the foods which we eat on Shabbos to celebrate in *olam hazeh*.

In many Ashkenazi homes, it is customary to eat fish on Friday night as the appetizer, followed by chicken soup, and then the main dish, chicken. At Shabbos lunch, we eat all types of meats such as cold cuts, liver, and cholent meat. Is there a meaning behind this order? Yes! Since all of Shabbos is "*zecher l'maasai bereishis*—in remembrance of the work of Creation," the menu is therefore designed to reflect this. Thus the courses are served in chronological order of creation: Fish were created on the fifth day, followed later that day by birds, and only on the sixth day were the animals created. Hence, even our menu on Shabbos is synchronized with the creation remembrance message of the day.

The *Bnei Yissaschor* suggests that since fish received a blessing on the fifth day of Creation, and humans received a blessing on the sixth day, and the Shabbos day is likewise blessed, we create the ingredients of a triple blessing when we eat fish on the seventh day. This is particularly meaningful since we are taught, *"Hachut hameshulosh lo bimheira y'natek—* the triple cord will not be speedily severed" [*Koheles* 4:12].

There are other explanations for the custom of eating fish on Shabbos. The *Yerushalmi* [*Shabbos* 15:3] states that Shabbos was given to Bnei Yisroel for the study of Torah. To drive home this message, we begin each meal with fish, which live in water. Symbolically, water represents Torah, as it says, *"Ein mayim ela Torah—*Water only refers to Torah" [*Bava Kama* 82a]. Rav Naftoli of Ropshitz adds that since fish emit no audible sound, we eat it on Shabbos to remind us to guard our speech on Shabbos.

Perhaps we also eat fish on Shabbos so that we'll remember our responsibility to the poor on Shabbos—fish in Hebrew is spelled with a "gimmel" and "daled," which the Gemara teaches us stands for the directive, *"gomel dalim—*bestow kindliness to the poor" [*Masechtas Shabbos* 104a]. Indeed Klal Yisroel's virtues shine brightly through such organizations as New York City's Tomchei Shabbos, which takes care of the needs of poor Jews in anticipation of the holy Shabbos day. Fish is also a symbol of purity for, unlike meat or poultry, it doesn't need any ritual such as slaughter or salting to render it kosher. Finally, even when fish are asleep, fish keep their eyes open. So, too, on Shabbos we testify to our belief that Hashem never takes His eyes off of Klal Yisroel!

Commemorating the Manna

In the beginning of *Hilchos Shabbos* [242:1], the Rama writes about the *minhag* in certain towns on Shabbos to eat meat crepes. This commemorated the manna which had a heavenly layer of dew underneath it and on top of it. (Another example of this would be the sandwich cookie!) The *Mishnah*

Berurah wonders why the manna would be remembered on Shabbos when no manna fell on Shabbos. The Chofetz Chaim cites the aforementioned *Toras Chaim* where it is written that since Shabbos is a semblance of *Olam Habah*, and since the Gemara notes that in the future world the righteous will eat manna, therefore, we remember the manna on Shabbos. (It is interesting to note that the Chofetz Chaim did not ask about the practice of covering the challah, which is done to show that the manna had a layer on top and on bottom. Perhaps this is because when we cover the challah we commemorate the double portion of manna given to Bnei Yisroel for the Shabbos. This is an understandable topic for Shabbos symbolism. And once the challahs are representing the double portion of manna, it's appropriate to remember the miraculous "dew covering" as well.)

Related to this connection between Shabbos and *Olam Habah*, we can suggest a novel reason why there are special zemiros sung on Shabbos—singing praises of Hashem will be the occupation of the righteous in the future world.

Perhaps we can suggest an alternate explanation for the custom of eating meat crepes cited by the Rama. The Gemara tells us that the expenses incurred for our celebration of Shabbos are not deducted from the yearly allowance allocated to us in Heaven on Rosh Hashanah [*Baitza* 16a]. So, in reality, what we enjoy on Shabbos is truly like the manna: A gift from heaven.

The only problem with this explanation is that the Chofetz Chaim states clearly that this custom was not practiced on Yom Tov but, according to my explanation, it should have been instituted for Yom Tov as well.

Creating a Shabbos Legacy

We are commanded, *"V'shomru Bnei Yisroel es Hasha-*

bbos, la'asos es HaShabbos l'dorosom—Bnei Yisroel should guard the Shabbos, to perform the Shabbos for generations" [*Shemos* 31:16]. Why, you may wonder, is the word Shabbos repeated?

Rav Yitzchak Elchonon Specter, zt"l, answers with an important lesson about Shabbos. It is not enough to *keep* the laws of Shabbos. We have to celebrate Shabbos in a way that ensures it will remain intact throughout all future generations. The posuk warns us to guard the Shabbos so that it will have a lasting effect on our families! To do this, we must take a blunt look at the way we spend our Shabbosim. Then we must ask if our observances will make a strong spiritual impact upon our children, or if they are empty rituals consisting of eating and drinking, plenty of sleeping, and reading the paper. Such Shabbos observance will not leave a long-term effect on our descendants!

Shabbos Enjoyment

"*U'shmartem es HaShabbos ki kodesh hi lachem*— Guard the Shabbos for it is holy for you" [*Shemos* 31:14]. In the Gemara's discussion [*Pesachim* 68 a/b], everyone conclusively agrees that on Shabbos you must engage in personal enjoyment—*lachem*.

Still, the Rebbe, Reb Nochumke, zt"l, explains that the Torah counsels, "*kodesh hi lachem*—it is Holy" and that the word *lachem*, personal enjoyment, should be invested and infused with holiness. Thus, the Shabbos cholent and the delectable chicken soup should be accompanied by thoughts of gratitude to Hashem for creating such an astonishing world and giving us such a beautiful day. We already mentioned that Shabbos is a semblance of *Olam Habah* and, in the future world, all enjoyment will be of a spiritual nature!

The Sweetness of Shabbos

In our Shabbos *bentching* the words, *"v'lanuach b'a-hava*—to rest with love"* are added. The *Devar Aharon* on the Haggadah observes that we also insert the word *b'ahava* in our Yom Tov liturgy (when Yom Tov falls out on Shabbos) because the mitzvah of Shabbos was given at Mara, before Matan Torah. Hence, unlike the rest of the Torah which was given under the threat of *"Kafa aleihem har k'gigis*—Holding the entire mountain over our heads"* [*Avodah Zarah* 2b], the mitzvah of Shabbos was accepted without any pressure whatsoever. Thus Shabbos is something we do wholeheartedly, out of love.

This is the perhaps the reason we sing (in the second verse of *Baruch Keil Elyon*, a well-known song of Shabbos), *"Eezein bani'mim*—He made it to hear it with pleasantness."* The *Ohr Shmuel* explains that Shabbos was given at Mara, and not later at Har Sinai with the rest of the Torah. This was because Hashem knew that if we tasted Shabbos' sweetness first, we would experience its ecstasy, and we would then be sure of the excellence of Torah and would thus be encouraged to make the commitment *"Na'aseh v'nishma*—We will do and we will listen."*

Thus, when we try to win back Jews who have gone astray, we often use a Shabbaton experience, which exposes people to the sweetness of Shabbos first (before other more rigorous observances), utilizing the same proven method that Hashem *Yisborach* used in the desert. This is also one of the reasons why a bris milah is not performed until the eighth day: It ensures that on whichever day the baby was born, he will experience a Shabbos before entering a pact with Hashem.

We discover in *Megillas Esther* [8:16] that after the victory over Haman and his cohorts, the Jews were in a state of *orah, simcha, v'sasson, v'ykar*. The Gemara elucidates that this refers to Torah festivals, bris milah and tefillin [*Masechtas Megillah* 16b]. One may wonder why Shabbos is not included on this list of cardinal mitzvos revitalized after Mordechai's heavenly coup. However, the absence of Shabbos is readily understood, since the Gemara in *Masechtas Shabbos* [88a] explains that the new spiritual level of the Jews after Haman's downfall was depicted earlier in the same posuk: *Kimu v'kiblu*, which Rava interprets to mean, *"Kimu ma shekiblu k'var—* they accepted lovingly what they originally accepted under pressure" [*Megillah* 7a]. Hence the change during Mordechai's time occured only in those mitzvos initially accepted under duress at Har Sinai. Since Shabbos was given beforehand (as previously mentioned), with love, there was no change during the Megillah era, and hence it wasn't included in the posuk.

The "Mouth" Connection

On Shabbos we should also be careful regarding what we say. The *Navi* teaches, *"V'chibadto ma'asos drachecha mimtzo cheftzecha, v'daber davar—*And to honor the Shabbos by avoiding working, going about our needs, and speaking in the usual manner" [*Yeshaya* 58:13]. The Gemara explains the restrictions on speech, *"Shelo y'hei diburcha shel Shabbos k'diburcha shel chol—*Our speech on Shabbos should not resemble our speech during the rest of the week" [*Shabbos* 113b]. In short, this means on Shabbos we shouldn't discuss any of the things which we are prohibited to do on Shabbos. (The ridiculous preface of, *"Nisht oif Shabbos geret,"* does not help a whit.)

Why is there such a special emphasis on resting our speech on Shabbos? The answer may lie in the fact that Shabbos commemorates Hashem's rest from creating the world. From what did Hashem actually rest? The Mishna states clearly,

"*B'asarah mamaros nivra'u haolam*—With ten utterances the world was created" [*Pirkei Avos* 5:1]. In addition, in *Tehillim* [33:6] we find that, "*B'dvar Hashem Shamayim na'asu*—The heavens were made by the word of Hashem." Thus, we see that Hashem rested from speaking. Therefore, it logically follows that when we commemorate Hashem's rest on Shabbos, we should put a special emphasis on resting our speech as well.

I think the Chassidic custom (for some) of making kiddush on whiskey on Shabbos morning connected to this. Why do they choose whiskey and not wine—the drink of choice for sanctifying Hashem? While some say the custom started when there was a scarcity of wine, I'd like to propose something more novel. Perhaps it was the wish of the Chassidim to sanctify the Shabbos using the blessing said over whiskey, "*Shehakol nih'yeh b'dvaro*—That everything comes about through His word," which emphasizes that it was with His word that Hashem created the world.

In addition, throughout Shabbos we are gifted with a *neshama yeseira* (an extra soul). The Targum teaches us [in *Bereishis* 2:7] that our *nefesh chaya* (spirit of life) is defined as a *ruach m'malla* (spirit of speech), so when we are given an extra portion of this spirit, it should be utilized with special care. Thus when one takes to heart this restriction on speech, the barometer of whether someone is fulfilling the mandate of *v'daber davar* (not speaking in a usual, weekday manner) is when an observer can readily discern that it is Shabbos from our speech. If our conversation and remarks are radically different from during the week, we know we are fulfilling this directive.

Yarei Shabbos

The Chida teaches that if we make an anagram of the first word of the Torah, "*Bereishis*," we will discover that it also spells *Yarei* Shabbos (those who fear the Shabbos). This is one of the great principles of the Torah. One should have a healthy fear and awe for the holiness and laws of Shabbos. To prove this concept, the *Imrei Noam* cites, "*Es Shabsosai tishmoru, v'es mikdashi tira'u*—You should guard my Shabbos, and fear my temple" [*Vayikra* 19:3]. From the proximity of the two words, Shabbos and *mikdashi*, he infers that one should have the same attitude of fear and reverence for the Shabbos that one would have towards the Holy Temple.

The Chofetz Chaim also emphasizes this theme in his *sefer, Likutei Amorim* [chapter 8]. He states that one is able to quantify the severity of a sin by the depth of its penalty. When the hierarchy of punishments is examined, one finds that they begin (at the low end)—with physical punishments to the body from imposed lashes, to death brought by the hand of heaven, to *kares* (spiritual excommunication), to the lesser death sentences of strangulation and burning, to the extremely severe death sentence of stoning. When one reflects that willful Shabbos desecration carries the death sentence of stoning (a penalty worse than the one meted out for murder!), one can appreciate how immensely serious is our obligation to properly keep Shabbos. The Chofetz Chaim points out that only regarding transgressions of Shabbos and transgressions pertaining to idolatry do we state that the transgressor is considered like someone who trampled upon the entire Torah!

The following anecdote from the life of the saintly Vilna Gaon, zt"l, vividly portrays this theme. The Gaon was once sitting at his Shabbos table when he inadvertently moved a nutshell. Now, a nutshell is considered *muktza* (forbidden to be moved) on Shabbos since it has no purpose once the nut has been eaten. When it came to his attention that he had dislodged it, he fainted on the spot! After his family revived him, he noticed the shell again, and fainted a second time. When they revived him the next time, his Rebbitzen suddenly popped the shell into her mouth and started munching upon it, showing the Gaon that it was fit to be eaten *al y'dei hadchak* (in desperation), and hence, that the shell wasn't *muktza* after all. This is a snapshot view of the awe that our great leaders held for the holy Shabbos.

With this in mind, we should be galvanized to action by the words of the saintly Chofetz Chaim who, in the preface to his *Mishnah Berurah* [volume 3], quotes from the *sefer Yaros D'vash*, where it is written that it is impossible for someone to avoid desecrating the Shabbos unless he spends time studying its intricate laws! What an incentive to make time for the study of Hilchos Shabbos.

Greater Inhibition

I stress, finally, that by no means is an attitude of reverence and awe for the Shabbos day restricted to the Gedolei Hador. Historically, even the lowly *am haaretz* had a healthy appreciation and respect for the sanctity of Shabbos. This can be seen from the first mishna in chapter four of *D'mai*, where the Tana teaches that an otherwise not credible person is believed if he testifies on Shabbos that his produce was tithed. The *Bartenura* explains that such a person is more afraid to lie and commit a transgression on the Shabbos than he would be during the rest of the week. Therefore, we must honestly ask ourselves if we feel a greater inhibition about yelling, or lying, or speaking *loshon hara* on Shabbos than we might during the rest of the week. If we do not then, sadly, we have descended lower in this area than even an *am haaretz* of old!

Shabbos and the Yetzer Hara

Nowadays, thank G-d, most of us feel no temptation to

violate the Shabbos. Indeed, Rav Yaakov Kaminetsky, zt"l, commented that fifty years ago (when many anti-discrimination laws were not yet in place) the prevalent *yetzer hara* in America was the challenge of not desecrating the Shabbos. Some fifty years later, we are spared this trial, thank G-d.

Now, he observed, our test is how we keep Erev Shabbos. Do we rush into our house at the very last minute, taking a shower like a speeding bullet, or do we arise early in the morning to begin a full day of Shabbos preparation even if we are busy at work for much of the day? The Gemara teaches that we should not expect Eliyahu to arrive on Erev Shabbos to herald Mashiach, because he would never disturb the Shabbos preparations of the Yidin! This demonstrates how valuable our Friday preparations are considered.

To give an idea of the greatness of Shabbos preparations, Rav Yonah MiGerona writes in *Shaarei Teshuva* that when one sweats while preparing for Shabbos, Hashem considers the sweat like tears. Thus, a woman bathing her children, or cooking over four burners in the hot kitchen, has earned the potent merit of tears (the gates of tears are never closed).

I would like to add another challenge for today's Shabbos observer. At the end of *Masechtas Shabbos* [150b], the Gemara relates a fascinating story. Once during Shabbos a certain chosid noticed a breach in his fence. Mentally, he decided to repair it. Later, when he realized that he had inadvertently made plans for a weekday activity on Shabbos, he decided never to fix the hole in his fence. At this point, the Gemara continues, Hashem intervened and made a miracle: A caper bush grew (a wondrous bush described by the Gemara as having completely edible leaves, branches, and berries) to cover the breach. From its produce, the chosid was able to support his entire family.

The lesson is clear. One should try to rest from even

thinking about forbidden things on Shabbos. Indeed, this is the way to ensure that one's Shabbos is absolutely and truly spiritual, and unmistakably distinctive from the remainder of the week. If we don't have control over our thoughts, and instead let our minds linger on the stock market or next week's chores, we are really not resting from the drudgery of the work week. Furthermore, if we are involved with the mundane rumination of the work week, we are not permitting Shabbos to be a facsimile of the afterlife in this world. This is the sentiment we mentioned earlier: With the arrival of Shabbos, we should feel as if all our work has been totally completed.

You might ask, "In the popular daytime Shabbos song, *Mah Yedidus,* don't we sing, '*hirhurim mutarim*—thoughts are permitted?' Isn't it only *words* of a weekday nature (and not *thoughts*) which are forbidden?"

I once heard Rav Avigdor Miller, *shlit"a,* stating that the only reason the Gemara permits *thoughts* of a weekday nature on Shabbos is because of "*Lo nitna Torah l'malachei hashares*—The Torah wasn't given to celestial angels" [*Yoma* 30a]. This is a Talmudic rule which explains that the Torah does not demand from us humans that which is too difficult. (As an aside, since we were sure that Hashem wouldn't give us more than we could handle, this is the reason Bnei Yisroel was able to say, "*Naaseh v'nishma*—We will do and then listen" at Har Sinai. As it says in Chazal, "*Ein HaKodesh boruch hu bah betrunia in briyosov*—Hashem doesn't ask from a person more than he can deliver" [*Avodah Zarah* 3a].) Thus, in our case, it would be considered an unreasonable expectation that we entirely erase our weekday plans, worries, and chores from our minds. However, given human limitations, when at all possible, one should try to maintain a tight reign on one's thoughts. Even a sincere attempt will dramatically elevate one's *kedushas* Shabbos.

I hope this essay helps to enhance the quality and pleasure of our Shabbos observance and, in this merit, we should be *zocheh* speedily to the, *"Yom shekulo Shabbos, umenucha l'chayei olomim*—the time when everyday will be Shabbos, for all eternity!"

Bentching—Saying Thanks To Hashem

Birchas HaMazon, or *bentching* as we familiarly call it, is habitually said in about two or three minutes at the end of a meal at which bread was eaten. However, this glorious prayer thanking Hashem for all that we've eaten is far more profound than just a simple formula to say as we leave the table.

The *Be'er Heitev* [185:1] quotes the *Ateres Zekeinim*, who points out that if we study the *Birchas HaMazon*, we will see that all the letters of the "aleph-beis" are included except for one. The "fei sofis" (final "fei") is nowhere to be found. The *Ateres Zekeinim* [185:1] concludes that if we are careful how we *bentch*, we will be spared all the words that end with the "fei" such as the words, *af* and *ketzef*, two adjectives often used in the Torah to describe Hashem's anger.

When a family goes through difficult times, whether it is sickness, loss of *shalom bayis* or loss of income, they experience manifestations of *af* and *ketzef*. Imagine we could save ourselves and our families from this with the proper *kavanah* when we say *Birchas HaMazon*! Indeed, the *Mishnah Berurah* concurs [185:1], saying that whoever says the *Birchas HaMazon* with *kavanah* will be richly rewarded with sustenance *b'revach* (in plenty) and *b'kovod* (with dignity) all the days of his or her life. In these times, when so many people do not have a livelihood, and others, although they are earning money, have difficulty making ends meet, we should pay special attention to *Birchas HaMazon*. For those among us who are doing well financially, we should thank Hashem even more, praying with *kavanah* that our sustenance will continue.

———•———•———

It really doesn't take much effort to concentrate on *bentching* with *kavanah*. For an investment of perhaps three extra minutes, we gain so much. I like to refer to it as the "three minute advantage!" Where else can a mere three minutes earn us such rewards as dignified financial success? The *Mishnah Berurah* [ibid.] quotes the *Bayis Chodosh*, the Bach, who tells us that the best way to *bentch* is while looking at the words in the *bentcher* and not, as so many do, by heart. I've also heard it said the name of Rav Elazar Menachem Shach, *shlit"a*, that *bentching* while looking into a *bentcher* is a *segula* (Divine assurance) for longevity.

We are unquestionably a society on the run. Many of us usually do two or three things at once. When it comes to *bentching*, however, we should change our pace and simply concentrate on each of the *brachos* we are saying. The *Kitzur Shulchan Aruch* [44:6] advises us that when we sit down to *Birchas HaMazon*, we should do so *b'eima u'vyirah* (with reverence and awe). No other activity should be done while reciting these blessings. Everything else should be put aside during these five minutes.

I heard from my good friend, Rabbi Shmuel Dovid Friedman, a superb example of appreciating the power of *bentching*. He related that his mother, z"l, would sigh at how people preferred *mezonos* bread (i.e., bread that isn't technically bread, and thus it might not be necessary to wash or *bentch*) to avoid the time-consuming need to wash and *bentch*. Aside from the halachic questions that arise from *mezonos* bread, such as being *kovei'a seudah* (establishing a meal) with it, or that it too closely resembles *hamotzi* bread, (i.e., bread that you have to wash and *bentch* for) the *hashkafah* (philosophy) behind the *mezonos* bread upset her. Even when she was ailing from the debilitating effects of chemotherapy, she would force down a *k'zayis* of bread (a portion large enough to require *bentching*) so that she would be able to *bentch*. One has to question making a meal with *mezonos* bread, when it causes the loss of a wonderful opportunity to recite *Birchas HaMazon*.

We ought to ask ourselves, "Do we eat in order to make a *bracha* or do we make a *bracha* in order to eat?"

━ • ━ • ━

In *Devarim* we find, *"Va'ahalela Hashem b'chayai—* And I will praise Hashem with my life" [6:13]. The Rambam asks how can we accomplish this? He says that if we eat in order to *bentch*, then even through our eating we are praising Hashem, since the purpose of our eating will be to sing His praise. We should all be aware that at the end of 120 years when we stand before the Heavenly Tribunal, and we are asked why we didn't always daven with *kavanah*, we may respond, "I had to keep up with the minyan," or "I was really in a rush and had to leave for early meetings with clients." But what excuse will we find when we are asked why we didn't *bentch* properly on Shabbos? Could we say that instead of a two-hour and fifty-five-minute nap on Shabbos afternoon, we hurriedly *bentched* so that we could enjoy a three-hour nap? Couldn't we give Hashem those five minutes? We should follow the example of the great men of the previous generation. Reb Yaakov Kaminetsky, zt"l, for example, never varied in the amount of time he spent *bentching*, whatever the situation. And the Manchester Rav, Rav Yehudah Zev Segal, zt"l, would never wash and make *hamotzi* on a meal if he felt he would have to rush his *bentching*.

———•———•———

It helps to keep in mind that the mitzvah of *Birchas HaMazon* is *min haTorah*. Only three tefillos are from the Torah: *Shema*, *Birchas HaTorah*, and *Birchas HaMazon*.

It is a highly recommended practice for a father or mother to *bentch* aloud with the children. This way we train our children from the very beginning to say the words slowly and with feeling. It also ensures that they will remember the importance of *bentching*. This beautiful practice will, in all likelihood, remain with them when they set up their own *batei ne'eman*.

———•———•———

So let's seize the wonderful opportunity of *bentching* and give heartfelt thanks to Hashem for all the goodness He has showered upon us. Let's break the habit of just zipping through *bentching*. Let's instead condition ourselves to *bentch* slowly with concentration in a way that is suitable and worthy of one who is voicing thanks to the "King of kings." In this merit may we continue to enjoy Hashem's kindness for many years to come!

How To Deal
With Fear

We have been bombarded by the media with scenes of horror—from multiple tragedies in Eretz Yisroel, which leave us numb with shock, to, *lehavdil*, the much-talked about death of the Princess of Wales. This preoccupation with death can pry on our minds and permeate our lives. So, too, we grow anxious when we hear reports of young people finding lumps, *rachmono litzlon*, on their bodies, or having sudden heart attacks. The Torah can help alleviate some of this fear and worry, or at least, put it in perspective.

The Gemara relates a revealing incident about a disciple who was walking behind Rabbi Yishmael, the son of Rabbi Yossi, in the marketplace of Tzion. Rabbi Yishmael noticed that the student was anxious and commented, "You are a sinner," for it states, 'Sinners are fearful in Tzion'" [*Masechtas Brachos* 60a]. We see from here that fear is considered a sin.

The Gemara relates further [*ibid.*] that Yehuda Bar Nosson was once walking behind Rav Hamnuna. Rav

Hamnuna heard Yehuda Bar Nosson sigh (because of his worry and fear) and commented, "Do you want to bring suffering upon yourself? In *Iyov* [3:24] it states, '*Ki pachad pachad'ti vayehsayeinee*—I have been fearful, and that which I feared came upon me.'"

This sentiment is echoed by the great Chassidic master, the *Pele Yoetz*, who asked, [on the word *daaga*] what will a person gain through fear and worry? If it (what he is worrying about) is the decree of Hashem, then his worry won't help a whit, and if not, then he is simply saddling himself with the aggravation of needless fear and distress. Furthermore, the *Pele Yoetz* says, sometimes one brings upon oneself the exact thing which one was worrying about simply because of the worry itself! So we see that it is not only sinful to worry, it is downright dangerous!

Puzzling enough, the *Navi* sings the praises of fear! In the wisdom of *Mishlei* [28:14], it says, "*Ashrei adom m'facheid tamid*—Fortunate is the person who is always fearful!" The Talmud in *Brachos* [60a] observes this apparent contradiction, and responds that it is different when one worries about Torah. On the simple level this means that if we worry that our learning may be forgotten and this prompts us to review our studies, then this is a productive worry.

The Maharsha elaborates that worrying about Torah is not the only manifestation of permissible worry. Rather, any worry and fear which is positive and fruitful is to be commended. Rashi [in Tractate *Gittin*, 55b] comments on the above mentioned verse, "*Ashrei adom m'fached tamid*," that this refers to a person who worries about what the future might bring because of his or her behavior, and takes precautions to avoid any action which could cause future repercussions. In *Mishlei* commenting on the above verse Rashi states succinctly that this refers to someone who is afraid of punishment and therefore distances himself or herself from sin.

For example, someone who fears the statement, "A door which doesn't open for the poor will have to open for a doctor," [*Kitzur Shulchan Aruch*, Laws of Tzedakah, 34:1], will be motivated by this positive fear, and always take action to tend to the needs of the poor.

Such positive fear will result in greater vigilance towards many of our mitzvos. Thus, obviously it is certainly not recommended to avoid eating because of a fear of choking on food. But, if this prompts one to make a more meaningful *bracha* of *"shehakol nihye bidvaro,"* or if this adds another element of thanks to one's *bentching,* or if it makes one more wary about talking *loshon hara* at the table, then this is indeed meaningful fear! Similarly, if the fear of food poisoning, mad cow's disease, or catching an infectious disease from a food handler prompts someone to be more careful with kashrus, that too is wonderful!

Similarly, if one is afraid of burglars at night (particularly someone whose security may have been shattered by a previous break in), and this prompts one to say *Krias Shema al Hamitta* with concentration (because of the Gemara where it states that *Krias Shema* protects one from the "damagers" of the night [*Brachos* 5a]), and if one also says the blessing during *Maariv "haskiveinu Hashem Elokeinu l'shalom"*—i.e., asking Hashem to allow us to sleep in peace with intent, then this, too, is a productive fear. This equally applies to someone who fears car crashes and thus always recites *tefillas haderech* with fervor before leaving on a car trip!

The *Pele Yoetz* adds that although one should not sit around and worry, it is appropriate to be concerned and cautious. If steps of protection exist, they should definitely be taken. Thus, he says, we should engage in preventive prayer. Therefore, someone who worries about cancer, *rachmono litzlon,* should continually pray for good health, as the Gemara advises, "*L'olam y'vakesh adom shelo yecheleh*—One should always pray not to become sick." Parents should also pray every morning that their children will be safe when going on and off their school bus! So, too, people whose financial worries cause them to have sleepless nights should pay particular attention to their prayers during the blessing of *Bareich aleinu* in the *Shemoneh Esrei*.

In the same vein, the *Metzudas Tzion* in *Mishlei* [*ibid.*] gives a practical explanation to the verse, "*Ashrei adom m'facheid tamid.*" The *Metzudas Tzion* says, in essence, that someone who takes steps to avoid the dangers of what he fears is to be praised. Thus, someone terrified by reports of drownings should never venture into a swimming pool or lake without a lifeguard. A woman who hears about the escalating numbers of women with breast cancer should schedule a mammogram at regular intervals. Similarly, someone who frets about inoperable lung cancer should make sure that no one in the family smokes! Fear of car accidents should generate the use of seat belts, and fear of muggings should make one more alert concerning where one travels at night.

Avos D'rabbi Nosson [9:5] teaches, "Do not despair from retribution. Rather, one should worry each day that perhaps today or tomorrow one's sins will catch up with them." This is considered fruitful worry, for it motivates us to be continually engaged in doing teshuva, which will erase our misdeeds and obviates the need for punishment.

Initially, we cited the Gemara in *Brachos* where it said that unproductive fear is considered a sin. However, it is unclear which sin it is referring to. Perhaps, the source of the sin is the lack of *bitachon* (trust in Hashem). Indeed, the *Pele Yoetz* cites, to counter fear, the verse, "*V'habotei-ach B'Hashem chesed yesov'venhu*—one who trusts in Hashem is always encircled by kindness!"

The Hebrew word for worry is *daaga*. This word has a noteworthy oddity. Four of the five first letters of the Hebrew alphabet are used in its spelling. Of "aleph", "beis", "gimmel," "daled," and "hei" it is missing only the "beis." Perhaps this is to signify that if the "beis"—which stands for *bitachon*—is missing, then there is worry!

May Hashem bless us all with a life of good health, happiness, and prosperity both spiritually and in gashmius!

In Loving Memory
Of Reb Moshe

The name Reb Moshe evokes a plethora of emotions and recollections: Awe and reverence for his encyclopedic knowledge, amazement at his unwavering diligence, longing for his warmth, incredulity for his devotion to all aspects of Jewish life the world over, and finally an ever-present sadness that he is no longer with us.

As a young talmid, I merited to serve him for about ten years, when he came to the Yeshiva of Staten Island and during the summers at Camp Yeshiva Staten Island in Kerhonkson, New York.

When I was thirteen years old I asked an older boy (Moshe Bodner, to whom I am forever grateful) who was then serving the Rosh HaYeshiva, zt"l, to allow me to carry the milk bottle whenever he went to serve Reb Moshe. And so, I tagged along holding milk and soda bottles, relishing the opportunity to observe the leader of world Jewry at close quarters. Then Moshe Bodner left the yeshiva and I, *boruch Hashem*, slipped into his place.

Indeed, there were times during the decade in which I attended my Rebbe when I had to dodge attempts to replace me. There were several logical reasons these attempts were made. First, I was a mere "younger bochur," hardly deserving to serve the Gaon of the generation. Furthermore, some people believed that, in my formative years, such activities would distract me from my learning. Yet I stubbornly persisted, subtly hinting that, if they wanted to replace me, they would have to take it up with the Rosh Yeshiva. The fact that no one ever did this perfectly illustrates the Rosh Yeshiva's credo which was to almost never cause anyone's removal, no matter how unworthy he or she may be. Thus, the concept of throwing a boy out of yeshiva because his parents didn't pay tuition was absolutely foreign to him.

My close contact with Reb Moshe has had a powerful effect on my life. Recently, for instance, I visited a shul for the first time and I automatically began calculating the maximum capacity of people the shul could hold for a shiur or a drosha. It struck me that probably no one else in the shul harbored such thoughts. I wondered why, almost instinctively, I always do this when I visit a new shul. Later, it dawned on me, that I must have absorbed this from Reb Moshe. In the preface to one of his *seforim*, the *Dibros Moshe* on *Bava Kamma*, Reb Moshe explains why he had the "temerity" (he was also a Gaon in humility) to write a *sefer*. He explains that when a person goes up to heaven, it will be assessed whether he spread Torah as far and as wide as his potential. Hashem would thus ask Reb Moshe, "Why did you just teach Torah in MTJ (Mesivtha Tifereth Jerusalem), and not spread Torah around the world and to future generations?" In preparation for this moment, and in order to be able to answer affirmatively to this question, Reb Moshe wrote *seforim*. It took a decade after his passing for me to become aware that I had absorbed this lesson from him by osmosis.

I believe this is a great lesson. The *Medrash Rabbah*, [*Bamidbar* 22:1] cites the posuk *"U'vo sidbak*—You should cleave to Hashem" [*Devarim* 10:20], and asks how is it possible to cleave to G-d, Who we cannot see and Who is a consuming fire? The *Medrash* explains we should cleave to true Torah sages, and in this way grow closer to Hashem. Similarly, the Mishna in *Pirkei Avos* [1:4] recommends, *"Hevei misabek bafar ragleihem*—Get dusty from the earth beneath their feet." This signifies that proximity to sages and exposure to Torah giants is powerfully beneficial even for young people.

Indeed, the Mishna teaches us: *"Shimon b'no amar, Kol yamei gadaltee bein hachachomim v'lo matzasee l'guf tov m'shtika*—Shimon his [Reb Gamliel's] son said: All my days I lived among the sages and I haven't found anything better than silence" [*Avos* 1:7]. This preface by Rabbi Shimon conveys not only that silence was the most impressive trait which he had observed in these great people, but it describes his life among scholars. It teaches us that one absorbs lessons by observing and assimilating the behavior of extraordinary people. Indeed, we are like giant sponges and we soak up the conduct of people who are around us, people we choose to surround ourselves with. It is therefore of the utmost importance that parents make sure that their growing boys and girls have exceptional Torah models to emulate in their formative years. When choosing a yeshiva or bais yaakov school, this should be one of the most important criteria!

Although the Rosh Yeshiva thought in global terms, and wrote Torah novellae for the ages—deciding practical halachah, in subjects as varied as the permissibility of organ transplants and Shabbos elevators, from artificial insemination to the plight of agunos—he also found time to focus on each individual who came to him. At Reb Moshe's funeral, Rav Alpert, z"l, mentioned the amazing amount of "help" letters that the Rosh

Yeshiva signed, encouraging others to give a hand to untold numbers of individuals in trouble. Over the years, the mentally unstable found extraordinary patient tolerance in Reb Moshe. I vividly recall one morning when a mentally disabled man entered the Beis HaMedrash at Camp Yeshiva Staten Island in upstate New York. It was right in the middle of the morning seder, around 10:30 a.m., and the man began to say a *hoiche* (loud) *Shemoneh Esrei*. When the man got up to Kedushah, the Rosh Yeshiva stood up and responded to his Kedushah prayer. Of course, all the talmidim followed suit. It was a lesson in patience and profound tolerance which I have never forgotten.

Reb Moshe's devotion to the individual was repeatedly demonstrated by his attendance at countless simchas—sometimes he attended up to four weddings a night! This synthesis of using every moment for Torah and still having all the time in the world for other people—without making them feel rushed (a talent so essential for a busy rabbi or doctor)—was something that Reb Moshe practiced impeccably. He gave equal attention to an inquiry that would affect millions and to an individual's trouble. This special quality was a small part of the reason he was venerated the world over.

And, through the same osmosis, I still find myself propelled to open a *sefer* and learn while waiting for the next aliyah during Krias HaTorah, or while I wrap up my tefillin. Thousands of talmidim remember with awe his incredible *hasmoda* (diligence), the way he learned Mishnayos at every (allowable) break during davening, and repeatedly finished Shas before our very eyes. Similarly, he thoroughly reviewed Tanach, often carrying the precious Tanach he received from Rav Shisgal, *alav hashalom*. Reb Moshe learned from it at extra moments, while waiting for a car or taking a walk, etc. As students exposed to this behavior we learned how to utilize time and how small increments of time could add up to huge accomplishments!

For many people, seizing moments for learning is the only way they can fulfill their quota of learning in the midst of a hectic life (as the Chasam Sofer explains, *"Kavata ittim La-Torah*—Steal time for Torah" [*Shabbos* 31a]). Not so Reb Moshe! His entire life was learning Torah—with breaks in the middle when something else needed care. He was the quintessential example of *"Lo yamush sefer haTorah hazeh m'picha, v'hageesa bah yomam v'layla*—Never turn away from this Torah, and think about it both day and night" [*Yehoshua* 1:8].

Ahhh! Reb Moshe's profound warmth, deep feeling and radiant smile! When he shook your hand, he used both of his hands—turning this simple gesture into something resembling an embrace more than a handshake. His special glow for a talmid was something we were all proud of. He was the living embodiment of why the Torah is referred to as fire—as seen in the verse *"mi-y'mino eish das lamo*—from his right hand, a fiery law to his people" [*Devarim* 33:2]—and in the fact that the menorah was a symbol of Torah study. A lit menorah—like the Torah—not only illuminates the darkness of this world and burns away the evil inclination, but it invests those immersed in it with loving warmth.

Reb Moshe also gave honor to all people he met! He, who towered far above others, lifted himself off his chair to show honor to Rebbeim and Askonim fifty years younger than he. To everyone he came in contact with he showed respectful attention and deferential treatment. He was the embodiment of the Mishna in *Avos* [4:1], *"Eizehu m'chubad? Ha-m'chabeid es kol adom*—Who is honored? He who honors all men."

By observing Reb Moshe's davening habits one could also learn a remarkable amount. Although no one appreciated learning more than he, this didn't interfere with his quality time for praying. He would stand the entire *p'sukei d'zimra*. During both the silent *Shemoneh Esrei* and the chazan's repetition, his standing would take on yet another amazing dimension. It would be ramrod straight without *any* shuckling. What a lesson it was to witness Reb Moshe as the *shaliach tzibbur* repeated the *Shemoneh Esrei*. He concentrated as if he were saying another silent devotion! (It was Reb Moshe's opinion that one was not allowed to learn at such times, even if it were possible to concentrate.) Quite often he had names with him of those who needed cures, shidduchim, children, jobs, *shalom bayis*, etc.

His legendary powers of *psak* left all who knew him dumbfounded. People were astounded not simply by his ability to apply all of Shas to any given question, but when he cited a source from the Gemara, his application demonstrated an intricate understanding of all the Gemara's complexities at a level which we could only hope to understand after perhaps studying that particular Gemara, non-stop and in depth, for two weeks! This bestowed upon all those who heard him a profound respect for how much care and scholarship is necessary in the making of any halachic decision. Reb Moshe's involvement in every Jewish concern, from Chinuch Atzmai to Agudah, from the plight of the Russians, to forced autopsies, etc., was legendary. May he intercede now for all world Jewry, and help bring the Mashiach *tzidkeinu*, speedily in our days!

Developing A Daily
Desire For Mashiach

At one time or another, all of us have anxiously waited to take an exam. Whether it's a high-school regent, a bar examination, or a bechina to enter a yeshiva, the common denominator is agonizing trepidation and mounting tension. Many of us have even fantasized ways of legally obtaining the test questions beforehand! How this would ease our burden and calm our nerves!

Similarly, we are all aware that one day the time will come for our ultimate test and reckoning, when we are all destined to stand before the Almighty. In this most important of tests it's even more crucial to discover everything about the nature of the questions that will be asked of us. Our eternal happiness will depend on our ability to answer these questions properly. Thus knowing these questions in advance will enable us to dedicate our life to ensuring that we pass this critical test with flying colors. Therefore, we can fully appreciate the bonanza in *Masechtas Shabbos* [30a] which informs us in advance of

Hashem's test questions!

The Gemara states that the first question the Heavenly Tribunal will ask is, "Did you perform your business dealings faithfully and honestly?" Then, the Divine Court will inquire if we regularly devoted time to the study of Torah. The Celestial Judge will then inquire if we properly engaged in raising a family.

Now, up to this point, many of us may breathe a sigh of relief, quite secure that we are on safe ground. The next question may very well knock us off balance, since we may not be able to answer this correctly, *"Tzipisa l'yeshsuah*—did you hope for Mashiach?" What are we going to answer? Are we going to scratch our heads and mutter, "Oops, I didn't think of that. Give me another chance?" Alas, there will be no other chances!

Let's be honest. What are our true aspirations, our dreams, and goals? Is it to be able to finally buy an exquisite dress, to purchase a late model Cadillac or Lexus, a fancy couch, a string of diamonds, a big house, to travel on a dream vacation, or to get a long-awaited promotion? Sadly, the list of our hopes and ambitions might just be composed of items such as these! To be fair, we can add to this classical American dream list some Yiddishe dreams as well; *nachas* from the children, wonderful son-in-laws, grandchildren and the like. However, Hashem expects us to add to our list of dreams one vital addition! He us daily to pine for the Mashiach and the eventual redemption!

This is not surprising if we take a deeper look at the *Shemoneh Esrei* and study the nineteen blessings which constitute this prayer. The *Shemoneh Esrei* contains only one blessing each for such vital needs as health, wealth, and peace. The *Shemoneh Esrei*, however, features seven entire blessings concerning the future ingathering of the Jews, the redemption, rebuilding of Yerushalayim, the restoration of the kingdom of

Dovid, the eventual punishment of the wicked, the revival of the great Jewish court, and the return of the *Shechina*! This is more than a third of our total requests to Hashem in the *Shemoneh Esrei*. The Anshei Knesses HaGedola, who authored the *Shemoneh Esrei*, placed these blessings at the heart of our daily beseeching. What does this teach us about the importance of hoping for these events?!

Yet, unfortunately, too many of us space out when we say these blessings. After all, the restoration of the Kingdom of Dovid has no great meaning to us since we've never known Dovid's monarchy. However, we talk to Hashem daily in our prayers and, mindlessly and without real feeling, we mouth seven of the nineteen requests. Wouldn't it make more sense to dig a little deeper? Why is it that so many of us seem unconcerned about the dream of redemption and restoration of the Bais HaMikdash? The fault, you may think, lies in our education. No one emphasized these hopes and dreams. The real reason, I think, is more profound.

Imagine you are relaxing on your couch when you hear a loud noise piercing the quiet. At first you assume it's the local fire alarm. As it continues you may guess that someone's store must have been burglarized. As it persists and grows in crescendo you may realize—to your absolute amazement—that it must be the shofar of Mashiach. Now, as you are visualizing this scenario, ask yourself honestly—what would be your reaction at that moment? It could be—"Yikes, I'm not yet ready for Mashiach!" or "Why did he have to come now? I'm going to be marrying off a child soon and this will ruin everything!" or "Why did he have to arrive in the summer, just when I've got some time off," etc. How many of us would authentically feel, "Thank G-d, I've been waiting for this for so long?!" Shouldn't *this* be our reaction? After all, we pray a full three times a day, *"Teka b'shofar gadol"* (Please blow the great shofar)! Our reaction should be, it's about time! The unfortunate truth, however, is that many of us, deep down, are scared of the Mashiach. Many of us are not sure if we'd like the lifestyle changes he will bring. We are content with our accustomed life. Other people may feel that they are spiritually unprepared for his coming, they still need a few more decades to improve themselves and get ready for his arrival.

This is, of course, the wrong way to view this subject. Particularly if we acknowledge the phrase we repeat daily to Hashem in the *Shemoneh Esrei*, *"ki leeyshuascha keeveenue kol hayom*—for Your salvation I hope every day!" One of the Rambam's *Thirteen Ikkarim* (essential Jewish beliefs) is that every Jew should feel, "I believe with a complete belief in the coming of Mashiach, and although he is slow in coming each day I hope that he might come!"

And even if we have reservations concerning our state of readiness for the Mashiach, we must invest increased trust in our Creator. If we acknowledge that Hashem invariably wants the best for us then we must realize that if He tells us to pray for the coming of the Mashiach, it must be the most ideal thing that can possibly happen to us. So next time you pray and come upon the request for redemption, take this as a golden opportunity to upgrade your life by adding to your daily spiritual repertoire a heartfelt desire for the redemption.

The evidence of the importance of this subject is overwhelming. Even amidst the joy of a wedding ceremony a glass is broken to remind us of our lack of a Bais HaMikdash! This teaches us that—even at the pinnacle of our pleasure of either finding our own happiness or bringing our children to the chupah—we intentionally make sure that our happiness does not blur our constant and unwavering hope for the restoration of Yerushalayim. To ensure that we don't forget our ultimate wish —even during one of the happiest moments of our life—we do something to jog our memory. Thus it's obvious how momentous is our consuming passion to see the return of the *Shechina*!

Additional proof of how intimate our feelings should be towards the Bais HaMikdash can be found if we examine our behavior on Tisha b'Av. On Tisha b'Av observant Jews sit either on the floor or on low boxes. We don't greet anyone and we even refrain from general Torah study. This is done because on this day we behave as mourners sitting shivah (the seven days of absolute mourning following the death of one's next of kin). When you consider this, it's astonishing! The loss of our Temple is treated almost identically to the loss of our next of kin. Once again, it's vividly clear how deep our feelings are meant to be for the rebuilding of the Temple and the coming of Mashiach!

How can we make the Mashiach a greater part of our daily life? One immediate way is to pay more attention to these requests in our daily prayers. For example, in the latter part of *Aleinu*, which we recite three times daily, we fervently pray, "*Al kein n'kave lecha, Hashem Elokeinu, liros meheira b'siferes uzecha*—Therefore we hope to you, Hashem our G-d, to see speedily Your glorious might." And, in the *Shemoneh Esrei*, we say, "*Ki lee'shuascha kivinu kol hayom*—for Your salvation we hope the entire day." In addition, every time we respond Amen to the moving Kaddish prayer, we are asking for the magnification of Hashem on earth.

But, as we all know, hoping for the Mashiach is not enough. A child can long to become a medical doctor, but, if he doesn't do well in school and then go through the lengthy training of medical school, his hopes will never materialize. A patient may desire to get well, but, if she doesn't follow her physician's recommendations, it probably won't happen. Similarly, hoping alone won't bring the Mashiach. We must act! We must do whatever we can to hasten his arrival.

What can we do to bring the Mashiach? When will

Mashiach come? The Gemara tells us, "Due to our unworthiness, all the predestined times for the coming of Mashiach have already passed and now it's entirely up to us" [*Masechtas Sanhedrin* 97b]. In addition, Chazal give us specific recommendations, in various places, to hasten the Mashiach's arrival. For starters, the *Medrash Tanchuma* [*Beshalach*, chapter 6] tells us that the final redemption will come only in the merit of *emunah* (belief in Hashem). Thus, we can quicken the redemption by strengthening our convictions via *sifrei mussar*, by attending *hashkafah* lectures, and through serious spiritual meditation.

In a famous Gemara we are told that the Mashiach will only come through the merit of charity [*Bava Basra* 10a]. Therefore, even when we're not being prompted by an appeal at shul or by an outstretched hand, we should endeavor to give tzedakah on our own initiative. In the *Medrash Rabbah* [*Devarim*, chapter 5], Chazal tell us that Hashem will herald in the Mashiach only when Jews are at peace with one another. The *Medrash Tanchuma* shares this same sentiment when it tells us that the Mashiach won't arrive until we are all one agudah, one completely united group. We could begin to achieve this by divesting ourselves of any prejudices we have about any specific groups in Klal Yisroel, and by teaching our children to care for every Jew.

The Gemara stresses how important building a family is in our attempt to usher in the Mashiach. The Mashiach will not arrive until all the children who are supposed to be born are brought into the world [*Pesachim* 109a]. Let us not, *chas v'shalom*, place our careers before the supreme obligation of building a "*bayis ne'eman b'Yisroel*—a faithful Jewish household." And in the process, while raising a family, we will be quickening the coming of Mashiach!

There's a well-known Talmudic dictum in *Masechtas Shabbos* [118b] that if all Jews kept only two Shabbosim, the redemption would immediatcly arrive. Knowing this, shouldn't we be busy brushing up on the halochos of Shabbos, and getting into the habit of asking questions of our Rovs when situations arise of which we are in doubt? This would definitely be in order for a prescription to bring the Mashiach.

The *Medrash Rabbah* [chapter 7-3] also disclosed that the only way all of the Jews scattered across the four corners of the earth will be reunited is through the merit of learning Mishnayos. Can we motivate ourselves (and our children!) to establish the habit of a daily dosage of Mishnayos? This, more than anything else, will help free our unfortunate brethren from the dangers in Eastern Europe and the horrors of Iran and other Arab countries.

Well, it seems that we have our work cut out for us. The next time someone impatiently asks, "When is Mashiach coming already?" tell them to roll up their sleeves (figuratively speaking) and get to work. May it be the will of Hashem that we should be *zocheh* that there should be no more sickness, no more suffering, and may Hashem bring the Mashiach *Tzidkeinu* speedily, in our days!

Glossary

Glossary

Achdus—togetherness, brotherhood, Jewish unity.

Achron achron chaviv—expression denoting that the best is saved for last.

Ad Me'ah V'esrim Shana—literally, s/he should live to one hundred and twenty years.

Admor—an acronym for a Chassidic leader.

Adom Gadol—a great person.

Adom Harishon—the first man, Adom.

Afikomen—the final matzah eaten at the seder.

Af—anger.

Agudah—a unity of people.

Agunos (plural) **Agunah** (singular)—women who cannot remarry because they have not received a Jewish divorce.

Ahava—love.

Al Hamichya—a blessing recited after eating certain foods.

Al Y'dei Hadchak—in a time of need.

Alav Hashalom—may he rest in peace.

"Aleph"—first letter of the Hebrew alphabet.

Aleinu—the last prayer said at all public daily services.

Aliyah—to be called up to the Torah to make a blessing.

Am haaretz—a man devoid of Torah learning.

Amen—affirmative response to another saying a blessing.

Amoraim—one of the participants of the Talmud.

Ananei HaKavod—the heavenly clouds which guided and protected Bnei Yisroel in the desert.

Aniyim—the poor.

Aron Kodesh—the ark which holds a Torah scroll.

Arusah—a betrothed maiden.

At–Bash—a gematria similar in nature to a children's code, where the first letter of the "Aleph-Beis" ("aleph") is substituted for the last ("tuf"); the second letter ("beis") is substituted for the second to last ("shin"), and so on. The numerical values of the letters are then calculated in the normal manner.

Asher Yotzar—a blessing said after using the restroom.

Askonim—those who do for the community.

Avodah Zorah—idol worship.

Avodas Yisroel—the service or prayer of Jews.

Avos—patriarchs.

B'kovod—with honor.

Baalei Mussar—masters of ethical discipline.

Bachatzos Halayla—at midnight.

Bachurim—yeshiva students.

Bais Yaakov—Jewish schools for girls.

Bakashos—requests (from G-d).

Balabustah—homemaker.

Bamidbar—in the desert; the fourth book of the Torah.

Batei Medrashim—houses of learning.

Bayis Chadash—a newly establish household.

Bedikas Chometz—the search for chometz on the night before Pesach.

Bein HaZemanim—intercession between school semesters.

Beinonim—average people.

Beis Din—Jewish court or tribunal.

Beis HaMikdash—the Temple in Yerushalayim.

"Beis"—the second letter of the Hebrew alphabet.

Bentch Licht—blessing and lighting Friday night or Yom Tov candles.

Bentcher—a booklet which contains the blessings after a meal.

Bentch—say Grace after Meals.

Bereishis—in the beginning; the first book of the Torah.

Bezras Hashem Yisborach—with the help of Hashem, may He be blessed.

Bimah—the platform from which the Torah is read.

Birchas HaTorah—blessings made on the Torah or on Torah learning.

Bitachon—trust.

Bli Ayin Horah—without an evil eye.

Bll Neder—without making a vow.

Bnei Yisroel—the sons, or children of Yisroel.

Boruch Hashem—thank G-d.

Bris milah—Jewish circumcision ceremony.

Bracha—a blessing.

Chachomim—people learned in Jewish law.

Chas V'shalom—G-d forbid.

Chosid—a pious individual.

Chazal—acronym for *Chachamenu, Zichronam Levracha*—our sages of blessed memory.

Chazan—a prayer leader.

Cheilek—portion.

Cherubim—the angelic figures on the ark in the Temple.

Chesed—a righteous act.

Cheshbon—calculation or an accounting.

Chiddush—novel Torah interpretation.

Chilul Hashem—desecration of G-d's name.

Chinuch—education and initiation.

Chiyuv—an obligation or one who is obliged to perform a certain action.

Chochom—a wise man.

Chodesh—month.

Chol Hamoed—intermediate days between the first and last holiday days of Pesach and Succos.

Choleh—a sick person.

Cholent—a hot food usually consisting of meat, potatoes, and beans regularly eaten at the Shabbos day meal.

Chometz—leavened food, of which even a minute amount is forbidden on Pesach.

Chumash—five books of Moshe.

Chumros—stringencies.

Chupah—wedding canopy under which the couple stands during the marriage ceremony.

Churban—the destruction of the temple.

Daaga—worry.

Daf Hayomi—learning schedule by which the same, single folio of Talmud is learned on a daily basis around the globe.

Dag—fish.

"Daled"—the fourth letter of the Hebrew alphabet.

Daven—pray.

Deoraisa—Jewish law coming directly from the Torah.

Derabbanan—Torah law enacted by the rabbis of former times.

Derech Eretz—commonly used to denote proper behavior and manners.

Devarim—the fifth book of the Torah.

Dibbur—speech.

Din V'cheshbon—a judgment and an accounting.

Divrei Torah—words of Torah.

Dor HaMidbar—the generation which left Egypt and lived in the desert for forty years.

Drosha—exposition of a Torah subject.

Emunah—belief in Hashem; faith.

Eretz Yisroel—land of Israel.

Erev—evening.

Frumkeit—the practice of Torah Judaism.

Gadol Hador—a great sage of the generation.

Galus—exile from the land of Israel.

Gan Eden—Garden of Eden.

Gashmius—materialism.

Gehinnom—purgatory.

Gemara—Talmud.

Gematria—an interpretive device which assigns a numeric value to each of the Hebrew letters.

Goyim—non-Jews.

Haggadah—the telling of the story of leaving Egypt read at the Pesach seder.

Hakdamah—preface.

Hakoras Hatov—appreciation, gratitude.

Halachah—Jewish law.

Hamapil—blessing said before going to sleep at night.

Hamotzi—blessing said before eating bread.

Har Sinai—Mount Sinai.

Harbotzas Torah—disseminating Torah.

Hashem—literally means the Name, G-d.

Hashkafah—philosophy.

Hasmada—Torah diligence.

Hatzlocha Rabbah—(a wish for) great success.

Havdalah—sanctifying the Shabbos with wine at its conclusion.

Hechsher—(kosher) certification.

Heter (sing.) **Heterim** (pl.)—allowances because of a contingency.

Hiddur—a beautification.

Hishtadlus—to make the proper attempt.

Hisorerus—an awakening.

Imahos—matriarchs.

Ivri—literally, a Hebrew; a Jew.

Iyov—Job.

K'vitlach—notes (usually with a request) given to a great rabbi.

K'zayis—a measurement the size of an olive.

Kaddish—a prayer said for the deceased.

Kal Vechomer—a fortiori, deriving a lesson from that which is lenient to that which is more severe.

Kares—spiritual excommunication.

Kashrus—the observance of Jewish laws regarding food, including specifications about meat, milk and meat, etc.

Kavanah—concentration in prayer.

Kavod—honor.

Keitz—the time of redemption.

Kesuvah—wedding document.

Kibud Av V'eim—the lofty mitzvah of honoring a father and mother.

Kiddush Hashem—sanctification of G-d's name.

Kiddush—the prayer usually said over wine, which sanctifies the Shabbos or Yom Tov.

Kiruv Rechokim—bringing people closer to G-d.

Kisei HaKavod—the heavenly throne of glory.

Klal Yisroel—the community of Israel.

Kohen—priest.

Kollel—advanced learning center for married men.

Korbonos—sacrifices.

Kotzer Ruach—literally, weakness of spirit.

Kovei'a Seudah—to establish a meal.

Krias Shema Al Hamitta—saying *Shema* before retiring at night.

Krias Yam Suf—splitting of the Red Sea.

L'shem Shamayim—for the sake of heaven.

Lehavdil—to differentiate.

Leiv—heart.

Letzonos—the act of mockery.

Leviim—the tribe which attended to the kohanim, the priests.

Livyoson—the legendary fish which will be eaten by the righteous in the afterlife.

Loshon Horah—evil gossip.

Luchos—the tablets of the law brought down from Mt. Sinai by Moshe.

Maariv—the evening prayer service.

Maasim Tovim—good deeds.

Machlokes—argument and conflict.

Madreiga—a certain level.

Maggid Shiur—Torah lecturer.

Maidel—Yiddish expression for a young Jewish girl.

Malach HaMaves—the angel of death.

Malachim—angels.

Masechtas—a volume of the Talmud.

Mashgiach—a rabbi in a yeshiva who oversees the spiritual growth of the students.

Mashiach—bringer of the final redemption.

Matan Torah—giving of the Torah at Mt. Sinai.

Mayim—water.

Mechanchim—Torah educators.

Mechaneches—a female Torah educator.

Mechiras Yosef—the sale of Joseph by his brothers.

Medrash—a collection of derived lessons from the Torah.

Mefarnes—to sustain or nourish.

Meilitz Yosher—an intercessor.

Mekadesh—to sanctify.

Melavah Malka—meal eaten after Shabbos, in its honor.

Melech—king.

Menahel—spiritual guide.

Menorah—Chanukah candelabra.

Meshulach—messenger, often engaged in collecting money for charitable causes.

Mesorah—the oral transmission of Torah law.

Mezonos—non-bread pastries, cakes and cookies.

Mezuzah—Scriptural sections placed on door-posts of a Jewish home.

Midbar—a desert.

Middos—literally measurements, commonly used to refer to an individual's character traits.

Mikvah—a ritual bath.

Milah—a ritual circumcision.

Minhag—custom passed down through the generations.

Minyan—group of ten Jewish males over bar mitzvah age.

Mishlei—proverbs of King Solomon.

Mishloach Manos—gifts of food given to friends and acquaintances in the observance of Purim.

Mishna Yomis—a schedule of learning the Mishna with the goal to finish a certain time.

Mishna—the oral law as codified by Rabbi Yehuda Hanasi.

Mishpacha—family.

Mispar katan—a gematria which reduces the numeric value of all numbers to a unit value from zero to nine. In this system, the letters "aleph" through "tes" are valued as they are in the most common form of gematria. Then beginning with the letter "yud", which is normally ten, becomes one in *mispar katan*. Likewise, "chof" which is normally twenty, becomes two; "lamed" normally thirty becomes three, and so on.

Mishpat—law.

Mispallel—person who prays.

Mitzrayim—Egypt.

Mitzvah—a Torah commandment.

Mizbeiyach—the altar in the Temple.

Modim D'rabonon—a prayer of thanksgiving said by the congregation during the chazan's recital of the *Shemoneh Esrei*.

Mohel—a Jewish male specially trained to perform a Jewish circumcision.

Mun or Manna—food which came down from heaven to Bnei Yisroel for forty years in the desert.

Moreh D'asra—the rav of a city or a synagogue.

Muktza—an item which is forbidden to be moved on Shabbos.

Mussaf—additional prayer service on Yom Tov and Rosh Chodesh which corresponds to the additional sacrifices brought on these occasions in Temple times.

N'tilas Yadayim—ritual hand-washing in the morning and before eating bread.

Nachas—reaping Jewish enjoyment.

Navi—prophet.

Ner—candle.

Neshama—soul.

Niftar—to pass away.

Nisikatnu Hadoros—the diminishing of the generations since receiving Torah at Mt. Sinai.

Nisyonos—trials.

Nivul Peh—foul speech.

Nusach—a specific version of prayer.

Ohl Torah—the yoke of Torah.

Olam Habah—the World to Come.

Olam Hazeh—this world, in distinction to the World to Come.

Onah—the mitzvah of marital relations.

Oneg—delight.

Oni—a poor person.

Os—a sign.

P'sukei D'zimra—a collection of praises to Hashem recited during the morning prayer service.

Pachad—fear.

Parnasa—livelihood.

Parshah—section of the Torah.

Payat—part of the Yom Tov liturgy.

Perek—chapter.

Pirkei Avos—Ethics of Our Fathers.

Pirya V'rivya—the mitzvah to reproduce children.

Posuk—a verse in the Torah.

Psak—a halachic ruling.

Rachamim—mercy.

Rachmana Litzlon—literally, "may heaven save us," colloquially used to say "G-d forbid."

Ratzon Hashem—the will of G-d.

Rebbitzen—a rabbi's wife.

Rechilus—slander.

Refuah Shelaimah—the wish that one should receive a complete recovery.

Reshaim—wicked people.

Ribbono Shel Olam—Creator of the universe.

Rosh Chodesh—the new moon, first day of the Hebrew month.

Rosh HaYeshiva—head of a Talmudic academy.

Ruach—spirit.

Sanhedrin—the Jewish high court.

Schar—reward.

Sefer—a holy book.

Sefira—counting the days from the second day of Pesach until Shavuos.

Segulah—a helpful device.

Seuda Shlishit—see shalosh suedos.

Shacharis—the morning prayer service.

Shaim v'Eiver—the academy at the time of the patriarchs.

Shalom Bayis—marital harmony.

Shalom—peace.

Shalosh Seudos—the third meal eaten on Shabbos.

Shas—the entire Talmud.

Shechianu—a blessing on something new, or a special happening that only comes from time to time.

Shechina—the Divine Presence.

Sheitlach (pl.) **sheitel** (sing.)—a wig worn by a married woman.

Sheliach—messenger.

Shema—a prayer accepting the yoke of heaven.

Shemesh—sun.

Shemoneh Esrei—literally eighteen, a term that designates a collection of (actually nineteen) prayers constituting the silent devotion.

Shemos—literally "Names," the second book of the Torah.

Shidduch—an effort of matchmaking.

Shir Shel Yom—song of the day.

Shiur—a Torah lesson.

Shivah—the seven days of absolute mourning held when one's next of kin dies.

Shlit"a—an acronym meaning that one should live a long and good life.

Shofar—ram's horn.

Shor Habor—a legendary wild ox to be eaten by the righteous in the afterlife.

Shteig—to excel.

Shuckle—shake.

Shulchan—table.

Shul—synagogue.

Shver—a father-in-law.

Siddur—prayer book.

Simcha—happiness.

Siyyum—a festive meal on the occasion of completing a body of learning.

Tachanun—a beseeching prayer said with head lowered during the morning service.

Talmid—student.

Tanach—an acronym for portions of the written Torah liturgy, which includes the *Torah* (five books of Moshe), *Neviim* (the books of the prophets), and *Kesuvim* (holy writings).

Targum—a translation.

Techiyas Hameisim—the resurrection of the dead.

Tefillah—prayer.

Tefillas Haderech—prayer for travelers.

Tefillin—phylacteries.

Tehillim—psalms.

Teshuva—literally to return, used to designate repentance.

Teva—nature.

Tichya—to live.

Tikkun Chatzos—a prayer said at midnight in mourning over the Temple.

Tishah b'Av—the ninth of the month of Av, a Jewish fast day commemorating the destruction of both Jewish Temples and other Jewish tragedies.

Tochacha—admonitions.

Tomchei Shabbos—a voluntary organization in New York City which provides food for the needy for Shabbos.

Torah Lishma—Torah for the sake of heaven.

Tosefos—early commentary on the Talmud.

Totty—Yiddish expression for father.

Treifah—colloquialism meaning non-kosher.

Tumah—ritual impurity.

Tzadik—a righteous person.

Tzedakah—charity.

Tzitzis—ritual fringes on a four-cornered garment worn by Jewish males.

Tznius—modesty in dress and behavior.

Vort (sing.) **vertlach (pl.)**—a short Torah exposition.

Yaaleh V'yavo—an additional paragraph added to the *Shemoneh Esrei* on Rosh Chodesh and Chol Hamoed.

Yashrus—straightness.

Yayin—wine.

Yehudim—Jews.

Yemach Shemam—literally, may their names be erased.

Yerei Cheit—those who fear sin.

Yeridah—to fall.

Yerushalayim—Jerusalem.

Yeshiva Bochur—a male student of a Torah academy.

Yetzer Hara—the evil inclination.

Yetzias Mitzraim—the exodus from Egypt.

Yiddishkeit—Judaism.

Yid (sing.) **Yidin (pl.)**—Jew; in Yiddish.

Yiras Hashem—fear of G-d.

Yom Hadin—the day of judgment.

Yom Tov—a Jewish holiday.

Yomim Noraim—high holy days.

Zechus (sing.), **zechusim** (pl.)—merit.

Zemiros—songs.

Zt"l—acronym for *zecher tzadik l'vracha*—literally, may the memory of the righteous one be blessed.

Zugos—pairs.

Partial Bibliography
Of Sources Quoted

Partial Bibliography
Of Sources Quoted

Abramsky, R' Yecheskel—Head of bais din of Great Britain and Rosh Yeshiva of Slabodka Yeshiva in Bnei Brak (1886-1976).

Afraksta D'anya—Responsa of R' Dovid Sperberg (1875-1962).

Agudas Aizov—Commentary on the Pesach Haggadah by R' Avraham Ahron Friedman of Tshopp, Hungary (c. 1938).

Aruch HaShulchan—Elaboration of the *Shulchan Aruch* by R' Yechiel Michel Halevy Epstein (1898-1908).

Ateres Zekeinim—Commentary on *Shulchan Aruch* by R' Menachem Mendel of Krotchin, a student of the Bach.

Avodah Zarah—A Talmudic tractate dealing with the subject of idolatry.

Avos D'Rabbi Nasson—Commentary on *Pirkei Avos* by Talmudic sage R' Nasson (c. 210 C.E.).

Avudraham—Commentary and laws on prayer by R' Dovid ben Yosef (1420-1494).

Baal Shem Tov—R' Yisroel ben Eliezer, founder of the Chassidic movement (1700-1760).

Bach—Commentary by R' Yoel Sirkis (1561-1640) on the Arba Turim.

Bava Metzia—A Talmudic tractate dealing with the subject of property ownership, wages and civil law.

Be'er Heitev—Commentary on *Shulchan Aruch* by R' Yehudah Ashkenazi, rabbi of Tiktin, Poland.

Beitzah—A Talmudic tractate dealing with the laws of the Jewish festivals.

Ben Ish Chai—Work containing Jewish laws, customs and lectures by R' Yosef Chaim of Bagdad (1835-1909).

Ben Yehoyada—Commentary on the Aggadic portions of the Talmud by R' Yosef Chaim of Bagdad (1835-1909).

Biur Halachah—Commentary on *Shulchan Aruch, Orach Chaim* by R' Yisroel Meir Kagan of Radin (1838-1933).

Bnei Yissaschor—Book of chassidic thought by R' Hirsch Elimelech of Dinova, Poland (1795-1851).

Bostoner Rebbe—R' Levi Yitzchok Horowitz of Boston, Massachusetts and Jerusalem.

Brachos—A Talmudic tractate dealing with the laws of blessings and prayer.

Chaim of Volozhin, R'—Illustrious disciple of the Vilna Gaon, founded and headed the Yeshiva of Volozhin, "father of all yeshivos" (1749-1820).

Chasam Sofer—R' Moshe Schreiber (1762-1839), Rabbi of Pressburg was known by this name after he authored works of responsa and novellae with this title.

Chazon Ish—R' Avrohom Yeshaya Karelitz (1878-1953) of Bnei Brak was known by this name after he authored halachic works with this title.

Chemdas Shlomo—Responsa by R' Shlomo Zalman, R' of Warsaw (early 17th century).

Chidah—Acronym for R' Chaim Yosef Dovid Azulai, reknowned Kabbalist and author (1724-1806).

Chofetz Chaim—R' Yisroel Meir Kagan of Radin (1838-1933) was known by this name after he authored a work with this title on the subject of proper speech.

Chovos Halevovos—Work of Jewish Ethics by R' Bachya ben Yosef Ibn Pekudah (1050-1120).

Dibros Moshe—Commentary on several tractates of Talmud by R' Moshe Feinstein (1895-1986).

Eitz Yoseif—Commentary on Midrashim by R' Chanoch Zundel.

Emdin, R' Yaakov—Respected scholar and author of a commentary on the siddur as well as halachic responsa. (1697-1776).

Eruvin—A Talmudic tractate dealing with the subject of creating areas for carrying on Shabbos.

Feinstein, R' Moshe—(1895-1986) Rosh Yeshiva of Mesivta Tifereth Jerusalem in NY. Halachic authority and one of the foremost leaders of American Jewry.

Frand, R' Yissochar—Noted lecturer and Rabbi in Yeshivas Ner

Yisroel in Baltimore, Maryland.

Friedman, R' Shmuel Dovid—Author of *Metzuveh V'oseh* and *B'air Basadeh* amongst other works. He lives in Brooklyn, New York.

Hirsch Elimelech of Dinnova, R'—Rabbi of Dinnova, Poland, Chassidic Rebbe and noted author (1795-1851).

Hirsch, R' Shamshon Raphael—Rabbi of Frankfurt am Main, prolific author, one of the foremost leaders of German Jewry (1808-1888).

Kaminetsky, Rabbi Yaakov—(1891-1986) Rosh Yeshiva of Torah Vodaas in Brooklyn, New York and recognized leader of American Jewry.

Kav Hayashar—Work of ethics by R' Tzvi Hirsch Codnaver, Rabbi of Frankfurt am Main.

Kiddushin—A Talmudic tractate dealing with Jewish marriage practices.

Kitzur Shulchan Aruch—Condensed compendium of Jewish law written by R' Shlomo Ganzfried of Ungvar, Hungary (1804-1886).

Knesses Hagedola—Halachic work by R' Chaim Benveniste of Constantinople, Turkey (1603-1673).

Kotler, R' Shneur—Rosh Yeshiva of Beis Midrash Govoha in Lakewood, New Jersey (1918-1982).

Kotzker Rebbe—R' Menachem Mendel of Kotzk (1787-1859) widely known and respected Chassidic rebbe.

Kraiyna D'igrasa—A collection of responsa by R' Yaakov Yisroel Kanievsky, known as the Steipler Gaon.

Krohn, R' Paysach—Noted Mohel and renowned Maggid who lives in Kew Gardens, Queens.

Ksav Sofer—R' Avraham Shmuel Binyomin Schreiber (1815-1879), a leader of Hungarian Jewry was known by this name after he authored a collection of responsa and commentaries with this title.

Levin, R' Aryeh—His piety made him known as the "tzaddik of Jerusalem" (1885-1969).

Likutei Amorim—Part of the Tanya by R' Schnur Zalman of Ladi (1745-1813).

Lopian, R' Elya—Prominent mussar personality whose lectures were compiled in the work *Lev Eliyahu* (1876-1970).

Machane Chaim—Responsa from R. Chaim Sofer, Rav of Budapest (1822-1886).

Maharsha—Acronym for Moreinu HaRav Shmuel Aidels (1555-1631) of Poland. Author of famous commentary on the Talmud.

Mataeh Moshe—Halachic compendium by R' Moshe Mos of Premysl (1540-1606).

Me'am Loez—Monumental commentary on Tanach by R' Yaakov Culi (1689-1732). Originally printed in Ladino, it has been translated into

Hebrew and English.

Megillah—A Talmudic tractate dealing with the holiday of Purim.

Menochos—A Talmudic tractate dealing with the Temple meal offerings.

Mevaser Tov—Responsa by R' Meyer Isaacson of Staten Island, N.Y.

Miller, R. Avigdor—Contemporary Rabbi and Rosh Yeshiva of Bais Yisroel Torah Center, noted lecturer and author who lives in Brooklyn, New York.

Minchas Yitzchok—Responsa by R' Yitzchok Yaakov Weiss (d. 1989).

Mishna Brurah—Commentary on *Shulchan Aruch, Orach Chaim* by R' Yisroel Meir Kagan of Radin (1838-1933).

Moadim U'zmanim—Halachic discussions pertaining to holidays by R' Moshe Shternbach.

Naftoli of Ropshitz, R'—(1760-1807), Prominent Chassidic leader in Galicia and disciple of Reb Elimelech of Lizensk.

Nedarim—A Talmudic tractate dealing with the subject of vows and promises.

Ohr Hachayim—Kabbalist and scholar R' Chaim ben Moshe Ibn Attar (1696-1743) of Morroco and Israel was known by this name after he authored a commentary on the Torah with this title.

Orchos Chaim L'harosh—Mussar work by R' Asher ben R' Yechiel (1250-1328).

P'eir Aharon—See Agudas Aizov.

Pele Yoetz—Mussar work written by R' Eliezer Papa.

Pesachim—A Talmudic tractate dealing with the holiday of Pesach.

Pirkei Avos—"Ethics of Our Fathers"—a Talmudic tractate dealing with ethical and moral practices.

Rabbainu Bachaya—Commentary on the Torah by R' Bachya ben R' Asher.

Radvaz—Acronym for R' Dovid Ben Zimra (1480-1573), Chief Rabbi of Egypt and author of a work of responsa.

Rama—Acronym for R' Moshe Isserles (1530-1572), Rabbi of Cracow and Torah leader of East European Jewry. Author of many works including *Sefer Hamapeh*—annotations on *Shulchan Aruch*.

Rambam—Acronym for R' Moshe ben Maimon, also known as Maimonidies (1135-1204) of Spain and Egypt, one of the leading authorities in all areas of Jewish law and thought. He served as personal physician to Saladin, Sultan of Egypt and Syria.

Ramban—Acronym for R' Moshe ben Nachman also known as Nachmanidies (1194-1270) of Spain. He was a leader of world Jewry and a prolific author of numerous works on Bible, Talmud, philosophy, Jewish law, kabbalah and medicine.

Rashi—Acronym for R' Shlomo Yitzchaki (1040-1105) of Troyes, France. Rashi is considered the "father of commentators" and is famous for his commentaries on the Torah and the Tamud. About two hundred supercommentaries have been written on his commentary on Chumash, attesting to its greatness.

Rokeach—Code of Jewish law and ethical practices by R' Elazer of Garmiza (1164-1232). He authored many works including a commentary on the Torah.

Safer Hamakneh—R' Eliezer Zusman Sofer's work on the laws of ownership.

Sanhedrin—a Talmudic tractate dealing with the subject of the Jewish court system.

Satmar Rebbe—(1887-1979) R' Yoel Teitelbaum, Rebbe of Satmar Chassidim.

Schwab, R' Shimon—Rav of Cong. K'hal Adas Yeshurun of Washington Heights, New York; a foremost leader of American Jewry (1908-1995).

Sefer Chasidim—Work of laws and customs of "Chasidei Ashkenaz" written by R' Yehudah Hachasid (1150-1217).

Segal, R' Yehudah Zev—(1910-1993) Rosh Yeshiva of Manchester Yeshiva in England.

Sfas Emes—R' Yehudah Leib Alter (1847-1905), the third Rebbe of Ger was known by this name after he authored a commentary on Torah and Talmud with this title.

Shaarei Teshuva—Mussar work on the subject of repentance by R' Yonah of Gerona (d. 1263).

Shabbos—A Talmudic tractate dealing with the subject of the Sabbath.

Shach, R' Eliezer—Current Rosh Yeshiva of Ponevez Yeshiva in Bnei Brak.

Shelah—Acronym for *Shnei Luchos Habris*, a work of Jewish laws, customs and ethics by R' Yeshaya Horowitz of Prague (1560-1630).

Shmulevitz, R' Chaim—(1902-1978) Rosh Yeshiva of Mirrer Yeshiva in Shanghai and Jerusalem. Author of *Sichos Mussar*.

Shulchan Aruch—Universally accepted compendium of Jewish law compiled by R' Yosef Karo (1488-1575).

Sifsei Chachomim—Commentary of Rashi by R' Shabse ben R' Yosef Bass.

Specter, R' Yitzchak Elchonon—Rabbi of Kovno, Lithuania and leading halachic authority of his time. He died in 1886.

Steipler Gaon—R' Yaakov Yisrael Kanievsky (1899-1985) of Bnei Brak.

Succah—A Talmudic tractate dealing with the holiday of Sukkos.

Ta'amei Minhogim—Work by R' Avrohom Yitzchok Sperling expaining reasons for Jewish customs.

Taanis—A Talmudic tractate dealing with the subject of fast days.

Tur—R' Yacov Ben R' Asher, author of Arba Turim on *Shulchan Aruch* and the Tur commentary on the Torah (1270-1343).

Twerski, R' Dr. Abraham—Noted psychiatrist of Pittsburgh, Pennsylvania and author of numerous self-help books.

Vayikra Rabbah—Anthology of Aggadic interpretation on the book of *Vayikra* compiled c. 450 C.E. Editorship is attributed to R' Hoshea Rabbah.

Vilna Gaon—R' Eliyahu ben Shlomo Zalman of Vilna (1720-1797). He was a leading authority in all fields of Torah study and authored more than seventy works on varying subjects in Judaism.

Vital, R' Chaim—Reknowned kabbalist and student of the Arizal (1543-1620).

Yaros D'vash—Anthology of lectures by R' Yonasan Eibshitz (1690-1764) noted author and kabbalist and chief rabbi of the triple community of Altona, Hamburg and Wandsbeck, in Germany.

Yehuda Hachasid, R'—Head of yeshiva in Regensberg and author of *Sefer Chasidim* (1150-1217).

Yeitev Lev—Works by R' Yekusiel Yehudah of Siget (1808-1883).

Yevamos—a Talmudic tractate dealing with marrying one's widow.

Zohar—classic work of Kabbalah from the school of R' Shimon Bar Yochai (c. 120 C.E.).

Dedications

THIS SEFER IS ALSO DEDICATED

In loving memory of my wife's wonderful parents

ר׳ אהרן בן ר׳ משה Gelbtuch ז״ל

who survived the war and came to America
as a devoted Kopishnitz and Boyana chosid.
In his advanced age he succeeded in
raising a beautiful Torah mishpacha.

And his wife

דבורה בת ר׳ אריה ליב ז״ל

Who was a woman of
incredible piety and chesed.
She was a superb mother
and was very dedicated to Ezras Torah, working closely
with the great Rav Henkin, zt"l

ת.נ.צ.ב.ה

נדבת יחיאל דוד ורעיתו צעדער

⬥•⬥•⬥

לעילוי נשמת אבי מורי
ר' שמעון זאב ע"ה ב"ר יחיאל ע"ה הי"ד צעדער
נפטר בשבת קודש י"ז כסלו תשנ"ג
לעילוי נשמת אמי מורתי
מרת חנה צפורה ע"ה
בת ר' אליעזר שמחה בונים ע"ה צעדער
נפטרה בשבת קודש ח מר חשון תשנ"ד

⬥•⬥•⬥

גם לזכר נשמת הקדושים שנהרגו על קידוש השם בימי השואה
הוריו ר' יחיאל ב"ר נתן דוד
מרת פייגע נחה בת ר' ישעיהו אהרן ובניהם
יהודה אריה, יעקב שמואל, נתן דוד, אבנר, אליעזר

⬥•⬥•⬥

ולזכר נשמת ששה מיליון יהודי אירופה
שנהרגו ושנשרפו על קידוש השם ע"י הרשעים
הארורים ימ"ש בימי השואה ת"ש - תש"ה
השם ינקום דמם
תנצב"ה

⬥•⬥•⬥

לעילוי נשמת
ר' אברהם לייב ב"ר ישעיהו הכהן ע"ה גרינבוים
נפטר ט באב תשנ"ז
תנצב"ה

נדבת יחיאל דוד ורעיתו צעדער

בית גור

הרה״ק רבי יצחק מאיר מגור זצוק״ל
בעל חידושי הרי״ם
כ״ג אדר תרכ״ו

הרה״ק רבי יהודה אריה לייב מגור זצוק״ל
בעל שפת אמת
ח׳ שבט תרס״ה

הרה״ק רבי אברהם מרדכי מגור זצוק״ל
בעל אמרי אמת
בחג השבועות תש״ח

הרה״ק רבי ישראל מגור זצוק״ל
בעל בית ישראל
ב׳ אדר תשל״ז

הרה״ק רבי שמחה בונים זצוק״ל
בעל לב שמחה
ז׳ תמוז תשנ״ב

הרה״ק רבי פינחס מנחם מגור זצוק״ל
בעל פני מנחם
ט״ז אדר תשנ״ו

In honor of

Rabbi Moshe Meir Weiss

Morris & Lilian Lieberman

לזכרון עולם בהיכל ה׳

לע״נ משה בן שמואל יהודה Rozenek

by Mr. & Mrs. Ephraim Niernberg

לזכרון עולם בהיכל ה׳

מוקדש לזכר ולעילוי נשמת האשה החשובה

יהודית סערקע בת ר׳ יצחק אייזיק גאלדבערג ע״ה

נפטרה י״ט שבט תשנ״ד

מאת בניה ונכדיה שיחי׳

ר׳ יצחק בן ציון ורחל גאלדה קורצער

אהרן, חיה שרה, קלמן אברהם, איטא מלכה,

שמואל מנחם, יהודית סערקע, משה נח

לז"נ סעדיה אליעזר בן יהושע ניסן Zakarin
לז"נ הר׳ יהודה לייב חייקל בן יצחק Shifrin

by Dr. & Mrs. Averick

❖ ⬦ ❖

אייזק לייב בן יעקב דוד Rosenbaum
צפורה בת מרדכי Rosenbaum

by Mr. & Mrs. Richard Gordon

❖ ⬦ ❖

לז"נ
רחל בת אליהו Benson

❖ ⬦ ❖

לע"נ
Baila bas Faiga Friedman

❖ ⬦ ❖

Chaya Sora Miriam bas Yonah HaKohain Zeitlin, z"l
Yehuda Lev ben Yeruchem Fischel Zeitlin, z"l

❖ ⬦ ❖

ר׳ אליעזר יהושע בן טוביה ז"ל פליגעל
אסתר בת ר ניסן ז"ל פליגעל
ת.נ.צ.ב.ה
מאת משפחת פראפעסאארסקי